JOSÉ LIMÓN AND LA MALINCHE

Joe R. and Teresa Lozano Long Series in
Latin American and Latino Art and Culture

JOSÉ LIMÓN AND LA MALINCHE

The Dancer and the Dance

Edited by Patricia Seed

UNIVERSITY OF TEXAS PRESS   AUSTIN

A different version of Chapter 1 appeared as "Limón's *La Malinche: Negotiating the In-Between," Dance Research Journal* 37/1 (2005): 75–93.

An earlier version of Chapter 2 appeared as "Jose Limón's *La Malinche,*" *Dance Chronicle* 26/3 (Jan. 2003): 279–309.

Parts of Chapter 5 were adapted and abridged from Chapters 2 and 3 of Susan Kellogg, *Weaving the Past: A History of Latin America's Indigenous Women* (2005, Oxford University Press) with permission from Oxford University Press, Inc.

Requests for permission to reproduce material from this work should be sent to:
    Permissions
    University of Texas Press
    P.O. Box 7819
    Austin, TX 78713-7819
    www.utexas.edu/utpress/about/bpermission.html

♾ The paper used in this book meets the minimum requirements of ANSI/NISO Z39.48-1992 (R1997) (Permanence of Paper).

Library of Congress Cataloging-in-Publication Data

José Limón and La Malinche : the dancer and the dance / edited by Patricia Seed. — 1st ed.
    p. cm. — (Joe R. and Teresa Lozano Long series in Latin American and Latino art and culture)
  Includes bibliographical references and index.
  ISBN 978-0-292-71735-0 (cloth : alk. paper)
  1. Limón, José.   2. Malinche (Choreographic work : Limón)   I. Seed, Patricia.
  GV1790.M35J67 2007
  792.8'092—dc22
  [B]

2007015648

TABLE OF CONTENTS

8. The Director: Thoughts on Staging José Limón's *La Malinche*
Sarah Stackhouse   154

ACKNOWLEDGMENTS

I would like to thank the Center for Humanities and the Center for the Study of Writing and Translation at the University of California, Irvine, for their generous support of Manuel Gómez's translation of "José Limón and La Malinche in Mexico: A Chicano Artist Returns Home." I would also like to thank editor extraordinaire Kathleen Much for her advice at all stages of writing the manuscript. Sonia Hernández provided valuable research assistance at the start of the project, and Ingrid Wilkerson did so at the end. Susan Armsby created the layout for the illustrations in the book.

INTRODUCTION

José Limón and La Malinche

Patricia Seed

During the 1950s and 1960s, one of the great Mexican American art- ists of the century traveled to more than a dozen countries in Europe and Latin America as a cultural ambassador of the United States. He trained a generation of students at New York's famed Juilliard School in his technique, received two of the highest honors in his field, and created theatrical pieces that even today remain widely performed. Yet despite all these achievements, outside of a tightly knit community of artists few people know his name.[1]

José Acadio Limón (1908–1972) attained renown in a new twentieth-century art form. Apprenticed to Charles Weidman and Doris Humphrey, two major figures in the second generation of the modern dance movement, Limón assumed his place as the lone Mexican American among an elite circle of twentieth-century modern dancers—a field whose founders were mainly female and included Isadora Duncan, Martha Graham, and Mary Wigman as well as the talented African American choreographers Pearl Primus and Katherine Dunham. While excellent studies of the early impact of female and African American choreographers on modern dance have appeared,[2] relatively little has emerged on the distinctive impact of the first Mexican American dance composer.[3]

Born in Mexico to a middle-class family, Limón fled north with them to avoid the turmoil of the Revolution. Like many immigrants to this country, his family lost their financial security in the move north. In the northern Mexican province of Sinaloa, Limón's father, Florencio, had directed the state band. But state governments in the United States do not hire full-time musicians, let alone musical directors. Rather, artists depend primarily on private philanthropy, occasionally supplemented by grants from government agencies. In the highly competitive world of U.S. orchestras, a musical director from a northern Mexican provincial town did not have a chance of assuming a position of equivalent status. As a result, the family struggled to make ends meet as Florencio taught music to individual students, an uncertain living in the best of circumstances. Occasionally he played in small Mexican bands that performed on holidays and special occasions.

José Limón's economically insecure family moved first to Arizona and then to East Los Angeles in 1923, where they joined the swelling Mexican American community. While only a handful of immigrant families in East Los Angeles had started out, like the Limóns, in the middle class, economic prosperity eluded his family, as it did most others in the 1920s and 1930s.

Los Angeles was not particularly welcoming to new Spanish-speaking arrivals. Viewed largely as a source of cheap labor by the ruling Anglo community, most newly arrived Mexicans and Mexican Americans struggled to eke out a living amid competition from workers from other ethnic communities—Filipino, Japanese, and African American—seeking similar jobs. But the larger numbers of Mexican Americans made them easier targets for antiforeign sentiment, feelings that were fueled by the declining number of jobs during the Depression. In 1931 the Immigration Service began large-scale roundups of hundreds of Mexican Americans, deporting them regardless of their immigration status. Over the next nine years an estimated forty thousand people, including many legal residents, were deported to Mexico. Even those who had entered the country legally had to spend years reestablishing their legal right to reside in Los Angeles.[4] Life for Mexican Americans in 1920s and 1930s Los Angeles was, at the very least, precarious.

Succeeding despite the double burdens of poverty and discrimination, José Limón graduated from high school. He studied art for a semester at the University of California, Los Angeles but abandoned college and headed east to establish a career as an artist. Initially he planned to paint, having demonstrated a talent for drawing from an early age. But after seeing El Greco's masterpieces in New York, he despaired of making a career in art. A chance ticket to accompany a friend to a modern dance concert and an equally lucky visit to a modern dance classroom, however, showed Limón where his true vocation lay. From his very first lesson, he demonstrated a remarkable ability to use his body as a means of artistic expression.

Only a year after having taken his first dance class, Limón was performing professionally. This feat alone is remarkable. Most people begin dance training when they are young; a few have succeeded after beginning in their early teens. But Limón was nineteen before he even knew what modern dance was and twenty when he began performing on stage.

Limón commenced his professional artistic career with his first teacher, Charles Weidman. Together with Doris Humphrey, Weidman had created one of the two leading modern dance companies of the 1920s and 1930s. Limón soon began performing regularly with the company, and he toured the United States with it in 1935. During the 1930s he also began to choreograph, demonstrating yet another talent in the field of dance. The Second World War interrupted Limón's dancing career, but he returned to it in 1946. That year he again joined forces with Humphrey, who by that time had split from Weidman. When financial misfortune overtook Humphrey's company, Limón founded his own company with her as its artistic director. The newly formed dance troupe would take his name, and thus the José Limón Company was born. That company and its dances would propel this young man from East Los Angeles to stages throughout the world and to international renown within the field of modern dance.

Writings and films about Limón, while relatively few, have rightly focused on his considerable artistic achievements. The dance writer and former Limón dancer Daniel Lewis has produced an outstanding guide to the techniques for learning modern dance that Limón developed during his career. Two well-regarded essay collections and a biography have analyzed the trajectory of his career as an artist, properly celebrating his artistry as a performer and as a choreographer.[5] His deft interpretations of Shakespearean classics in dance have been appropriately celebrated, including his interpretation of Othello in *The Moor's Pavane*. The dance historian Ann Vachon produced an excellent documentary film, *Limón: A Life beyond Words*, containing valuable insights into Limón's life as well as his work.[6]

Yet we know very little about the impact his Mexican heritage had on his artistic imagination, in part because during his lifetime Limón publicly remained relatively reticent.[7] Vachon's film, for example, contains the surprising revelation that in the makeup box he took with him to every performance Limón carried a picture of Mexico's illustrious nineteenth-century president, Benito Juárez, the *mestizo* son of a Spanish man and a Oaxacan Indian woman. Throughout most of his career, Limón refused to answer questions about the identity of the figure in the portrait he carried with him, revealing that information (without elaboration) only as his career neared its end.

In his own elegantly composed published writings Limón remained equally taciturn regarding the impact of his Mexican and Mexican American background on his artistry. In his unfinished autobiography Limón recounts his early childhood in Mexico, the hair-raising journey across the border, and his early struggles to learn English, but he passes over his life in Arizona and California and leaps forward to the time he describes as his rebirth in the dance studio. In only one of the well-designed essays he composed does he allude, very briefly, to his Mexican American and Catholic heritage before passing on to the subject of modern dance.[8]

In order to understand how Mexico figured in Limón's artistic imagination, the essays in this book will turn to the set, costumes, music, unpublished choreographic notes, and historical content of his most famous Mexican-themed dance, *La Malinche*. From these diverse records emerges a clearer picture of the role his Mexican heritage played in his artistic creation. Limón's initial forays into choreography included several themes from Mexican history, including the Conquest and the Mexican Revolution as well as historical figures such as Hernando de Soto and Hernán Cortés. Furthermore, Limón first realized he had a gift for choreography when creating the *Danzas Mexicanas* (Mexican Dances), the predecessor of *La Malinche*, early in his career.[9] Mexican and Spanish art influenced the costumes and set design he created,[10] and his memories of the Mexican music he had heard as a child inspired the music he commissioned for his production of *La Malinche*.[11] Limón's Mexican heritage remains most strongly embedded in his dances.

Limón employed overtly Mexican themes in seven of the dances he choreographed after forming his company.[12] Four of those pieces were created in Mexico, which he visited at the invitation of the artist Miguel Covarrubias, then director of dance at the National Institute for the Arts, partly to create a set of dances for a new national modern dance company. Composed relatively rapidly in early 1951, these four works combine the artistic interests of Limón with those of his hosts, many of whom were Mexico's leading intellectual advocates of artistic nationalism.[13] One of his dances drew upon a well-known novel entitled *Los Redes* (The Nets) by the gifted José Revueltas, whose writings have remained little known or appreciated outside of Mexico.[14] A second piece, *Dialogues*, drew upon Mexican history by contrasting the struggles between Hernán Cortés and Montezuma during the Conquest with a corresponding conflict between two prominent nineteenth-century figures, President Benito Juárez and Emperor Maximilian. Two other dances he choreographed while in Mexico drew upon the country's indigenous pre-Conquest history, a favorite theme among artistic nationalists of the time. In Limón's interpretation of Aztec mythology Quetzalcóatl became the god of civilized people battling Tezcatlipoca, depicted as a god of barbaric tribes, in a dance entitled *Los Cuatro Soles* (Four Suns). In their struggles the earth was created and destroyed four times—hence the title.[15] A church in the tiny Mexican provincial town of Santa María Tonantzintla decorated by sixteenth-century Indian artists inspired the last of the dances created in Mexico. With the exception of *Los Redes*, the themes of these dances came from Mexican history and art.

As the Mexican dance historian Margarita Tortajada notes in her essay in this book, three of the four dances Limón created in Mexico seemed unfinished at the time. His host and principal Mexican patron, Miguel Covarrubias, would later describe one of these works as "premature" and another as an "interesting experiment." Despite the disappointment of the dances produced during his stay,[16] Limón memorably exhorted Mexican choreographers to try for greatness, and he encouraged them to find their visions of Mexico from within their artistic creativity, rather than beginning with the popular, politically motivated nationalist interpretations of Mexico's past.

Of the three Mexican-themed dances Limón choreographed for his company in the United States, one, *La Piñata*, is a lighthearted tribute to the mainstay of Mexican American birthday celebrations of his childhood. That dance along with several preliminary compositions from 1951 has vanished from the repertory. Two of Limón's dances on Mexican themes have survived as regular pieces in the repertory, both drawing upon well-known episodes of Mexican history. One historical dance dealt with the ill-fated couple Maximilian and Carlota, who briefly became the monarchs of an independent Mexico only to be ignominiously deposed in 1867. Unfortunately, Limón succumbed to cancer only a few months after this piece debuted, leaving *La Malinche* as the most frequently and widely performed treatment of a Mexican subject during his lifetime.

In *La Malinche* Limón revisited the history of Mexico's Conquest and its most famous female participant and cultural icon in a uniquely vivid dance form. Presented first in the United States, then in Mexico, and subsequently in Russia, Canada, Western Europe, and the Middle East, *La Malinche* remained for decades among the company's most popular presentations overseas. Though its critical reception in those countries remains buried in newspaper archives around the world, members of the company recall the enthusiastic reception given the dance.[17] Having circulated so widely around the globe, Limón's representation of *La Malinche* merits consideration as an artistically important interpretation of a Mexican subject conceived and rendered in the United States.

Another reason for examining *La Malinche* resides in the importance of the actual historical figure as a cultural touchstone for Mexicans and Mexican Americans alike. According to Rosario Castellanos, a prominent Mexican writer, Malinche, along with two others—the seventeenth-century poet Sor Juana Inés de la Cruz and the Virgin of Guadalupe—ranks as the central female character in the contemporary Mexican cultural imagination.[18] Furthermore, as Sonia Hernández writes in this book, the historical figure remains equally well remembered among recent as well as longtime Mexican immigrants to the United States.[19] In that sense Malinche remains a shared female cultural icon bridging the boundary between Mexican and Mexican American culture.

The gender of the title character is noteworthy for yet another reason. Limón often drew upon history and literary classics to inspire his dance,[20] and he might simply have retold the Conquest of Mexico as a battle between Spanish men on the one side and indigenous men on the other. However, he chose to center the dance on the more enigmatic female figure, La Malinche, who stood between the two, perhaps as Limón saw himself standing between Mexico and the United States.[21]

As Cortés's mistress and interpreter, the historical Malinche was present during all of Cortés's encounters with Montezuma and other native leaders. Malinche also spied for Cortés, providing him with crucial military intelligence without which he and his men might not have survived. A woman from a Nahua family, Malinche (who converted to Catholicism) demonstrated unswerving loyalty to the man who led the troops that would eventually raze the capital of the Nahua empire.

Malinche appeared five hundred years ago during a military struggle, but unlike much of history that passes by in a readily forgotten dusty cloud of dates and facts her story was kept alive, albeit primarily in unpublished, native-informed accounts in the decades following the Conquest.[22] Although her tale largely faded from written Spanish accounts of the Conquest, she continued to appear occasionally in colonial painting. The narrative of her story reemerged in Mexico's literary tradition as the eighteenth century neared its close.[23] In the years leading up to independence from Spain in 1821, Mexican intellectuals, as part of a larger effort to distinguish themselves from their Spanish overlords, became increasingly interested in indigenous themes. Reversing the previous neglect of Malinche's role in the Conquest, the late colonial Jesuit historian Francisco Javier Clavijero transformed her into a romantic heroine.[24]

Nevertheless, this Indian woman who sided with the Spaniards presented post-Independence writers with an interesting conundrum—whether to celebrate her indigenous background or condemn her for allying with Cortés.[25] As Sandra Messinger Cypess notes, the first literary appearance of La Malinche cast her as a villain, while another (Cuban) author from the same period envisioned her as romantically involved with Cortés, a tragic victim rather than a villain.[26] The romantic tendency in literature in Mexico, as elsewhere, extended through the end of the nineteenth century, sweeping representations of La Malinche along with it.[27]

Historical literature continued to paint the romantic, heroic portrait of Malinche that Clavijero had popularized. William Prescott, the U.S. historian whose *Conquest of Mexico* (1843) enjoyed tremendous popular success in both the United States and Mexico, depicted her as a grande dame, elegant yet soft-spoken, and even included a suitable fictitious reconciliation with her family of origin. This upper-class family fiction became one of three nineteenth-century versions of the romance.[28]

In the second, spiritual version of the romance, Malinche becomes enamored of the true faith, setting an example to all other natives by renouncing idolatry and embracing Catholicism.[29] Other versions of Malinche as a Catholic heroine have her leading Native Americans to the faith by example. Fernanda Núñez Becerra characterizes this interpretation as Malinche the catechist.[30] A slightly different reading transformed Malinche into Cortés's ethical conscience, a most suitable nineteenth-century woman's role.[31]

This spiritual version of Malinche had also appeared earlier in a different artistic medium, folk dance. Beginning in the late eighteenth century, indigenous dancers from central and southern Mexico regularly depicted the Conquest in dance. While Malinche always appeared to lead her people into Christianity, in separate performances she accomplished that goal differently. In one rendering she did so by allying with Cortés and in another by betraying an idolatrous Montezuma (who, oddly, appears as her husband). In these folk arrangements she chose to side with Cortés out of religious conviction.[32]

More earthly nineteenth-century romantic portraits envisioned Malinche as being swept away by her all-encompassing love for Cortés. In the words of one author, "It was without a doubt extreme passion that inspired her from the first moment."[33] To other writers in the same vein, the romantic passion signified that she could be forgiven for the treason she committed by aiding the Spaniards.[34]

Of the three romances—the upper-class family, the spiritual, and the sexual—the first two faded as the nineteenth century waned, leaving the sexual variant as the prevailing perspective. Several early versions of this romance condemned Malinche for her lascivious conduct in having a relationship with Cortés.[35] The novelist Ireneo Paz stressed a novel dimension of Malinche's sexual relationship with Cortés, the birth of a son whom Cortés acknowledged as his own. Malinche thus bridged the gap between Spaniard and Indian by giving birth to a mixed race (mestizo) child.[36]

The outcome of the sexual romance—a mixture of Spaniard and Indian—began to inspire a new political vision for the nation during the second decade of the twentieth century. The first such works saw the Spaniard becoming submerged in the Indian, then gradually becoming an equal partner with him.[37] The renowned Mexican political writer José Vasconcelos celebrated the mestizo in his widely read book *La raza cósmica* (The Cosmic Race) (1920), a paean to mixed-race peoples in which Spaniards did not appear entirely as villains but were lauded for having brought Catholicism to the country.[38]

Yet not all Mexican writers of the early twentieth century shared this celebratory attitude toward the mestizo as the apparent resolution of the conflict between the Spanish and Indian heritage of modern Mexico. Miguel Ángel Menéndez saw the birth of this offspring as the result of a relationship Malinche did not choose, but one which, as Cortés's slave, she had no option but to enter. As a result, the appearance of the mestizo remained a sorrowful rather than celebratory event.[39]

Focus on the mestizo offspring of the sexual relationship, however, continued to dominate Mexican political and cultural discussions of Malinche through the middle of the twentieth century. As the ethnohistorian and Nahuatl scholar Susan Kellogg notes, sexual relations between Spaniards and Indians ranged from consensual to coercive. Thus a mestizo could as easily have been conceived in love as in violence. At midcentury, Octavio Paz strengthened the critical view espoused earlier by Miguel Ángel Menéndez. Setting aside interpretations of the sexual relationship as consensual or structurally enforced he also declared Cortés's relationship with Malinche to be a form of rape. In his widely read essay "El laberinto de la soledad" (The Labyrinth of Solitude), Cortés's violating of Malinche meant that she and her offspring (and all others of mixed race) were literally screwed.[40]

Shortly before Paz's portrait of Malinche as sexual victim appeared, another opinion about her was gaining popularity and soon became bound up with Paz's. In this perspective, Malinche was not victimized, but actually had chosen an unpopular alliance with the overseas invaders. Beginning in the 1930s, her name became used as an adjective—*malinchista*—to malign individuals who displayed a seemingly irrational admiration of foreigners.[41] In this respect dislike of Malinche stemmed from the perception that she had allied with a foreigner in preference to her own people. Swelling nationalistic, antiforeign sentiment from the 1940s to the 1970s sustained this image of a politically treacherous Malinche.

Limón created his dance in 1949, two years after Paz composed his now-famous essay on La Malinche (and her offspring) as both victim and traitor and amidst prevailing Mexican nationalistic antagonism to a disloyal figure. His own interpretation, however, differed both from Paz's and from the prevailing popular political view in Mexico. In the dance only three characters appear: the Conquistador, Malinche, and El Indio. Bearing a cross in the shape of a sword, the Conqueror defeats El Indio with Malinche at his side. After his defeat, the Indian reproaches Malinche, who, realizing what she has done, weeps and then reunites with the Indian.

Unlike the nineteenth-century romantics, who mentioned but often sidelined her, Limón made Malinche central to the story of Conquest. She remains on stage throughout the entire performance. As Carol Maturo shows in her essay in this book, Limón's interpretation parallels visual portraits of the sixteenth-century indigenous Tlaxcalans, whose stories also portray her as central to the Conquest.

The finale to Limón's dance, however, provides a cryptic resolution to the conflict between Conqueror and Indian by reuniting all three characters, who dance offstage together. This enigmatic conclusion is open to multiple interpretations. Three essays in this book, in fact, offer three divergent interpretations of the ending. One of two dance historians, Shelley Berg, sees Malinche's joining with the Indian as a form of unresolvable cultural hybridity. Carol Maturo sees reconciliation in the visual imagery of Malinche's mestizo costume and the ending a moment of hope. The dance director Sarah Stackhouse, who has frequently staged the dance for various companies, sees the three characters reconcile as performers, linking arms on the way to another performance.

When Limón was invited to Mexico he had already choreographed *La Malinche*, which he performed for Mexican audiences. The dance historian Margarita Tortajada Quiroz notes in her essay in this book that the almost universal praise for Limón's choreographic and performing talent in the land of his birth did not extend wholly to *La Malinche*. Reactions at the time ranged from adulation to dismissal, the music (despite its indigenous inspiration)[42] coming in for the harshest criticism.

Local hostility may have stemmed from Limón's failure to adopt the prevailing Mexican popular view of Malinche as expressed in Paz's essay. Limón's Malinche is no victim; she joins willingly with the Conqueror against the Indian, and no hint of treachery mars their association. Limón's attitude toward the mestizo also fails to follow the nationalistic political agenda of the time. His dance itself alludes to the mestizo political solution only at one dramatic moment, when the Indian disappears beneath Malinche's skirts only to be reborn. The ambiguity of the identity of the individual renewed through this rebirth—either an Indian or a mestizo—suggests a more equivocal resolution to the conflict between Spaniards and Indians, hinting at the potential reawakening of a not entirely defeated indigenous culture after the Conquest.

Since its initial performance (and revision in the 1960s) Limón's composition has continued to be performed. The ongoing appeal of the dance lies first of all in its artistic achievements, many of which are spelled out in this book. But a second reason for the continued attention to the dance derives from the ongoing appeal of the subject matter— Malinche's continuing role as a contested cultural icon.

Different interpretations of her character have continued to unfold since 1950 in literature and in political struggles both in Mexico and the United States. During the 1950s and 1960s, few Mexican writers differed significantly with Paz's position on Malinche. Several theatrical productions returned to the theme of the Conquest but usually foregrounded the relationship between men—Spanish and Indian—(unlike Limón), relegating Malinche to a peripheral role. Other productions presented an updated version of the nineteenth-century romantic construction of the relationship between Malinche and Cortés.[43]

The 1970s saw interpretations of the myth taking a different direction in Mexico: Malinche was rehabilitated from her twenty-year-old status as a traitor and sexual victim. In the hands of Carlos Fuentes, Rosario Castellanos, and other prominent recent Mexican authors, Malinche became the more powerful figure, manipulating Cortés and in the process defending her people.[44] Several of these writers employed satire to establish

Malinche's power.[45] Although Limón's interpretation anticipated this new attention to her strength, his remains a sober, not satirical, piece.

Also during the 1970s, Malinche captured the attention of yet another group of writers, this time in the United States. The first generation of Mexican American women intellectuals turned to the figure of La Malinche in part because the 1930s term *malinchista* (traitor) was being used largely to defame Mexican American women (but not men) who consorted with American partners. Women who challenged (male) political authority or who had any intellectual or other ambition beyond the local community were also smeared with the same label.[46] Seeking to challenge this sexist usage, Chicana feminists revived the image of Malinche as translator between two cultures—in their interpretation, however, she also mediated contending Mexican and American influences instead of just warring Indians and Spaniards.[47]

Like Mexican feminist writers of the same decade, Chicana intellectuals also constructed Malinche as more powerful than she had been depicted previously. To some she also symbolized sexual independence, a rejection of two previously popular images equally: the sexually enslaved nineteenth-century romantic heroine and Paz's mid-twentieth-century rape victim. In Carmen Tafolla's "Yo soy La Malinche," (I am La Malinche) (1978) Malinche alone understands how her mestizo offspring will redefine the future.[48]

In one sense, Limón's Malinche anticipated these writers' belief in the Indian woman's strength. Susan Kellogg finds a similar strength in the historical record. Aztec women exercised real authority and power in their communities.[49] Whereas many Chicana authors and Shelley Berg viewed her as a negotiator (paralleling their own experiences), I see her differently, powerfully using her talents alternately for one side and then the other, seeking but never finding a final moment of hybridity.[50]

As a Mexican-born Mexican American choreographer, Limón introduced these perspectives to modern dance. Unlike early African American performers, who often integrated spirituals and dance steps into their pieces, Limón incorporated into the new dance medium not dance steps or a specific song genre but themes from Mexican art and history. Although his personal early artistic vocation may have inspired his use of Mexican art for scenery and costuming, his choice also reflected the historical artistic traditions of Spain, indigenous America, and the great twentieth-century Mexican mural renaissance.[51] His preference for themes from the past, while likely also personal, additionally reflects the unique way in which historical memories—of the Conquest in particular—continue to feature prominently in both contemporary Mexican and Mexican American cultural imaginations.

While bringing history and artistic traditions to modern dance, Limón also incorporated both a Mexican and Mexican American twentieth-century cultural fascination with a historical female cultural icon.

From grande dame to slave, from national inspiration to rape victim, the image of Malinche has changed greatly since its revival at the end of the eighteenth century. Although Limón's *La Malinche* was choreographed more than half a century ago, its subject seems likely to continue to intrigue observers, as she continues to fascinate and attract many outside of literary and intellectual circles. Her status as a cultural icon in Mexico is likely to continue to evolve in years to come.

Yet she is not just a Mexican symbol, but a Mexican American one as well. In today's Mexican American communities in the border states of California and Texas, the image of Malinche remains complex and full of contradictory points of view, not unlike Limón's. Alternately embraced and rejected, Malinche appeared as heroine and rape victim. As Hernández notes in this book, the name Malinche continues to be widely recognized. Even recent Mexican American immigrants she interviewed, people who had never attended school past third grade in Mexico, knew La Malinche and had an opinion about her.

In Mexico, several of the dancers who had seen or performed with Limón in the early 1950s remain divided over which side of the border his portrait of Malinche originated in. Some of those interviewed for the first time in this book saw his Malinche as the product of an exile from the homeland. One well-known dancer declared that Limón was not unlike many who left Mexico yet "keep their roots and feel part of a culture that supports them, but this becomes a ghost, a childish ghost," and their creations are hybrids, products of a "third culture, valid and valuable, but a non-Mexican one." Yet others interviewed believed his *La Malinche* to be wholly Mexican. The famous Mexican dancer and actress Rocío Sagaón declared that Limón had captured "the core of the Mexican dilemma, of the woman that is caught in between the Spanish and the Indigenous. I have never seen anything so perfect and stylized that goes straight to your heart. One does not need flags or uniforms to say that 'this is Mexican', and José was able to capture it with his North American education on his back." In this respect, Limón's *La Malinche* appears as a different kind of mestizo, one both Mexican and Mexican

American. In the end, the DVD that accompanies this book will allow readers to make up their own minds.

The essays that make up this book will look at the sources from which Limón drew his inspiration, his artistic contributions, and public reaction to his portrayal of the character; finally, they locate his interpretation between the historical and art historical knowledge of Nahua women like Malinche and identify contemporary Mexican American attitudes toward her.

The contributors to the book are a diverse lot. Three are professional dancers (Berg, Harrington Delaney, and Stackhouse), a fourth (Tortajada) is a well-known Mexican dance historian. Two of the dancers (Harrington Delaney and Stackhouse) and a musical conductor (LaMarche) have staged *La Malinche* for performances and draw upon that experience to provide readers with their own understanding of the character. Tortajada uncovered all of the published Mexican reviews of Limón's performances in Mexico City. In addition, she interviewed all the surviving Mexican modern dancers who either saw or performed *La Malinche* with Limón in Mexico in the 1950s. The other three nondance contributors are historians of varying backgrounds. Carol Maturo examined all the images of Malinche in the most famous indigenous pictoral account of the Conquest, the Lienzo de Tlaxcala.[52] Susan Kellogg places Malinche's life in the context of Native women of her class and time. The Mexican American historian Sonia Hernández, whose field is twentieth-century Mexico, interviewed present-day Mexican Americans in the border states to explore their understanding of La Malinche. The results of this collection do not form a single story, but rather a set of ten prisms through which José Limón and his dance can be viewed. It shows not a single Mexican or Mexican American voice, but many, and among those many the choreographic voice of one of the preeminent artists of the twentieth century can be heard.

NOTES

1. The exception is Jose E. Limón, "Greater Mexico, Modernism, and New York: Miguel Covarrubias and José Limón," in Kurt Heinzelman, *The Covarrubias Circle: Nickolas Muray's Collection of Twentieth-Century Mexican Art* (Austin: University of Texas Press, 2004). The author develops an interesting thesis about the artistic ties between Mexican artists in the United States and those in Mexico. Melinda Copel, "José Limón, Modern dance and the State Department's agenda: The Limón company performances in Poland

and Yugoslavia, 1957," *Dancing in the Millennium, Proceedings of the Society of Dance History Scholars, 2000*, 88–94.

2. The African American choreographer Katherine Dunham incorporated Caribbean dance steps while both she and Pearl Primus turned to themes of slavery, sharecropping, and lynching. Alvin Ailey utilized spirituals for two of his most famous pieces. Julia L. Foulkes, *Modern Bodies: Dance and American Modernism from Martha Graham to Alvin Ailey* (Chapel Hill: University of North Carolina Press, 2002), 68–77, 141, 164–68, 183.

3. Two articles on the subject have appeared. Ann Vachon, "Limón in Mexico, Mexico in Limón," in Dunbar, ed., *The Artist Reviewed*, and Lucia da Costa Lima, "Performing Latinidad: Dances and Techniques of José Limón," *Dancing in the Millennium, Proceedings of the Society of Dance History Scholars*, 115–18. Vachon sees Limón's emphasis on weight and breath related to styles of Mexican dance; Costa Lima does not distinguish among the European, Spanish, Mexican, and Native American themes in her discussion.

4. Francisco E. Balderrama and Raymond Rodriguez, *Decade of Betrayal: Mexican Repatriation in the 1930s* (Albuquerque: University of New Mexico Press, 1995). See also George Sanchez, *Becoming Mexican American: Ethnicity, Culture, and Identity in Chicano Los Angeles, 1900–1945* (New York: Oxford University Press, 1993).

5. Daniel Lewis, *The Illustrated Dance Technique of José Limón* (New York: Harper and Row, 1984); June Dunbar, ed. *José Limón: The Artist Reviewed* (Singapore: Harwood Academic Publishers, 2000).

6. Ann Vachon (Producer) and Malachi Roth (Director) *Limón: A Life beyond Words* (New York: Antidote International Films, 2004).

7. Ruth St. Denis and Ted Shawn had earlier composed dances that exoticized and romanticized other cultures. Their outsider's perspective is usually identified as a form of orientalism. For a Latin Americanist perspective on orientalism, see Patricia Seed, "Colonial and Post Colonial Discourses," *Latin American Research Review* 26 (1991): 181-200.

8. José Limón, *José Limón: An Unfinished Memoir*, edited by Lynn Garafola (Hanover, N.H.: University Press of New England [1998]); José Limón, "Rebel and the Bourgeois," in Jean Morrison Brown, ed., *The Vision of Modern Dance in the Words of Its Creators* (Princeton, N.J.: Princeton Book Co., 1979); Barbara Pollack and Charles Humphrey Woodford, *Dance Is a Moment: A Portrait of José Limón in Words and Pictures* (Pennington, N.J.: Princeton Book Co., 1993).

9. Patty Harrington Delaney, "José Limón's La Malinche," in this book.

10. Carol Maturo, "Visual Communication," in this book.

11. "The Music: Interview with David LaMarche," 50, and Sarah Stackhouse, "The Director: Thoughts on Staging José Limón's La Malinche," 154, both in this book. However, Limón did not construct his choreography around the rhythms of traditional Mexican music, as early African American choreographers did around spirituals.

12. Lynn Garafola, "Works Choreographed by José Limón," in *Unfinished Memoir*, 133–149. I counted the two versions of *Redes* as a single performance, and the unfinished and finished "Unsung" as a single piece for a total of fifty-five. His first run at a Mexican theme, *Danzas Mexicanas*, was choreographed before he formed his company.

13. Ironically, the promotion of Indian themes in Mexican art and cultural life has resulted in some native communities abandoning their indigenous identities for national ones. David L. Frye, *Indians into Mexicans: History and Identity in a Mexican Town* (Austin: University of Texas Press, 1996).

14. José Revueltas, *El luto humano* (Editorial México, 1943). When performed for a second time in Mexico the work was retitled *O Grito* (*The Scream*). A recent critique of Revueltas's literary contributions is Philippe Cheron, *El árbol de oro: José Revueltas y el pesimismo ardiente* (Ciudad Juárez, México: Universidad Autónoma de Ciudad Juárez, 2003).

15. The "barbarian" Toltecs associated Quetzalcóatl with civilization. In Nahua cosmogony he intervened in the creation of the Earth, rescuing ancient bones and creating the men and women of the Fifth Sun. Enrique Florescano, "Quetzalcóatl: un mito hecho de mitos," in Florescano, ed., *La sociedad y sus mitos* (1995), 112–118.

16. For Covarrubias, see Tortajada, in this book. Ironically a revised *Los Cuatro Soles* was praised by the New York dance critic Walter Terry when it was revived. Adriana Williams, *Covarrubias*, ed. Doris Ober (Austin: University of Texas Press, 1994), 193.

17. The list of cities includes London, Berlin, Paris, Moscow, Kiev, Leningrad, Valladolid (Spain), São Paulo (Brazil), Quebec (1954), Piraeus (Greece), several Italian cities, Damascus, and Sarajevo. See also Melinda Susan Copel, "The State Department Sponsored Tours of José Limón and the Modern Dance Company, 1954 and 1957: Modern Dance, Diplomacy, and the Cold War" (Ed.D. thesis, Temple University, 2000), and ibid., "José Limón, modern dance and the State Department's agenda: The Limón company performances in Poland and Yugoslavia: 1957," in *Dancing in the Millennium, Proceedings of the Society for Dance History 2000*, 88–94.

18. Rosario Castellanos, *El eterno femenino* (Mexico City: Fondo de Cultura Económica, 1975).

19. Sonia Hernández, "Malinche in Cross-Border Historical Memory," in this book.

20. *The Exiles* relied upon John Milton's *Paradise Lost*, *Antigone* upon Greek tragedy, *Serenata* upon a poem by Federico García Lorca, *And David Wept* upon the biblical story of David and Bathsheba. *Barren Sceptre* returned to Shakespeare, but this time to *Macbeth*.

21. Limón may have picked La Malinche partly because he identified with her role as a translator since he personally saw himself as translating "the tongue of Castile into that of the Anglo Saxon." In this ballet, Limón's central character translates between Spaniards and Indians. Only one dance critic

has seen one of the male figures as central to the dance. Tortajada, in this book. Patty Harrington Delaney discusses the evolution of Limón's relationship to female dancers, in this book.

22. Spanish authorities rarely allowed these accounts to be published at the time they were composed. The Chimalpahin Codex was a pictorial manuscript composed ca. 1541–1542, originally attributed to Fernando Alvarado Tezozomoc under the title *Crónica mexicayotl*. An English translation exists, *Annals of his Time: Don Domingo de San Antón Muñón Chimalpahin Quauhtlehuanitzin*, ed. and trans. James Lockhart, Susan Schroeder, and Doris Namala. (Stanford: Stanford University Press, 2006). The Lienzo de Tlaxcala is another important manuscript—it is described in Carol Maturo's article in this book. Other early authors—either natives themselves or native informants—contributed to unpublished collections of the Conquest, including, most famously, the Florentine Codex. Suárez de Peralta in the *Tratado del descubrimiento de las Indias* (Noticias Históricas de Nueva España) SEP. 1949, 39–42, 119 [1589], Fernando de Alva Ixtlilxóchitl, *Historia de la nación chichimeca* (composed between 1610 and 1640), ed. Germán Vázquez (Madrid: Historia 16, 1985). Diego Durán, *Historia de Tlaxcala* (Mexico City, 1970), 509. For Spanish colonial art, see Jeanette Peterson, "Lengua o diosa? The Early Imaging of La Malinche," in *Chipping Away on Earth: Studies in Prehispanic and Colonial Mexico in Honor of Arthur J. O. Anderson and Charles E. Dibble*, ed. Eloise Quiñones Keber, 187-202 (Lancaster, Calif.: Labyrinthos, 1994).

23. For the few mentions she did receive, see Carmen Wurm, *Doña Marina, La Malinche: Eine historische Figur und ihre literarische Rezeption* (Frankfurt am Maim: Vervuert Verlag, 1996), 51–80, 97. The most prominent mention occurred in Agustín Vetancurt, *Teatro Mexicano [1697–1678]* vol. 1, facsimile edition (Mexico City: Editorial Porrua, 1971).

24. Francisco Javier Clavijero, *Historia antigua de México*, prólogo de Mariano Cuevas (Mexico City: Porrua, 1987), lib VIII, sec. 5. For commentary on this approach, see Fernanda Núñez Becerra, *La Malinche: de la historia al mito* (Mexico City: Instituto Nacional de Antropología e Historia, 1996), 41–45; Wurm, *Doña Marina*, 99.

25. One of the early condemnatory histories is Carlos Maria Bustamante, *Cuadro Histórico de la Revolución Mexicana* 1:251 and 3:71, 164, 352.

26. Sandra Messinger Cypess, *La Malinche in Mexican Literature from History to Myth* (Austin: University of Texas Press, 1991), 44–67.

27. For a parallel tendency in Spanish understandings of La Malinche, see Wurm, *Doña Marina*, 113–120.

28. Clavigero first invented the reconciliation (*Historia antigua de México*, lib VIII, sec. 5). The same theme reappears in Prescott's translator, Joaquín García Icazbalceta (1825–1894), *Opúsculos y biografías* (Mexico City: UNAM 1973), 68–70, and Carlos Pereyra, *Hernán Cortés* (Madrid, 1931). See also Núñez Becerra, *La Malinche*, 101–107.

29. Lucas Alamán, *Disertaciones sobre la historia de la República Megicana, desde la época de la conquista que los Españoles hicieron, a fines del siglo XV y principios del XVI, de las islas y continente americano, hasta la independencia México* (J. M. Lara, 1844–1849), 3 vols.

30. Núñez Becerra, *La Malinche*, 121–126. This tradition continued in a lesser fashion into the middle of the twentieth century. See Felipe González Ruiz, *Doña Marina, la india que amó a Cortés* (Madrid: Ediciones Morata, 1944).

31. Núñez Becerra, *La Malinche*, 144–149, 152–158, 168–173. In the same vein, Manuel Gamio's interpretation in *Forjando Patria* diminishes Malinche's Catholic leadership from an elevated status with Cortés to the fulfillment of a traditional feminine role as moral guardian of the home.

32. The document left by an unknown Dominican is known as the Códice Gracida. Bonfiglioli, "Visiones prohispanistas y proindigenistas de la conquista de México," 145–165, esp. 146–149. Helena Alberú de Villava, *Malintzin y el señor Malinche* (Mexico City: Edamex, 1995), Wurm, *Doña Marina*, 100–110.

33. Laurena Wright de Kleinhans, "Caonianal, Tenepal or Malinal," in *Mujeres notables mexicanas*, 17. See also Núñez Becerra, *La Malinche*, 58–64, 112–118, 151. The folklorist Max Harris, using a different bibliography, arrives at similar conclusions. "Moctezuma's Daughter: The Role of La Malinche in Mesoamerican Dance," *Journal of American Folklore* 109, no. 432 (Spring 1996): 149–177. He mentions a possible earlier association, 152.

34. Efren Rebolledo, *El águila que cae* (1916), in *Obras completas*, introd. edición y bibliografía por Luis Mario Schneider (Mexico City: Instituto Nacional de Bellas Artes, Departamento de Literatura [1968]).

35. Alfonso Toro, *Compendio de historia de México escrita para uso de las escuelas preparatorias de la república* (Mexico City: Sociedad de Edición y Librería Franco-Americana, 1926). It appeared in its eighteenth edition in 1966. The charge of lasciviousness had appeared earlier in a series of plays presented in Puebla between 1826 and 1829. Cristina González Hernández, *Doña Marina (La Malinche) y la formación de la identidad mexicana* ([Madrid]: Encuentro, c. 2002), 109.

36. Cypess, *La Malinche in Mexican Literature*, 68–90.

37. Andrés Molina Enríquez, *Los grandes problemas nacionales* (Mexico City: Imprenta de A. Carranza e hijos, 1909). Manuel Gamio, *Forjando Patria* in 1916 (reprint 1982), 66–183; Justo Sierra considered the mestizo equally Spanish and Indian, *Historia de México: la conquista* (Madrid, s.n. 1917), 117.

38. José Vasconcelos, *La raza cósmica: misión de la raza iberoamericana* (Paris: Agencia Mundial de Librería [1920?]). Margo Glantz adopts this perspective in *La Malinche, sus padres y sus hijos*, 7. Gloria Anzaldúa reinterprets Vasconcelos (but stays within his paradigm) in *Borderlands/La Frontera: The New Mestiza* (San Francisco: Aunt Lute Books, 1987), 77–91. For a critical perspective, see Alan Knight, "Racism, Revolution, and Indigenismo: Mex-

ico, 1910–1940," in *The Idea of Race*, ed. Richard Graham (Austin: University of Texas Press, 1990).

39. *Malintzin en un fuste, seis rostros, y una sola mascara* (Mexico 1964), 10–11, 19–20. Salvador Novo, *Cuauhtémoc, pieza en un acto* (Mexico City, 1962). This perspective was foreshadowed by Alfredo Chavero, *Historia antigua de la conquista*, vol. 1 of *México a través de los siglos*, Vicente Riva Palacio, ed., 4 vols. Núñez Becerra, *La Malinche*, 164–167.

40. Octavio Paz, *El laberinto de la soledad* (Mexico City: [Cuadernos Americanos] 1950 [c. 1947]).

41. Carlos Monsiváis, "La Malinche y el primer mundo," in *La Malinche, sus padres y sus hijos*, ed. Margo Glantz (Mexico City: UNAM, 1994), 139–147, esp. 145. The best-known example of this point of view is Carlos Fuentes, *Todos los gatos son pardos* (Mexico City: Siglo Veintiuno Editores [1970]). The idea of Malinche as traitor appeared in two works in the previous century, Carlos Maria Bustameante, *Cuadro Histórico*, and Alfredo Chavero, *Xochitl: drama en tres actos y en verso*, 3d ed. (Mexico City: G. A. Esteva, 1878), but their viewpoints had failed to become widely held.

42. For the indigenous origin of the components of the music, see my editorial remarks in "Interview with David LaMarche," in this book.

43. Cypess, *La Malinche in Mexican Literature*, 98–116. González Hernández maintains that Gorostiza and Fuentes continue the patriarchal versions of Malinche, *Identidad*, 164.

44. Ibid., 119–137. Castellanos, *El eterno femenino*.

45. González Hernández considers that both Castellanos's book and Sabina Berman's *El águila o sol* powerfully critique the patriarchal dimensions of earlier versions of Malinche. Jean Franco also characterizes the Mexican narrative of Malinche as sexist in *Plotting Women* (New York: Columbia University Press, 1989), 131.

46. Deliah Anne Storm, "Retextualized Transculturations: The Emergence of La Malinche as Figure in Chicana Literature" (Ph.D. diss., University of Illinois at Urbana-Champaign, 1994), 65, 76, 95, 138. Naomi Helena Quiñonez, "Hijas de la Malinche: The development of social agency among Mexican American women and the emergence of first wave Chicana cultural production" (Ph.D. diss., Claremont Graduate School, 1997), 189–190, 308. For the social roots of this movement, see Viki Ruiz, "'Star-Struck' Acculturation, Adolescence, and Mexican American Women, 1920–1950," in *Building With Our Hands: New Directions in Chicana Studies*, ed. Adela de la Torre and Beatríz M. Pesquera (Berkeley: University of California Press, 1993).

47. Cypess, *La Malinche in Mexican Literature*, 142–152; Norma Alarcon, "Traddutora, Traditora: A Paradigmatic Figure of Chicana Feminism," *Cultural Critique* 13 (1989): 77–87; Storm, "Retextualized Transculturations," 88; Quiñonez, "Hijas de la Malinche," 294–297, 303; Adelaida R. Del Castillo,

"Malintzin Tenépal: a preliminary look into a new perspective," in Rosaura Sánchez and Rosa Martínez Cruz, eds., *Essays on La Mujer,* 124–149; Tey Diana Rebolledo, *Women Singing in the Snow: A Cultural Analysis of Chicana Literature* (1995), 64–76, 125–127. Rebolledo and Eliana S. Rivero, eds., *Infinite Divisions: An Anthology of Chicana Literature* (Tucson: University of Arizona Press), chap. 5.

48. Carmen Tafolla, "Yo soy La Malinche"; Rebolledo and Rivero, *Infinite Divisions.* Sentiments similar to those of Rosario Castellanos appear in Norma Quiñonez, "Trilogy," Storm, "Retextualized Transculturations," 99–100, 108, 112. For some of the other ways in which Chicana writers have turned Malinche into an active figure, including turning apparent submissiveness into strength, see Mary Louise Pratt, "'Yo Soy La Malinche': Chicana Writers and the Poetics of Ethnonationalism," *Callaloo* 16, no. 4 (1993): 859–873, and Cypess, *La Malinche in Mexican Literature,* 138–152.

49. Mexican modern dancers also perceived Malinche's strength. Tortajada, in this book. Limón's use of a female character is unusual. Pratt, "Ethnonationalism," 870. José E. Limón also noted *La Malinche*'s closeness to modern Chicana perspectives, only in their criticism of her portrayal as a traitor. *Greater Mexico,* 92.

50. Limón, *Unfinished,* 8–9.

51. Carlos Pellicer, *Mural Painting of the Mexican Revolution,* 2d ed. (Mexico City: Fondo Editorial de la Plástica Mexicana, 1985), Jean Charlot, *The Mexican Mural Renaissance, 1920–1925* (New Haven: Yale University Press, 1963).

52. Carol L. Maturo, "Malinche and Cortés, 1519–1521: An Iconographic Study" (Ph.D. diss., University of Connecticut, 1994).

1. LA MALINCHE

The Inspiration for the Dance

Shelley C. Berg

The artist; disciple, abundant, multiple, restless.
The true artist, capable, practicing, skillful,
Maintains dialogue with his heart, meets things with his mind.
The true artist draws out all from his heart.[1]

As a choreographer, José Limón was often most eloquent in creating compact dance-dramas with archetypal, mythic, or literary characters: *The Moor's Pavane*, *The Exiles*, *The Emperor Jones*, and *La Malinche*. None is more powerful than the latter, the ballet created at the very start of Limon's career, reconciling his artistic ambitions with his Mexican American heritage.

Limón was born in 1908 in Culiacán, a city in the northern Mexican state of Sinaloa. His father, Florencio, enjoyed local prestige as the conductor and director of the State Academy of Music.[2] His mother, Francisca, came from a moderately well-off bourgeois family. Although his parents came from the same social class, their ethnic backgrounds differed, reflecting the dual identity he would perpetually struggle to reconcile: his European (Spanish and French) father and his mother with "a dash of Indian blood." In respectable provincial Mexican society of the early 1900s, Limón notes, it was not considered "quite nice" to be "tainted with the blood of the wild tribes of the mountains or deserts, the peons enslaved in the gigantic *haciendas* or *les plebes*, the degraded or poverty-stricken rabble of the cities."[3] Hence his mother's family did their best to disregard their Native American ancestry.

The violence of the Mexican Revolution of 1910 affected Limón personally. In his abbreviated autobiography, *An Unfinished Life*, Limón described how as an eight-year-old child he witnessed the dramatic death of his young uncle, Manuel, shot in the head at the beginning of the battle of Cananea during what had started as a peaceful family breakfast.[4]

Even his childhood games reflected the military violence around him. He and his friends would collect and trade spent cartridges from the ongoing street battles to reenact the shooting as pretend *federales*, or government troops, and revolutionaries. As a choreographer, he would transform these memories and images into *Danzas Mexicanas* (1939).

Despite the revolution raging around him, young Limón was able to observe ballroom dances, concerts, dramas, and *zarzuelas* because of his father's position as director of the Academia de Música. Years later, he could recall the "electrifying pound of castanets, the magnetic intricacy of the steps and figurations, the verve of the *taconeado* [heel tapping]" of the "glittering" Spanish dancers, as well as the elegant tango of a ballroom dance team.[5] The young Limón was also enthralled with local bullfights, which he would later describe as the "most Spanish of dances."[6]

With musical jobs increasingly scarce and his own position in jeopardy, Florencio Limón moved his family from Mexico to the United States, eventually settling in Los Angeles. The young Limón's skills in painting and sketching became very apparent even while he was still attending the schools of Los Angeles, and this interest prompted him to move to New York City to pursue a career in painting following the death of his beloved mother.

Not long after arriving in New York, however, Limón saw a performance by the German modern dancer Harald Kreutzberg that changed his life's ambitions. He no longer wished to paint, he wanted to dance. Referred by two friends of Charles Weidman's, Limón began to study at the Humphrey/Weidman studio, where he proved himself an apt and fervently committed pupil. Soon he joined the Humphrey-Weidman Dance Company and rapidly rose within its ranks. Limón performed many of the seminal works in the repertory, including Humphrey's *The Shakers* (1931), *New Dance* (1935), and *With My Red Fires* (1936).

Beginning in 1930, Limón began to create small-scale dances of his own, initially solos, duets, or trios with the Humphrey-Weidman dancers Eleanor King and Ernestine Henoch (later Stodelle). These early dances appear to have emphasized formal elements of dance composition. Seven years later Limón created his first full-length piece, the *Danza de la Muerte* (Dance of Death), inspired by the Republican cause during the Spanish Civil War.

Limón was certainly not the only artist who supported the Republicans in Spain. As the dance historian Ellen Graff notes, the Spanish Civil War "triggered an avalanche of artistic opposition to fascism."[7] Limón appeared in concerts sponsored by the leftist New Dance League in 1935 (formerly the Workers Dance League, whose slogan was "Dance Is a Weapon in the Revolutionary Class Struggle"). In 1936 he shared programs with William Matons and his Experimental Dance Group. Matons choreographed a May Day pageant that depicted "memorable scenes from Labor history," including the trial of Sacco and Vanzetti, thus garnering praise from the leftist *Daily Worker.*[8]

In his choreographic notebooks, Limón sketched the Prologue to the Dance of Death as "the heroism of dying for a cause," while personifying the "black trinity" of Hitler's Germany, Mussolini's Italy, and Franco's Spain through three dance sequences, one for each dictator. Hitler's "Prussianism" would appear "loud-cheap, ruthless, comical" even "pompous and neurotic" and would feature a speedy and precise military step. Limón's Mussolini, a "resurrected Imperial Caesar," would perform a "violent, pompous recitative." Franco, who embodied the "unspeakable elegance and urbanity of the degenerate overlord," would dance in a manner at once "majestic," yet also "shallow and utterly cruel."[9] In condensing the evils of fascism into three characters, Limón deftly employed illustrative motifs and themes. He would further refine the technique of compressing political principles into a single character in *La Malinche.*

Leftist movements in the 1930s sometimes associated themselves with calls for global revolution, but many often advocated nationalist causes instead. As Graff observes, at the height of the antiforeign sentiments of the 1930s, the Communist Party supported artists who were developing new American identities without effacing their ethnic roots or shunning their pasts. The leading figures of the modern dance movement, Martha Graham and Doris Humphrey, were self-evidently American, creating dances for a country that "encompassed all races and creeds in its past, in its present and in the future." Graff points out, however, that leftist dancers struggled "to join the American dream, to assimilate what were basically urban, foreign and radical visions into American historical myths and realities."[10] Limón, already feeling a conflict between his Mexican and Spanish heritage, saw his choreography as a way to embed his ethnicity within the evolving aesthetic of American modern dance.

Other factors may have prompted Limón's initial incorporation of Mexican themes in his choreography. Interest in Mexican art and artists surged in New York in the early 1930s. In October 1931, the Metropolitan Museum of Art hosted a major exhibition of Mexican art, an event that was "widely and most favorably noticed in the press"; it drew twenty-five thousand visitors.[11] Including both early and contemporary examples of fine and decorative arts, the exhibition proposed to illustrate "the origin and development of Mexican civilization from the Conquest to the present."[12]

At the same time, two prominent Mexican artists were invited to create murals in New York. In 1931, the prominent Mexican artist José Clemente Orozco completed a group of murals for the recently created New School of Social Research. Nelson Rockefeller commissioned another highly visible left-wing Mexican painter, Diego Rivera, to decorate his new office building, Rockefeller Center. Rivera's mural was titled "Man at the Crossroads Looking with Hope and High Vision to the Choosing of a New and Better Future." When Rivera included the face of Lenin in his mural, giving it a prominent place, Rockefeller dismissed the artist and ordered the face painted over. The controversy surrounding Rivera's mural spilled over into Orozco's activities.

In 1932 Dartmouth College in New Hampshire invited Orozco to create a series of frescoes to be entitled "The Epic of Culture in the New World." The commission of these frescoes ignited a firestorm of controversy. The *New York Times* reported that Dartmouth had "incurred the displeasure" of the National Commission to Advance American Art by employing a Mexican rather than an American artist.[13] So unhappy was the commission with the choice of Orozco that they established an official "regret list," with Dartmouth conspicuously at its head.[14] Despite this rather genteel imbroglio, Orozco completed the frescoes, which the *New York Times* art critic Edward Jewell described as "very possibly the finest mural accomplishment to date, from any hand, in the United States."[15]

In the summer of 1935, Limón, the once-aspiring painter, was dancing at Bennington College, just over one hundred miles from Dartmouth. His choreography notebooks reveal that while he was at Bennington that year he was thinking about dance compositions based on the Mexican Indian. Given the controversy, Limón may have made an effort to see the Orozco murals. The possible confluence of Orozco's artistic epic with Limón's early musings on Mexican thematic ideas—and his vision of the conquistador in his first Mexican historical dance—seems a tantalizing possibility.

Orozco's frescoes at Dartmouth depict the Mexican myth of Quetzalcóatl, a name that signifies the feathered or plumed serpent. An ancient Toltec god of knowledge and the arts, and the priest-king of the Toltecs whose rule began around 980, also bore the name Quetzalcóatl.[16] Orozco painted the second Quetzalcóatl, also identified as Topiltzin-Quetzalcóatl, as a "white-robed, blue-eyed sage, who first rouses the Indians from their mental and moral sleep."[17]

A second mural panel of Orozco's that may have influenced how Limón depicts Cortés, "in armor and sword in hand, standing amid a heap of slain bodies and the rubble of the destroyed Indian civilization."[18] Yet at the same time, the panel portrays Cortés as a "handsome bearded conqueror" surveying the scene "with a calm, intelligent gaze."[19] Jewell, calling the frescoes "splendid," lyrically described them in terms of musical composition. The murals have, he declared, a "breathtaking splendor of orchestration . . . as actually as a piece of music constructed of mighty chords, crescendos, diminuendos, the phrases, the movements, drawn into an often telling dramatic coherence by means of mural lines that, in its own modern fashion, convincingly bind together the various themes."[20]

Another four years would pass after his summer at Bennington, however, before Limón choreographed his first Mexican-based historical dance. *Danzas Mexicanas* comprised a suite of five solos based on symbolic figures in Mexican history: Indio, Conquistador, Peón, Caballero, and Revolucionario (see chapter 5 in this book). The choreographer describes El Indio as "a figure from Mayan and Aztec sculpture—hieratic, half-man, half-pyramid . . . existing in and because of a compelling rhythm, primitive yet complex . . . a canticle to Quetzalcóatl." The more complexly depicted Conquistador was "the image of Hernán Cortés. Despite his apocalyptic apparition, bringing doom and destruction, Cortés also wielded the double-edged symbol of redemption and death."[21]

In his memoirs, the choreographer reveals his ambivalence about his Mexican/Spanish heritage. He designs his dialectic around the central figure of El Conquistador (Hernán Cortés), who represents "the destroyer and despoiler of ancient native cultures" and Spain's three hundred years of "subjection, the enslavement and oppression of indigenous populations . . . and exploitation."[22] Nonetheless, Limón argues, Spain is also the mother country, responsible for bringing to Mexico the Catholic religion and "compassionate missionaries who consoled, healed and educated," all in the wake of "Don Hernán Córtez, gallant and honorable Christian knight, bringer of enlightenment to the benighted."[23] Over the decades, in his development as an artist, Limón would continue to wrestle with these contradictory perspectives of Spain's legacy in Mexico in general, and the Iberian inheritance and its role in his life and work in particular.

A decade after *Danzás Mexicanas*, Limón once again prepared to mine his associations with what he termed the "confrontation of the blood and the culture of the European and the American Indian," the dysphoric union that resulted in "centuries of unremitting conflict."[24] *La Malinche*, composed in 1949, was one of the first ballets the choreographer created for his company. In the dance Limón evokes the Conquest of Mexico through three characters: the conquistador Hernán Cortés, the Indian woman known as La Malinche, and the "disenfranchised" Indio.[25]

As the ballet begins, the three performers who enact the roles of El Conquistador, La Malinche, and El Indio enter the stage as a group of traveling players.[26] They first circle the performance space, both limiting and inscribing the circumference of their metaphorical world. Here the three are in every sense two-dimensional; they move forward like mechanical dolls or sideways as though their forms are flattened along the proscenium, insistently vertical, always moving their bodies in a single piece. Each character then performs a brief solo of introduction, establishing movement motifs used throughout the ballet. The solos allow each dancer to be, in a sense, reconstituted as a three-dimensional persona through the character's individual steps and gestures.

In the duet between La Malinche and El Conquistador that follows, Limón effectively conveys his conception of the arc of the Conquest: the encounter, ineffective struggle, and ultimate capitulation of the Aztec people. His use of signs and symbols, both in bodily forms and as artifacts, is especially potent. As the section begins, La Malinche runs softly across the stage to kneel and offer a flower to El Conquistador, who stands resolute, his sword staked in the ground before him, like a cross. The blossom serves as an emblem of Mexico as well as of La Malinche's innocence and femininity and symbolically suggests the idea of the indigenous Amerindian culture as a virginal civilization, as yet unspoiled by European incursions. Another meaning of the flower lies in Aztec history. At the time of the Conquest, the Tlaxcalan state was at war with the Aztecs in a series of battles known as the Flower Wars, which have been described as "ritualized war games in which both groups engaged in military battles as a means of providing the sacrificial victims needed to propitiate their gods."[27]

In Limón's duet, El Conquistador accepts the flower, circles his leg over La Malinche to straddle her, and places the sword he carries under her shoulders. The dancers are in profile, and La Malinche's arms are gently open as if in submission, the frame of her body matching the design of a cross. It is understood that the fruit of this union will be the half-caste, or *mestizo*, and that the fate of the Mexican people is often linked with La Malinche's association with Cortés. The historical destiny of the "sons of La Malinche" literally becomes her cross to bear.

The duet between El Conquistador and La Malinche exemplifies not only Limón's creative and complex imagery, but also the choreographer's instinctive understanding of the intricate relationships between the conqueror and the conquered. During Cortés's campaign, La Malinche became first his mistress and later a convert to Catholicism. For virtually everyone in the epic of the Conquest, "the site of the strategic symbolic oscillation between self and other is the body of this woman."[28]

The literary historian Sandra Cypess, in her consideration of the portrayal of La Malinche in Mexican literature, notes that several nineteenth-century narratives use the Indian woman as a metaphor for land and her sexual possession by Cortés as an allegory of his military and political Conquests.[29] The literary historian Stephen Greenblatt provides us with a metonymic analogy taken from a contemporaneous text entitled *The Conquest of New Spain*, a firsthand account of Cortés's campaign written by Bernal Díaz del Castillo. The greatest scene of wonder in the book, Greenblatt writes, "takes place on the straight and level causeway leading into the city in the immobilized moment before the Spanish embark on the path of penetration."[30] "I know very well," wrote Cortés, "that what I shall say . . . will appear so wonderful that it will hardly seem credible."[31] So might an ardent lover describe the moment of the *coup de foudre*. In the terminology of a Conquest, El Conquistador goes on to recount the glories of Tenochtitlán as a man might catalogue the attributes of a beautiful woman. Indeed, both the combative and passionate acts of possession have something of the same trajectory, sharing careful planning, strategic violence, submission, and the eventual shedding of blood.

As this duet in the dance continues, El Conquistador's sword supports La Malinche as both move in concert. He turns her so that the couple faces the audience, La Malinche still arching back, away from her aggressor. She is here literally both below and beneath him, but El Conquistador gently brings her to standing, facing him, and moves his sword to his left hand. La Malinche again arcs back, but now El Conquistador, giving the impression of rapprochement, gently cradles her. This movement is followed by a powerfully symbolic moment as La Malinche faces her conqueror, takes hold of the sword, and, kneeling and arching back once more, plunges it toward the earth. The placement of the sword between La Malinche and El Conquistador, between male and female, between the centers of their bodies, between two cultures, between heaven and earth, makes the weapon seem sword, stake, arrow, cross, and phallic sign all at once.

The resonance in this action for Limón might well have been acute. In Mexican culture, La Malinche had historically been associated with the image of La Chingada, the passive female who is seduced and vio-lated by the aggressive male. The Mexican poet Octavio Paz, in his es-say "The Sons of La Malinche" (1949), states that in Mexico the verb "chingar" is often associated with breaking or ripping open, and when it alludes to the sexual act, "violation or deception gives it a particu-lar shading."[32] He terms it a "masculine" verb, "active, cruel; it stings, wounds, gashes, stains." For Paz, the "chingón" is the "macho," the male who "rips open the chingada, who is pure passivity."[33] In both Limón's *La Malinche* and Paz's designation, the macho is personified by El Con-quistador, and, by association, the symbol of the violation perpetrated by the Conquest is La Malinche and her sons, the mestizo people.

Dance critics and historians often remark upon Limón's mastery of spatial patterns and motif designs, the geometry and imagery of his dances. Certainly it is a legacy from his mentor, Doris Humphrey, but it also derives from his knowledge of painting and sculpture. In the case of *La Malinche*, the richness of the choreography can also facilitate a metonymic reading of the dance text. Limón symbolically recasts the chronicle of Cortés in Mexico as his personal journey of self-discovery.

The oscillation of identification and transformation characterizes the entire ballet. The choreographer builds and manipulates movement themes and motifs, sharing them among the dancers. It is equally im-portant to the dramatic integrity of the ballet that each character lit-erally takes possession of these steps and images. Each dancer must appropriate, personalize, and vividly dramatize each element, for it is the accumulation and convergence of these signs that give the dance its narrative power.

Cortés conquered Mexico with the sword, but he also conquered with the cross. His military campaign accomplished only one goal of the Spanish enterprise of Conquest. The warriors from Castile addition-ally wanted to convert the Indians to the Holy Catholic faith. In Bernal Díaz's account, Cortés himself proselytizes, "preaching the immediate substitution of the Christian cult of sacrifice" for the Indians' form of worship.[34] Díaz reports that in Cozumel Cortés "spoke to [the Indians] about good and holy things" and gave them a cross, "which would al-ways aid them and save their souls."[35] In his zeal, the conquistador had the native idols smashed and trampled, setting the image of the Virgin and a cross in their place. There was no mimetic circulation here, no gradual process of identification and transformation, only the oblitera-tion of cultural symbols and the opening of an abyss of fear, anger, and mistrust.

By the conclusion of the dramatic duet, La Malinche has affixed her flower to El Conquistador's sword, their fates now conjoined. Through his duet with La Malinche, El Conquistador has performed a very literal "act of possession" to effect the Conquest, sexually, personally, and politically. In her transformation to Doña Marina, La Malinche dons a heavy skirt, onerous symbol of European dominion, and holds a scarf, which will come to represent the surrender of her body and of her people and finally the ineluctable ties of Spain and Mexico. Together with El Conquistador, she performs a rigid, arid, and stately pavane-like dance. With her body held taut and upright, La Malinche has assumed the posture and deportment of her Spanish conqueror.

The brief duet here is a symbolic and practical act of mimesis. If mimesis is the deliberate imitation of the behavior of one group of people by another, then Limón uses the pavane as a powerful gesture toward the process of cultural assimilation, and it is most appropriate for the choreographer's script that La Malinche's ultimate act of submission comes not in the physical act of love, but in the performance of a Spanish court dance.

As the duet concludes, Limón gives El Conquistador a macho dance of triumph. With his sword he first traces a circle around himself and La Malinche and then travels the circumference of the stage; the new world has been conquered for Spain, and he stands invincible at the center, with the spoils of his victory. The choreographer here establishes the simple but effective motif of a press walk for El Conquistador, as, holding the sword/cross directly before him, he thrusts one hip and shoulder forward as he advances directly downstage. His body is rigidly erect and monolithic, the figure of an implacable adversary armed for battle, for, it is "destruction that gives the Spanish *possession* of the empire" of the Aztecs.[36]

Having represented the arc of the La Malinche/Cortés relationship in the opening duet, Limón chooses El Indio to point a dramatically accusatory finger at La Malinche. In response, she dances an elegiac "Lament," still garbed in the heavy overskirt she wore to perform the pavane with Cortés. La Malinche assumes the same walking motif as that assigned to El Conquistador, but the movement here assumes a different aspect. Pressing one hand to her head, La Malinche walks haltingly, the overcurve of her back seemingly bent under the weight of her sorrow. The handkerchief she holds first hangs limply from one hand, allowing her tears to flow along its length and thus back into the soil of her native land.[37] Then, straightening her back, La Malinche pulls the handkerchief taut between her hands, the motion of her walk now more imperative as her body twists in a hieratic, two-dimensional design. At the close of the Lament, in a poignant and unexpected moment, Limón contrasts two vivid and startling images: first La Malinche literally covers the body of El Indio with her voluminous skirt and "gives birth" as he is forcibly expelled from this womb of his mother/whore. To reinforce the impact of this double vision of La Malinche for the observer, she later cradles El Indio in her arms, their bodies configuring a design reminiscent of a pietà.[38] Finally, El Indio pushes La Malinche into her upstage corner where she undergoes yet another transformation; she discards her overskirt and drops her handkerchief. The drama of Conquest has been played out, and El Indio claims center stage.

In this ballet, El Indio represents Mexico as well as the choreographer. Limón created the character of El Indio for himself, and the solo has the majestic sweep and raw power associated with his most dynamic performances. The dance is characterized by El Indio's execution of vigorous, carving shapes, precarious balances in flat, two-dimensional attitudes, and large beating and swooping arm designs and motifs—an entire dance of opposing designs and images. His movements reflect images of the Plumed Serpent, Quetzalcóatl, of Aztec mythology and the valiant Eagle Knight often represented in Aztec sculpture.[39] El Indio's multivalent symbol, too, is a cross, contextualized and amplified by the choreographic design; the sign of the hybrid, the mongrel, the Other. His cross is Saint Andrew's "X," a configuration that also replicates the design of the cartridge belts crisscrossed over the chests of the Mexican *revolucionarios* Limón remembered from his youth.[40]

For Limón, El Indio's emblem is no crafted artifact imposed by imperial force or ecclesiastical doctrine. It is unique, personal, of the body, forged in flesh and blood by the conflict and sacrifice of his ancestors. As if to emphasize the trajectory of the struggle of his people, Limón gives El Indio another configuration of El Conquistador's press walk; El Indio, however, performs it on his knees, with his hands clasped tightly behind his back. From subjugated and conquered infidel, El Indio becomes transformed into the Plumed Serpent, with his arms beating like wings. He then becomes the heroic mestizo warrior, his alliance to the soil reinforced when he drops to his knees and gives the ground an affirmative, resounding slap, arms crossed before him like a primitive symbolic device.

Limón used rhythm and sound as choreographic strategies in the last section of the ballet. In the 1939 *Danzas Mexicanas*, he had identified El

Indio as "existing in and because of a compelling rhythm."[41] Here, to enhance the impact of El Indio's dramatic alliance with La Malinche, the choreographer employs clapping, body percussion, and intricate *zapateado*, or foot tapping. As it is El Indio who first denounces and then rehabilitates La Malinche, it is he who sets the patterns for their call and response duet. Dancing together, their "voices" are translated as rhythm, a complex and subtle secret language that they transform into power.[42] They vanquish the deceitful Conquistador, here truly a victory of art over history. The final image, before the three players leave the stage, is that of La Malinche and El Indio together center stage, each pulling away from the other; between their two bodies, their joined hands hold the flower representing Mexico. Limón, it would seem, has heeded Paz's caveat; the writer insists that the Mexican who breaks his ties with the past and renounces his origins is sentenced to a life of isolation and solitude.

Paz, whose essay on La Malinche appeared in print in English the year that Limón choreographed *La Malinche*, also saw the resonance of the idea of betweenness in the oscillation of the identity of the mestizo, but in a more philosophical sense. In his foreword to the historian Jacques Lafaye's study *Quetzalcóatl and Guadalupe: The Formation of the Mexican National Consciousness 1531–1813*, Paz observes that the mestizo is neither Spanish nor Indian, nor is he a European who wants to put down roots in American soil: "He is a product of that soil, he is a new man." He achieves a kind of religious and historical syncretism "in an existential and concrete form." Paz concludes his foreword with this observation: "If it is no longer metaphysics but history that defines man, then we must put at the center of our meditations, in place of the key word *be*, the key word *between*. Man between heaven and earth, between water and fire at the center of time between the past and the future; between his myths and his acts."[43]

The Conquest of Mexico places its historical trajectory in the interstices between the complex grandeur of Aztec civilization and the creation of a new, blended culture, that of the mestizo. It is no surprise, then, that Limón, as an embodiment of bloodlines from Europe and the New World, would use the legend of discovery, Conquest, and transformation that is at the heart of the story of La Malinche as inspiration for the symbol of his new identity, that of leader/choreographer/creator of his own dance company. In *La Malinche* we have evidence that Limón did indeed come to terms with his European and mestizo heritage, and that, as Ann Vachon notes, all three roles in *La Malinche* embody aspects of the choreographer himself:[44] the macho power and imperiousness of El Conquistador, the Indian woman La Malinche, forever identified with the love/hate relationship between Spain and Mexico, and El Indio, symbol of a new culture and a new world.

The last two figures in this dance-drama, La Malinche and El Indio, are the most fully and powerfully realized. Limón renders a sympathetic portrait of La Malinche; in history she is a shadowy figure associated with passion and treachery, but here she is the quintessence of sad tales of seduction and betrayal. Unusually for a Mexican of his generation, Limón instinctively understood that La Malinche "serves not only as the supreme instance of the go-between in the New World, but as an emblem of the vast process of cultural translation that discovery initiated."[45] The choreographer declared that he himself played the perpetual role of the translator or conciliator, but in his ballet La Malinche becomes, through her partnership with El Indio, a positive force for the empowerment of the *indigenista*, a triumphant voice in the creation of the Mexican people.[46] But it is Limón's El Indio who finally is at the center of the drama. It is he who is the prophet, he who becomes the driving force in the reclamation of his heritage and resurgence of his people, a dynamic activist, moving from the margins of history through negotiations of the in-between to claim his cultural inheritance as the true and rightful son of La Malinche.

In his memoirs, Limón declared that he had found a harmonious resolution of these diverse streams of his heritage, even an acceptance and understanding. But he nonetheless recognized that he would always remain a translator, even a conciliator. It would be his perpetual task, Limón averred, to "reconcile many disparate and contradictory cultural habits and ways of living, and to resolve hostilities within and around me."[47] While the historical role of the artist as translator is well established and familiar, Limón's recognition of his European/Mexican heritage and its relationship to his artistic and creative life resonates, as we have seen, with Greenblatt's meditations on the Age of Discovery. Greenblatt concludes his study with a consideration of the role of Doña Marina, more widely known as La Malinche, and her importance to Cortés in his strategy of Conquest in Mexico. Indeed, as Greenblatt notes, "individuals and cultures tend to have fantastically powerful assimilative mechanisms that work like enzymes to change the ideological composition of foreign bodies. These bodies do not disappear altogether, but are drawn into the in between, the zone of intersection in which all culturally determinate significations are called into question by an unresolved and unresolvable hybridity."[48]

NOTES

1. Nahuatl text quoted by Benjamin Keen, *The Aztec Image in Western Thought* (New Brunswick: Rutgers University Press, 1971), 23.
2. José Limón, *An Unfinished Memoir*, ed. Lynn Garafola, with an introduction by Deborah Jowitt; foreword by Carla Maxwell and afterword by Norton Owen (Hanover: Wesleyan University Press, University Press of New England, 1999), 1.
3. Ibid., 2. [The battle was not Cananea but Mauricio Obregón's capture of Culiacán, in November 1913. Ed.]
4. Ibid., 3.
5. Ibid., 4–5.
6. When the José Limón Company made its New York debut in January 1947, Limón performed a searingly dramatic work created for him by Doris Humphrey, *Lament for Ignácio Sanchez Mejías*. The dance took both its title and its text from a poem by Federico García Lorca. The dance critic Margaret Lloyd described Limón's performance: "By his own energy of spirit and skill of execution he created drama without rhetoric in a dance of Spain that contained no formal Spanish dance; a dance about a bullfighter that exhibited no *verónicas* or other feats of the bullring. By modern movement alone, by some movements that had never been done on the stage before, he communicated the ambience of Spain, the emotions of the dying *espada*; he transmuted the outer into the inner event." Margaret Lloyd, *The Borzoi Book of Modern Dance* (New York: Knopf, 1949; reprint edition, Dance Horizons, 1974), 198
7. Ellen Graff, *Stepping Left: Dance and Politics in New York City, 1928–1942* (Durham: Duke University Press, 1997), 120.
8. Ibid., 148.
9. Pauline Lawrence, Limón Manuscripts *MGZMD 15, folder 198, New York Public Library Dance Collection.
10. Graff, Stepping Left, 21.
11. "The Mexican Exhibition," *American Magazine of Art* 22, no. 1 (January 1931): 3.
12. René d'Harnoncourt, "Mexican Arts," *American Magazine of Art* 22, no. 1 (January 1931): 5.
13. "Dartmouth Scored in Alien Art Row," *New York Times*, June 10, 1933, 15.
14. Ibid.
15. Edward Jewell, "The Realm of Art: Orozco's New Murals at Dartmouth," *New York Times*, February 25, 1934, 12X.

16. Keen, *Aztec Image*, 5–8.

17. Ibid., 532.

18. Ibid.

19. Ibid.

20. Jewell, "Orozco's New Murals at Dartmouth."

21. Limón, *Memoir*, 90–91. The "double-edged symbol" Limón refers to is the conqueror's sword, with its hilt in the shape of a cross. This prop would become a central element in the choreographer's evocation of La Malinche's story.

22. Ibid., 5.

23. Ibid.

24. Ibid., 90.

25. Deborah Jowitt, introduction, *Unfinished Memoir*, xvii.

26. Martha Graham had also employed the theatrical device of using three dancers as traveling players in her work inspired by the American Southwest, *El Penitente* (1940).

27. Sandra M. Cypess, *La Malinche in Mexican Literature from History to Myth* (Austin: University of Texas Press, 1991) 19.

28. Ibid., 139, 143.

29. Ibid., 89–90.

30. Stephen Greenblatt, *Marvelous Possessions: The Wonder of the New World* (Chicago: University of Chicago Press, Oxford: Oxford University Press, 1991), 135.

31. Keen, *Aztec Image*, 58.

32. Octavio Paz, *The Labyrinth of Solitude*, trans. Lysander Kemp (New York: Grove Press, 1961), 77. *El Laberinto de la Soledad* was published in Mexico in 1947, and it is certainly not inconceivable that Limón would have had access to the book. Octavio Paz, *El Laberinto de la Soledad* (Mexico City: Ediciones Cuadernos Americanos, 1947).

33. Ibid.

34. Greenblatt, *Marvelous Possessions*, 137.

35. Ibid.

36. Ibid., 134.

37. This is the image Sarah Stackhouse gave to the dancers when the work was staged at Southern Methodist University in 2001.

38. The establishment of the Catholic religion in post-Conquest Mexico gave rise to the cult of the Virgin Mary of Guadalupe. For a thorough discussion of this complex issue, see Jacques Lafaye, *Quetzalcóatl and Guadalupe: The Formation of Mexican National Consciousness 1531–1813*, trans. Benjamin Keen with a foreword by Octavio Paz (Chicago: University of Chicago Press, 1976).

39. See Keen, *Aztec Image*, 526.

40. Limón, *Memoir*, 6.

41. Ibid., 90.

42. The character of La Malinche is, in fact, represented by a female voice in Norman Lloyd's music score for the ballet.

43. Paz, foreword to *Quetzalcóatl and Guadalupe*, xxii.

44. Jowitt, introduction, *An Unfinished Memoir*, xvii.

45. Greenblatt, *Marvelous Possessions*, 145.

46. Limón noted that when *La Malinche* was performed in Mexico, it "aroused controversy." José Limón, "The Dance: A Visitor in Mexico," Dance Scrapbook, *New York Times*, July 22, 1951. Limón Manuscripts *MGZD 510 microfilm reel 14, folder 505, New York Public Library Dance Collection.

47. Limón, *Memoir*, 90.

48. Greenblatt, *Marvelous Possessions*, 4.

2. JOSÉ LIMÓN'S *LA MALINCHE*

Patty Harrington Delaney

La Malinche's role in the Spanish Conquest has been a constant source of conflict in Mexican society, wavering according to the sociopolitical climate of the time. Was she a trusting and resourceful victim of circumstance? or a self-serving temptress/traitor? When the Limón Dance Company performed *La Malinche* in Mexico in 1951, they were introduced to this conflict firsthand. Limón remembered, "Tempers flared in the audience and in the press both pro and con. Mexico's profound and tragic disunity is easily stirred."[1]

Limón portrayed La Malinche in much the same manner as Octavio Paz did in his essay *The Sons of La Malinche* (1947).[2] The violated mother of all mestizos, she embodies the struggle of women to have a voice in a patriarchal society. She is the axis around which Limón's choreographic commentary on political and religious persecution revolves.

The exact year of the premiere of *La Malinche* is in question. Dance historians believe it to be 1949, while those who danced for Limón question the fact that he would have created two major works, *La Malinche* and *The Moor's Pavane*, in the same year. However, it is certain that the gestation of the three characters in *La Malinche*, El Conquistador, La Malinche, and El Indio, began as early as 1935. A description of the dance itself will lay the groundwork for a discussion of this gestation.

The three dancers enter the stage as traveling troubadours. They bow to the audience and then introduce their characters through thematic movement taken from solos that appear later in the work. Important areas of the stage, such as the diagonal from upstage left to downstage right, the road of conquest, are identified in this section. The two upstage corners and the downstage right corner are also areas of pivotal dramatic transitions. For example, La Malinche is upstage left when she transitions from the Indian maiden to Cortez's mistress. Here, too, she transitions from the mistress to the legendary patroness of the Revolucionario. (In the course of the dance El Indio embodies three characters, the native Indian, the Peón, and the Revolucionario.) The "Prologue" ends as the dancers circle the stage, a device Limón uses to depict the passing of time, and occupy the focal corners: La Malinche upstage left, El Conquistador upstage right, and El Indio downstage right. The story begins as Limón presents the Conquest.

El Conquistador's large prop, which functions as both a sword and a cross, plays a central role as the extension of his character. He wields it first as a cross, which he forcefully presses upon La Malinche while at the same time caressing her. She accepts her fate by placing a flower, a symbolic representation of the land and spirit of Mexico, on the cross and then opening the vista of her country before him. They traverse the stage in a large circle, bringing the Conquest forward in time. During El Conquistador's solo, La Malinche watches as the cross becomes a sword and the attacks on El Indio begin. She begs El Conquistador for mercy. He again presses the cross upon her and then dominates her further by placing a European skirt and scarf around her waist. He magnifies his physical and emotional dominance by circling the stage, as he presses the cross toward the audience. The attacks on El Indio become more fervent, and La Malinche begs again for mercy. El Conquistador responds by trampling over her and driving the sword into El Indio. He assumes an arrogant, majestic pose in the downstage right corner. The section ends as El Indio points an accusatory finger at La Malinche, looks at his empty hands, and then slides them across the floor toward the audience.

As La Malinche's solo, "The Lament," begins, she pleads with El Indio for forgiveness, but he does not acknowledge her. She circles the stage and then pleads three more times. El Indio becomes more physical as he continually rejects her, finally forcing her back into the upstage left corner. La Malinche ceremoniously removes the skirt and lets it drop to the floor as El Indio crawls downstage, looking at his empty hands. In a moment of silence, she drops the scarf on top of the skirt. She watches expectantly as he performs his solo.

El Indio transitions from the subservient *peón* to the powerful *revolucionario*. He confronts El Conquistador three times, each time with a stronger, more powerful stance. His choreography is laden with imagery of the ancient Indian god, Quetzalcóatl, the Plumed Serpent. He is a bird of prey as he jumps, expanding his wings, and then turns to face El Conquistador in a predatory position. El Indio gains momentum as he circles the stage three times, with La Malinche joining him on the last circle. They then charge down the diagonal from upstage left to downstage right toward the arrogant Conquistador.

La Malinche and El Indio appear two-dimensional as they reveal only the front of their bodies and their profiles to the audience, as El Indio did in sections of his solo. It reminds the viewer both of Mexican folk art and the traditional drawings of Quetzalcóatl. As they converse through rhythmic stamps of their feet, El Indio forgives La Malinche and accepts her help in his battle with El Conquistador. They perform a stylized folk dance and then vigorously circle each other, striking their thighs and gesturing toward El Conquistador. They charge down the path of conquest toward him, as he slowly dies. La Malinche steps over his prostrate body and removes the flower from the sword/cross. She offers it to El Indio, who is at first reluctant, backing away. She follows him to center stage, where he takes the flower, bringing the story full circle. They both wrap one hand around the flower and lean away from each other in a position of mutual support.

In the "Epilogue" the dancers bring the viewer back to the present by circling the stage. They bow in character and exit.

The music that accompanies *La Malinche*, composed by Norman Lloyd, is simple in structure and is reminiscent of a Mexican village band. It is scored for a trumpet, representing El Conquistador, percussion for El Indio, a soprano voice for La Malinche, and a piano to tie the instruments together.[3]

THE DEVELOPMENT OF THE CHARACTERS FROM 1935 TO 1949

In Limón's early choreographic notes, which he titled "Libro de Ideas," there is a reference to Indio—"Indio" not "El Indio"—for the first time in 1935. Limón writes, "Two compositions based on the Mexican Indian—both religious in feeling—both votive offerings—the first gay—joyous—the second morbid—a votive offering refused."[4] Limón recorded his choreographic ideas with words and very expressive stick figures. He described the movement for Indio as disjointed, fragmentary, distorted, spasmodic, and jerky. Stick figures reveal pumping arm gestures with clasped hands and parallel leg gestures in front of the body. These studies were done at Bennington College in the early days of the American Dance Festival.

Indio appears again in Limón's choreographic work *Murals of Mexico*, which he later renamed *Danzas Mexicanas* (1939).[5] There were five solos, all danced by Limón, that were based on what he considered to be the most symbolic male figures in Mexican history: Indio, Conquistador, Peón, Caballero, and Revolucionario.[6] He describes these characters in his memoirs:

> *Indio.* A figure from Mayan and Aztec sculpture—hieratic, half-man, half pyramid; a rite of invocation to benign and destructive powers; a creature long risen from the savage state into a culture of barbaric splendor; existing in and because of compelling rhythm. A primitive yet complex; an adoration of the sun and the earth; a canticle to Quetzalcóatl.
>
> *Conquistador.* The vision of Hernán Córtez, as seen by José Clemente Orozco. An apocalyptic apparition, bringing doom and destruction, wielding the double edged symbol of redemption and death.[7]
>
> *Peón.* A creature of infinite pathos, lying in degradation on a bright crimson blanket, which is also a pool of his blood. His dance is a lament, the despairing cry of three centuries of bondage and servitude.
>
> *Caballero.* A creature of fastidious elegance and preciosity, the decayed descendant of the Conquistador, with all of his cruelty and none of his strength.
>
> *Revolucionario.* The contained fury of centuries finally unleashed; wildly explosive; an exultant crude shout of triumph.[8]

Danzas Mexicanas was captured in choreographic notes, short film excerpts of Indio, Peón, and Revolucionario,[9] and a collection of photographs[10] that capture only the figures of Indio, Peón, and Revolucionario. Fortunately, we do have Limón's drawings of all five of the characters.[11]

In Limón's drawing, Indio is bare-chested and is positioned much like the historical depictions of Quetzalcóatl, proud and fully two-dimensional. Indio has a thoughtful, sculpted expression, as if he is frozen in time. Photographs and films show the character kneeling on one knee, growing out of the earth, a possible reference to Quetzalcóatl's traditional role as the god of earth and water. Limón's choreographic notes speak of this relationship to the earth: "sit with arms folded—extend left leg straight to side—arms circle overhead to rt—& to floor."[12] Limón also describes Indio hitting the floor and then hitting his chest. Film excerpts of Indio reveal punctuated, quick, percussive footwork that has the qualities of Mexican folk dance. He uses dynamic downward gestures of the arms to accompany this footwork, which give him the appearance of a hunter.

As with Indio, Limón drew the character of Peón in a two-dimensional position. He stands parallel and wide with his eyes downcast, his serape over his right shoulder and his hat held in front of his body. He holds his left hand in a position halfway between a fist and an extended hand as if to show that his hand is empty. The films of Peón's character reveal a weighted, melancholy figure who takes his serape off his shoulder and places it on the floor in what Limón described as a pool of blood.[13] He crawls on his hands and knees in a circle around the blood, as if he is trying to contain it. Stick figures in Limón's notes illustrate a sequence beginning with the body crouched over in fourth position. The arms open to the side as the chest twists. Then Peón brings his knee to his chest, grabbing his leg as he falls forward into a deep lunge.

Limón's drawing of Revolucionario, also two-dimensional, shows the character with cartridge belts criss-crossed over his bare chest and his fist clenched tight in the air. In a very brief film clip of Revolucionario, he rebelliously travels the stage, stopping to strike a position and clench his fist. Limón's choreographic notes show numerous traveling patterns, which are depicted in floor plans, but contain few word notes and only two stick figures. In two of the floor plans, he moves on the diagonal from upstage left to downstage right, the path of conquest in *La Malinche*. In other floor plans he performs circling patterns, a spatial design that depicts the passing of time in *La Malinche*.

Limón drew Conquistador—"Conquistador," not "El Conquistador"—in the traditional Spanish military uniform of the early sixteenth century, in all of its high-collared elegance. With regal bearing, he carries a prop whose size and shape allow it to function as both a Catholic cross and a sword, "the double edged symbol of redemption and death."[14] In the drawing, Conquistador presents the full shape of the prop, so that its connection to Christianity is obvious. Limón crossed out the material in his choreographic notes for Conquistador (although they are legible nevertheless), indicating that the choreography was discarded. Three especially expressive stick figures appear to have had prominence in this discarded material. The movement has a rather primitive, savage appearance as the chest reaches forward with the cross/sword behind the body. The prop then swoops overhead to come forward as the body lurches forward. I will discuss below some possible conclusions concerning Limón's seemingly detached attitude toward this character.

Caballero is drawn in nobleman's attire with a long, double-breasted, high-collared waistcoat with puffed sleeves. He wears an ornate broach at his neck. The back of his left hand is on his hip, and the right hand is outstretched as if asking for money. His countenance is arrogant, his eyes half-closed in boredom. The choreographic notes for Caballero are filled with arm, hand, foot, and knee gestures, for example, "rt. arm gesture out to rt 6 cts—rt hand twist 6 cts—hands and foot 8 cts." Another passage reads, "accented mvt sequence—with finger wiggle and knee pulse—12 cts each."[15] There are also repeated references to an "ornate sequence" but no description of the movement. The most prominent stick figure in these notes depicts a wide fourth-position lunge with one arm thrust forward toward the floor and the other extended to the back, movement adopted by El Conquistador in *La Malinche*.

The figures of Indio, Peón, and Revolucionario from *Danzas Mexicanas* are distilled into one character in *La Malinche*, El Indio, who is the embodiment of the indigenous Mexican male. He begins the dance as Indio, is then confined to the role of Peón, and finally resurges as the powerful Revolucionario. These three representations of the Mexican male are inextricably linked by the cultural and religious imagery of Mexico, which I have traced back to Limón's earliest compositional studies. The cultural imagery speaks of Mexican folk art and folk dance, and the religious imagery harks back to the ancient god Quetzalcóatl.

El Conquistador embodies the Spanish influence on the Mexican male as he becomes a distillation of the characters of Conquistador and Caballero. Through his role as the conqueror, he represents the dominant patriarch in Mexican culture, who ensures his position of power through intimidation. The sword/cross El Conquistador carries is larger than the one Limón drew for Conquistador in *Danzas Mexicanas*. It is four feet tall and has a larger cross bar, which brings its role as a cross to more prominence. Even when El Indio and La Malinche defeat El Conquistador and he lies dead on the floor, the sword/cross remains standing, a seeming reference to the lasting power of Catholicism in Mexican culture. What is predominantly visible of Caballero in El Conquistador's character comes from Limón's description in his memoirs. The unbridled cruelty and greed of the Caballero can be seen as El Conquistador loses his majestic bearing and tramples over La Malinche to conquer El Indio.

Limón viewed the creation of *Danzas Mexicanas* as the point in his career when he truly became a choreographer. He writes in his memoirs,

Sometimes I would come upon a discovery exciting beyond words, and would experience, as if in recompense for the dull and even despairing hours such pure rapture that I was suffused with energies and powers I did not know were mine. Living became a sublime adventure. There were moments when I seemed to explode, and the fragile, fleshly envelope and the four confining walls were shattered into oblivion and the only reality was a convulsive, blinding consummation. I worked like a madman. There is pleasure in remembering that these dances were able to give those who saw them something of what went into their composition. There is pleasure, and even that more rare emotion, satisfaction, in knowing that while making them I grew up.[16]

John Martin wrote the following about *Danzas Mexicanas* in a *New York Times* article in 1943: "It is a very fine suite, indeed, not only for its individual dances (some of which are better than others) but for its development of its choreographic materials thematically in the direction of a general unity." Martin went on to identify Peón and Revolucionario as the two strongest characters in the work, saying, "The two related sections of Peón and Revolucionario are superb dances in themselves, and if the program had contained nothing else would have been sufficient to proclaim the presence of a dancer who is very much to be reckoned with." [17]

Two other works from this period of Limón's burgeoning choreographic talent are especially pertinent to the development of *La Malinche*. They are *This Story is Legend* (1941) and *Distant Ballad*, which was conceived sometime around 1946 but never fully choreographed. The importance of these works lies not only in their content, their use of imagery, and their spatial design, but also in their incorporation of a strong female protagonist.

This Story is Legend was based on "De Soto and the New World," a section of William Carlos Williams's book *In the American Grain*[18] (1925), which depicts the exploration of the American continent by the conquistador Hernando de Soto. Williams's piece referred to the continent as an alluring woman and to the explorer as an obsessed lover in search of her. May O'Donnell danced the role of the alluring Mississippi River opposite Limón as Hernando de Soto. The work had five sections: a seductive solo for the River, a solo for de Soto in which he reveals his restless need to discover and conquer, and a series of three duets. The first, entitled "Search and Counter-search," depicts de Soto's pursuit of the River and her riches as if she were a lover. The second duet, "Posses-sion," is like an impassioned love duet in which she purifies and prepares him for his destiny, death in the River. And finally came the "Consump-tion," in which he dies cradled in her arms, and she tenderly buries him. As the curtain falls, she broods over his watery grave.[19]

In describing *This Story is Legend*, Limón wrote, "The style of gesture and movement was worked out to give each protagonist an expressive domain as different as possible from the other's. May's movement was curved, flowing and fluid. Mine had hard irrepressible drive: it was an-gular and turgid."[20] Limón applied this process of developing characters through movement styles that contrast in *La Malinche*. El Conquistador moves regally in broad, powerful movements. La Malinche's movements are like the River's, curved and fluid and predominantly legato, until she joins El Indio and adopts his raw, driving, and percussive movements.

In a passage from his choreographic notes for the "Search and Counter-search" duet, Limón outlines movement very similar in style and emotional content to the duet between La Malinche and El Con-quistador: "May does a very slow back fall—[José] progresses forward in bold leg side to side pattern and walks over her—proceeds to rt. May caresses his leg—he continues."[21] Limón's notes also describe the use of zigzags, curves, and circles to depict de Soto's passage through space and time in his pursuit of the River and her riches, spatial manipula-tions similar to those in *La Malinche*.

Distant Ballad existed only in the conceptual phase. Although there is a detailed synopsis in Limón's personal notes, there is no evidence of a finished choreographic product.[22] The work was designed as a portrayal of the European/Mexican encounter of Benito Juárez and Carlota, the wife of Archduke Ferdinand Maximilian.[23] In Limón's notes he identi-fies Dorothy Bird as Carlota and himself as Juárez. The notes on the dance begin with a short synopsis:

> The Empress Carlota and President Juárez of Mexico. In the style of a tragic ballad it would juxtapose these two people as symbols of forces profoundly antagonistic to each other. The intent would be to show the drama of the conflict between these two and what each represented, but the devices for doing so would be entirely abstract and choreographic—Carlota's themes and motifs would stem from the European waltzes and polkas, etc, of the period, whereas Juarez' would be in violent contrast by their starkness and rude simplicity. The Empress at the start would be all elegance and arrogance and

power. Slowly the indomitable Juárez would dominate the scene and emerge triumphant, while the Empress would sink and disappear into defeat and oblivion.[24]

He named the sections of *Distant Ballad* after cultural dances, the "Waltz," "Polka," and "Courante" from Europe and the "Zandunga," "Zapateado," and "Jarabe" from Mexico.[25] At the beginning of the work, the stage is filled with a gigantic serpent (Quetzalcóatl), which Carlota arrogantly tramples to reach her throne. The scene changes as the serpent becomes a sacrificial altar whose victim symbolizes the Mexican people. A ballroom atmosphere is then created as Carlota dances with stilted elegance to a courtly waltz. Now, the god of the serpent rises again to save the sacrificial lamb by empowering Juárez. Carlota begins to flee from one end of the stage to the other as the waltz becomes a polka. She becomes madder by the moment. Juárez is, of course, triumphant over Carlota as he performs his "rampant, unbridled, cruel and primitive movement."[26] There are also two pages of specific movement notes and stick figures in Limón's choreographic journal that are simply titled "Ballad." Although these notes are separate from the synopsis, they are dated 1946. This would seem to indicate that they were describing *Distant Ballad* rather than *Three Ballads*, a work Limón choreographed in 1945. The stick figures depict movement that is similar in style to El Indio: the wide, two-dimensional second position, the deep lunge, and the crossed passé are all present, indicating that these notes may have been describing movement for Juárez.[27]

Limón returned to choreographing the story of Carlota and Juárez in one of his final works, *Carlota* (1972). In considering *Carlota* and *Distant Ballad*, it is most interesting to note that Limón carried a picture of Benito Juárez in his makeup kit. How long he had done so is uncertain, but many dancers who worked with him in the 1950s and 1960s recall mistaking the male figure in the picture for Limón's father until Limón clarified his identity.[28] Obviously, Limón admired this Mexican revolutionary who served as Mexico's president twice, first from 1861 to 1863 and then again, after ousting Carlota's husband, Maximilian, from 1867 to his death in 1872.

In looking specifically at the influence of *This Story is Legend* and *Distant Ballad* on the character of La Malinche, one can identify two main issues. First, the figure of the Mississippi River in *Distant Ballad* symbolizes the entire American continent and its indigenous peoples. La Malinche embodies the land as well as the spirit of Mexico in her character. The flower she carries further symbolizes this. Second, the River and La Malinche share the stylistic similarities of rounded, fluid movement and a nurturing, consistent presence. That Limón created *Carlota* in his last years demonstrates his continued fascination for using controversial historical female figures to express social commentary.

During the 1940s, Limón worked with some of the most prominent female dancers of the day, including May O'Donnell, Dorothy Bird, Beatrice Seckler, Letitia Ide, and Pauline Koner, the original La Malinche. All were consummate artists who became renowned teachers, choreographers, and artistic directors. Unfortunately Limón's memoirs trace his professional life only to World War II, so we are not privileged to Limón's personal account of working with all of these women. However, he does speak of working with O'Donnell on *This Story is Legend:* "Our ideas complimented and stimulated each other's. We would criticize, evaluate and modify with full appreciation of the other's efforts and abilities."[29] Koner describes a similar collaborative relationship with Limón in her autobiography, *Solitary Song.* In her description of rehearsals for *La Malinche* Koner said, "His movement would trigger a reaction on my part and mine on his. We went through those two hours singing the trumpet calls at the top of our voices and by 4 P.M., we had blocked the entire duet."[30]

Limón's respect for Koner's contributions is further evidenced in *Solitary Song:*

> Somehow, there seemed to be an instinctive understanding among us that, as a choreographer, I could save time and know what was best for my body by working on my solos alone. I used a yellow silk kerchief attached to the skirt to symbolize my tears, and found the desired quality of the very primitive carved saint figures in Mexican churches. I decided to be utterly simple, stark. I chose a stilted walk as my ground base and relied on an occasional hand gesture, with or without the handkerchief, and added head movement to create a lament. It was a plea to El Indio. Each time he pulled away from my touch, the walk and the gestures became more intense with inner agony, until with the final strength he finally pushed me away.
>
> At this point, I slowly walked upstage, discarding the symbolic skirt and becoming again the Indian.[31]

La Malinche owes much of her strength and clarity to Koner. Through her dramatic sensibilities, her unique movement style, and her experience with props and costumes, Koner helped to define La Malinche's psychological journey from the innocent victim of circumstance to the grieving women to the legendary strength of Mexico.

The other members of the original cast were Lucas Hoving (El Conquistador) and Limón (El Indio). Like Koner, they were gifted dramatic performers. They both credited the German expressionist dancer Harald Kreutzberg with inspiring them to dance. Kreutzberg, who came from the German dance lineage of Rudolph Laban and Mary Wigman, was primarily concerned with expressing the psychological conflict of his characters rather than presenting them in stereotypical gender roles. Hoving and Limón were drawn to this performance philosophy because it meant they were not limited to the melodramatic classical role of the virile male dancer. The contrast of both their physical appearance and their movement qualities made their collaborative expressions of human conflict very powerful. As Ann Murphy said in *José Limón: The Artist Reviewed*, "As a pair, they not only embodied physical and temperamental opposites, they manifested the poles of American society—the dark-skinned exotic indigenous man and the fair European who, through a kind of cultural primogeniture, would always be welcome."[32]

Hoving, a fair, tall, long-limbed, angular Dutchman, danced with a stately and elegant grace. Sarah Stackhouse, a member of the Limón Company in the late 1950s, wrote, "He had a sense of weight in his deep plié and the angular shaping of his legs. At the same time, he might use a light energy accenting with his remarkable arm and hand gestures. He kept his personal space, as he sent energy from his center. Lucas projected control, decision, power."[33]

In looking at how Hoving shaped El Conquistador, one need only refer to this description. Even in defeat he projects confidence that his influence will remain. Falling to the floor in controlled staccato movements, he holds the sword/cross so that it remains standing. Hoving brought the qualities to the character of El Conquistador that Limón had been seeking since *Danzas Mexicanas*. As noted, Limón crossed out his choreographic notes for Conquistador. He must have been striving to create choreography that expressed the European elegance and arrogance he had captured in his drawing of Conquistador. Limón understood the character completely, but his personal movement qualities were not compatible with those needed for Conquistador. On the other hand, Hoving had the exact qualities and the dramatic sensibilities needed to bring El Conquistador's character to fruition.

El Indio was the perfect vehicle for Limón. As a dancer, Limón presented an eloquent mixture of kingly stature and savage strength. His movements, especially when he was young, seemed raw and impulsive, and this gave his performance a sense of unpredictability. He moved with a powerful, grounded, and earthy quality and propelled himself through space, seemingly hurling his energy out of his center.[34] Limón's musical training[35] imbued his movement with a defined and often intricate musical structure in its rhythm and phrasing. Limón gave El Indio tragic nobility.

Although there are no films of the original cast performing *La Malinche*, there are photographs that graphically express the powerful interpretation of La Malinche, El Conquistador, and El Indio by Koner, Hoving, and Limón. The choreographic moments captured in these photos are very similar to the choreography we know today, indicating that the thematic movement material in *La Malinche* has remained intact over time.

Limón developed the characters in *La Malinche* over a period of some fourteen years. He began with compositional studies of Indio, probably because his own movement qualities were conducive to developing this character. In *Danzas Mexicanas*, Limón expanded his examination of the Mexican male to include Peón, Revolucionario, Conquistador, and Caballero.

Through his work on *This Story is Legend* and *Distant Ballad*, Limón not only discovered the importance of the feminine presence in social commentary, but also began to solidify his methodology for character development. He based his characters on historical figures so that he could provide a contextual framework in which to view them and then use the cultural imagery associated with their history to define them. In addition, he expanded his use of the architectural design of space as the framework for telling a story. In *La Malinche*, this methodology was codified.

In 2001, a documentation and preservation project sponsored by Southern Methodist University, the Limón Institute, and the Dance Notation Bureau was begun to ensure that *La Malinche* would be accessible to future generations. The project, which took three years to complete, produced a Labanotation score of the work, a performance of the work at Southern Methodist University, the educational DVD that accompanies this book, and a collection of reviews and articles that traces the history of the dance from its creation to the present. It is a tribute to Limón and to the lasting significance of one of his signature works, *La Malinche*, that all of these documentary materials now reside in the Library of Congress.

NOTES

1. José Limón, "The Dance: A Visitor in Mexico," *New York Times*, July 22, 1957.
2. Octavio Paz, *The Labyrinth of Solitude* (New York: Grove Press, 1985), 65–87. This is an English translation of his *El laberinto de la soledad* (Mexico: Cuardernos Americanos, 1947).
3. Norman Lloyd, "Composing for the Dance," *Dance Observer* (October 1973): 118.
4. Pauline Lawrence Manuscript(s). *MGZMD 15, folder 197, Jerome Robbins Dance Division of the New York Public Library for the Performing Arts.
5. Ibid.
6. José Limón, *José Limón: An Unfinished Memoir*, ed. Lynn Garafola (Hanover and London: Wesleyan University Press, University Press of New England, 1999), 90.
7. Ann Vachon's transcription of Limón's manuscript, which differs slightly from Garafola's in punctuation and other details, here reads "wielding the double edged symbol that served redemption and death by turns." Personal communication to the author, June 16, 2003.
8. Limón, *An Unfinished Memoir*, 90–91.
9. Knight, Helen (Producer). (1935–1939). Charles Weidman and Doris Humphrey [video recording]. Doris Humphrey (1935). [video recording]. Portia Mansfield also filmed excerpts of this dance.
10. *Danzas Mexicanas* Photos *MGZEB 80-3247, vol. 4, no(s). 9.1–9.23. Jerome Robbins Dance Division, New York Public Library for the Performing Arts.
11. Pauline Lawrence Manuscript(s), *MGZMD 15, folder 193. Jerome Robbins Dance Division, New York Public Library for the Performing Arts.
12. Ibid.
13. Limón, *An Unfinished Memoir*, 91.
14. Ibid.
15. Pauline Lawrence Manuscript(s), *MGZMD 15-197, folder 197. Jerome Robbins Dance Division, New York Public Library for the Performing Arts.
16. I have used Ann Vachon's transcription of Limón's manuscript, which is now in the Jerome Robbins Dance Division of the New York Public Library for the Performing Arts. Communication from Ann Vachon, June 16, 2003.
17. John Martin, "José Limón Comes Into His Own—Helen Tamiris and 'It's Up To You,'" *New York Times*, April 4, 1943.
18. William Carlos Williams, *In the American Grain* (New York: New Directions, 1956), 45–58.
19. The description of *This Story is Legend* is a compilation of information found in Limón, *An Unfinished Memoir*, 98–99, and in program notes from

performances in 1941. Limón Programs *MGZB, folder dated 1941, Jerome Robbins Dance Division, New York Public Library for the Performing Arts.

20. Limón, *An Unfinished Memoir*, 99.

21. Pauline Lawrence Manuscript(s), folder 197, Jerome Robbins Dance Division, New York Public Library for the Performing Arts.

22. Limón Manuscript(s) *MGZBD 510, microfilm reel 14, folder 505, Jerome Robbins Dance Division, New York Public Library for the Performing Arts.

23. Benito Juárez (1806–1872), who was of mixed native and Spanish descent, became a national hero and president of Mexico. Educated in law, he became governor of the state of Oaxaca in 1847 and was imprisoned by Antonio López de Santa Anna. When Santa Anna was overthrown, Juárez became the provisional president and then was constitutionally elected in 1861. After the French took power in Mexico in 1864 and put Maximilian on the throne, Juárez overthrew him and regained the presidency in 1867, dying in 1872 while still in office. Archduke Ferdinand Maximilian (1832–1867) and his wife, Carlota (1840–1927), ruled Mexico from 1864 to 1867. Maximilian was an Austrian archduke who was put on the throne of Mexico by the French in 1864. Napoleon III later withdrew his forces from Mexico and left Maximilian to his fate at the hands of Juarez, who ordered him executed in 1867. Carlota, who was a member of the Belgian royal family, went to Europe to plead (unsuccessfully) with Napoleon and the pope for support of her husband. She went insane and was institutionalized by her brother until her death.

24. Limón Manuscript(s) *MGZBD 510, microfilm reel 14, folder 505, Jerome Robbins Dance Division, New York Public Library for the Performing Arts.

25. The *zandunga* is a native dance of southern Mexico that resembles a slow waltz with its three-step pattern. The *zapateado* borrows from the flamenco lexicon with its articulation in the feet and sense of visual percussion. There are many regional versions of *jarabe* in Mexico; its general characteristics include light, percussive footwork, hopping, and patterns such as the figure eight, created by partners as they perform the dance.

26. Limón Manuscript(s) *MGZB d 510, microfilm reel 14, folder 519, Jerome Robbins Dance Division, New York Public Library for the Performing Arts.

27. Ibid.

28. On August 8, 2002, dance artists who had worked with Limón between 1958 and his death in 1972 gathered at the Limón Studio in New York to discuss their experiences with *La Malinche*. These artists included Daniel Lewis, Laura Glenn, Sarah Stackhouse, Ann Vachon, Dennis Nahut, and Carla Maxwell. Also included in these oral histories were Roxane D'Orléans Juste, who performed the role of La Malinche in the 50th Anniversary Concert

of the Limón Dance Company in 1997, and David LaMarche, who conducted the music for that performance. These oral histories were compiled as content for an educational DVD designed to provide a contextual framework in which to view *La Malinche*.

29. Limón, *An Unfinished Memoir*, 98.

30. Pauline Koner, *Solitary Song* (Durham: Duke University Press, 1989), 199.

31. Ibid., 198–199.

32. *José Limón: The Artist Reviewed*, ed. June Dunbar (Singapore: Harwood Academic Publishers, 2000), 62.

33. Sarah Stackhouse, "Thoughts on Setting: José Limón's *La Malinche*," lecture/demonstration. Presented to the Society of Dance History Scholars, Philadelphia, June 2002.

34. Ibid.

35. In his youth Limón studied music with his father, Florencio Limón, a musician, pedagogue, and conductor, and played the organ and piano.

3. THE MUSIC

Interview with David LaMarche, Musical Director, Limón Company and American Ballet Theater

Patty Harrington Delaney and David LaMarche

PATTY DELANEY: How would you describe your affiliation with the Limón Company?

DAVID LaMARCHE: I'm the music director of the Limón Company, and I believe I began my association with the company in their 50th anniversary season. I conducted the repertoire at the Joyce Theater, and we had a season shortly thereafter at Riverside Church. That was my very first exposure to the Limón Company.

I had conducted the *Moor's Pavane* for the Dance Theater of Harlem and that began my connection to Limón because I met Sarah Stackhouse through that experience. Then when the Limón Company needed a conductor for the season, I came into the picture.

PD: And now are you the resident musical conductor?

DL: When we have seasons in New York, I participate either by conducting or by playing solos, depending on the venue. The Joyce Theatre, which is the home of the Limón Company in New York, is a problematic place for live music in that the acoustic is not that good and there's not much space. So we try to use smaller ensembles.

PD: Could you tell us about your experience with conducting *La Malinche?*

DL: Well, the first time was during the 50th year anniversary season. There was a retrospective of famous Limón works: We did *Moor's Pavane, The Winged* to a new score, *A Choreographic Offering*, and others. There were a number of classic works. *La Malinche* was in there as well. The music is very simply put together—the motifs are simple, as a mirror to the story, which is a folk legend. We used musicians that year from the Juilliard School, a mezzo-soprano, trumpet player, percussion, and piano. It is not an incredibly difficult work musically, but it is a little bit challenging. It's exposed, because there are so few players. The rhythms are tricky, and it takes a little rehearsing to get that together.

PD: Could you talk about the actual structure of the music and how the instruments are used with the characters?

DL: There are three characters. First, the Conquistador. He is represented by the trumpet. I think Norman Lloyd chose the trumpet because of its association with military bands. The sound imparts a martial quality. Also, the trumpet is such a historic instrument in Mexico. It's used as the melody instrument in Mexican bands. [Ed. note: Native Americans used conch shells as wind instruments. Spaniards brought the trumpet to Mexico, where it replaced the conch shells. Hence the trumpet rightly belongs to the Conquistador's musical heritage.]

Then, second, Lloyd associated the Indio character with percussion, perhaps because of the earthy quality that drums convey. [Ed. note: Drumming featured prominently in many Aztec celebrations. The Aztecs played two drums: an upright, wooden, carved drum called the *huehuetl* and a hollowed-out, carved log, the *teponaztli*. Drummers used sticks on the loglike *teponaztli* but employed their fingers on the *huehuetl*.]

And of course the mezzo-soprano is La Malinche. [Ed. note: Song composers called *tlamatinime* in Nahuatl were highly regarded among the Aztecs. Many of the drawings in the Florentine Codex, which Limón may have used (see Carol Maturo, 55, in this book), depict Nahuatl women composing and singing. A famous woman composer named Macuilxochitzin (Five Flower), born in the Aztec capital of Tenochtitlán in 1435, invoked Xochiquetzal, or Quetzal Flower, goddess of the arts, dance, and song. The use of a voice linked one famous Aztec woman (Malinche) to another (Macuilxochitzin). Lloyd's melodies sound very much to me like free-floating Indian folk melodies. I think he might have done some research on Indian folk music or tried to imitate that kind of quality.

PD: What do you feel are the main musical challenges of the work?

DL: Singers aren't often accustomed to trying to blend into an ensemble as though they are another instrument. So you have to have a singer who has a beautiful, big, strong voice that's lyrical, but who is also very astute musically, because the rhythms are not normal; you have to know when to come in and count, and most singers aren't famous for that. That's one challenge.

The trumpet part is also hard; it's not incredibly difficult but it's a rather long piece for a solo instrument (fifteen or twenty minutes), and it ends going up to a high B, a tough note to reach at the end of a long solo stretch.

The percussion and piano parts are not that bad. It's just getting the entire ensemble to jell together, and the balances—and also getting the character right. The singer must figure out how it should sound, and likewise the trumpet. Those are the main challenges.

PD: La Malinche's part is referred to as the lament, and there is a sadness there. I can imagine getting the soprano to do that is a challenge.

DL: I think the performer has to be a singer who has had theatrical experience, someone who has either done opera or musical theater, so she can latch onto and express the idea, because there are no words, just "ahh's."

PD: Is there anything from the score that strikes you in particular?

DL: The motivic themes are very strong. When the characters come out in the beginning, the themes define them immediately.

PD: They're like theater performers, traveling performers, coming into a plaza in Mexico. They enter, present themselves, and take on the characters. And then they perform their play.

DL: Exactly. So the melody of the trumpet in the beginning is very simple, almost like a child's melody, but it sounds like a presentation—you know the show is about to begin. And that [melody] comes back later in the work. Besides regular march time and ¾ time, Lloyd uses compound meter, which is an uneven meter (⅝, ⅞, etc.). He does that, I think, because it presents conflict—it throws off the natural body rhythm. There is a lot of conflict in this story, so he probably did that to create tension.

PD: Was it hard to coordinate the musicians with the dancers when you had the changing meter?

DL: No, because the Limón Company is used to dancing to all different kinds of music. These particular dancers were so well rehearsed, and they learned it very well. So, that was not so much a problem. There are a lot of visual cues though. It's a very hands-on piece in terms of the connection between the music and the dancer: you really have to pay attention all the time. The score was written for the dance—it wasn't a piece of music written for a concert that someone later decided to dance to—so it has to be closely watched. If you used dancers who were unaccustomed to the music (not the Limón Company, but somebody else) the performance would probably require a good deal of rehearsal.

PD: That was one of the challenges we faced with the reconstruction at Southern Methodist University that Sarah Stackhouse worked on—just singing the music, which helped a lot.

DL: Right. It's probably a little challenging, I would imagine.

PD: Oh, very. But a good challenge.

DL: Also this past season at the Joyce Theater, we did *Invention*, the Doris Humphrey work that was also composed by Norman Lloyd, and we did a lecture-demonstration at Rutgers University. It is really a wonderful, wonderful score.

The thing about Norman Lloyd's compositions is that his musical ideas are fairly simple but he uses them economically in how the melodies blend into the rhythms. His background as a music theory professor comes into it, and you see how he's thinking of structure; it is not intellectual music, but you can tell there's a brain behind it.

PD: And that was a good fit, you think, for José?

DL: I think so, because Norman Lloyd's music shows that he studied the great composers: Bach, Mozart, and Beethoven, in the way he used materials. I think that probably appealed to José, because he respected those composers also. You can especially hear the influence of Bach in some of Lloyd's choices.

PD: Would you like to talk more about the "ahh's"? I diverted you from your journey through the score there.

DL: That's OK. In the melodic structure of the lament, the intervals are all based on fourths, a basic interval that's used a lot in indigenous folk music. I think that's probably why Lloyd used it. Also, it harks back to an earlier time. It has sort of an ageless quality, so I think that is why he used it for the [mezzo-soprano's] basic part. Then she goes into a melisma [holding one syllable for several notes].

PD: It sounds sometimes like weeping to me because there is such a strong sense of sadness and weight in the connection to the dance. One of the images that Sarah Stackhouse used [when teaching a dancer to perform La Malinche] was tears coming off the scarf. It's such a powerful way to think about the connection to that sadness.

DL: Oh, yes, exactly. And the way Norman used the percussion in the piece—it adapts to the character. Sometimes the percussion has a martial feel to it, like a marching band beat, but when the Indio dances, he's more apt to use the low sounds of the bass drum, which resemble the kind of crude drum that would be used in Indian folk music.

PD: The drum also creates a wonderful tension.

DL: It does. Lloyd sometimes uses it for the rhythms of a heartbeat. In fact, the score says at one point that the bass drum should be "Not heard, but felt." So you shouldn't be aware that you can hear it, but the presence is there . . . like that of a heartbeat. That's nice.

PD: There's a very organic, cyclical feel to it.

DL: Exactly! There are so many changes to the score. The rhythms change quite frequently, so that is one challenge. Also, you don't get stuck in a rhythm for very long, so you need to be aware of what's coming up. You have to know the piece very well before you perform it. It's not something you can just come in and rehearse a little, because it's tricky.

PD: There are a lot of fermatas [sustaining of a note, chord, for longer than the indicated time value], breath pauses, and silences. It seems that it would be a challenge to coordinate that with what's going on on stage and get that sense together.

DL: Yes, I think you need to know the dancers and know how they breathe. [Limón's dance technique notably employs breathing at specific times to change the way a movement flows.]

NOTE

This interview is a revised version of the oral conversation that appears in the accompanying DVD.

4. VISUAL COMMUNICATION
Props and Costumes

Carol Maturo

Religious images, cultural motifs, paintings, photos of significant events, films, film clips, television and computer programs, plays, and other performances, live as well as recorded, form the visual heritage of a civilization. Both the props and costumes of José Limón's *La Malinche* drew upon the rich visual tradition of Europe and the Americas in several different historical time periods—the sixteenth-century Spanish Conquest, the Spanish colonial era, the Revolution of 1910–1920, and the postrevolutionary cultural florescence to 1940. In its use of Spanish and Spanish colonial painting as well as Native American and Mexican art, *La Malinche*'s visual design offers subtle perceptions of history and human experience. Costumes and props designed for *La Malinche* link Limón especially to the famous twentieth-century Mexican muralists Diego Rivera and José Clemente Orozco as well as to the historical visual sources that touched their imagination. I will examine the visual sources that possibly inspired Limón's props and costumes for La Malinche.

The simple narrative of the dance appeals to all age groups and especially to children, who saw it performed many times by the Juilliard School. Limón recounts *La Malinche*'s story principally through movement. The stage is stark; the dancers wear simple costumes and employ only four props during the entire dance. The severity of the setting accentuates the dance, and it also intensifies the meaning of the visual accouterments that Limón and his wife, Pauline Lawrence, designed.

Yet when Limón created *La Malinche*, he had lived outside of his native land for thirty-four years. Limón originally heard the tale of Malinche as a folk story from his parents and grandmother,[1] but his relatives' tales did not provide clues for staging a performance. How did Limón connect with the visual heritage of Mexico to select the props and design the costumes for the dance? The immediate inspiration for *La Malinche*'s costumes and props probably derived from his years as a fledgling performer of modern dance in New York City, when several prominent Mexican artists appeared on the New York art scene. These painters' artistic visions, however, originated with political events in their homeland.

Cultural nationalism marked the artistic communities of early twentieth-century Mexico. Finding their inspiration in the country's Indian heritage, contemporary life, and aspirations, artists produced Indianist novels, art, and music. Even social science research was affected. Archaeologists, ethnologists, and social anthropologists reassessed the role of the Indian in Mexican history and society. The Mexican government established both the Departamento Autónomo de Asuntos Indígenas in 1936 and the Instituto Nacional de Antropología e Historia in 1939.[2] As a result, Indian sites were excavated and Indian artifacts preserved, and pre-Conquest, sixteenth-century, and contemporary Indian documents were published. Reflecting the prevailing enthusiasm for Indian culture, Mexican intellectuals linked these discoveries and materials to the achievements and the promise of the Revolution of 1910.

In addition to celebrating the nation's indigenous past, these new cultural nationalists celebrated their homeland as the land of the mestizo— the offspring of Spaniard and Indian. In 1925, José Vasconcelos published *The Cosmic Race*, in which he argued that mestizaje represented a progressive pan–Latin American embrace of racial and cultural mixture.

A decade after the start of the Revolution, a newly elected Mexican government hired artists to cover public buildings with paintings that would reflect the indigenist anthropological and historical themes associated with the Revolution. This art, intended to educate the people, unexpectedly produced a Mexican mural renaissance whose works transcended polemics. At a time when cubism appealed to the Western elite, Mexican artists captured popular attention worldwide by covering walls with their panoramic views of human history and progress as well as the development of science and technology.[3]

Among the group of talented Mexican artists at that time were Frida Kahlo, Rufino Tamayo, David Alfaro Siqueiros, Diego Rivera, and José Clemente Orozco. As a result of their growing overseas fame, Rivera and Orozco received invitations from wealthy U.S. art patrons and museums to undertake mural projects in the United States. During the 1930s, both Orozco and Rivera thus came to play a significant role in the cultural life of New York.[4] Ironically, these two famous Mexican muralists who influenced Limón were actually a product of the Revolution, from which Limón's parents had fled to the United States in 1915 with their seven-year-old son, José, and his siblings.

Rivera and Orozco painted in New York during the years of Limón's early dance training. In 1930, Orozco created a set of murals at the New School for Social Research. Although they were not specifically concerned with the subject matter of *La Malinche*, they did portray themes expressed in Limón's dance: universal fraternity, revolution, slavery, and work.

The following year the Museum of Modern Art held a retrospective on Rivera, by now the leading Mexican muralist. The retrospective would have introduced Limón to Rivera's murals, including one at the National Preparatory School in Mexico City that showed a figure exemplifying dance. Rivera's mural at the National School of Agriculture in Chapingo celebrated Native American agricultural heritage. Rivera's work at the National Palace in Mexico City and at Cortés's palace in Cuernavaca celebrated indigenous culture while condemning the Spaniards and their native collaborators, such as Malinche.[5]

In 1933 controversy erupted over Rivera's mural art when he painted a sixty-three-foot-long mural in the lobby of New York City's Rockefeller Center. Called *Man at the Crossroads Looking with Hope and High Vision to the Choosing of a New and Better Future*, it included a depiction of Soviet May Day celebrations with a portrait of Vladimir Lenin. Along with everyone else in New York, Limón undoubtedly saw the newspaper articles attacking the mural's anticapitalist subject, which prompted the sponsors of the Rockefeller project to destroy Rivera's work in 1934. Undaunted, Rivera moved to another project, the painting of panels on American history at the New Workers School, where he also gave lectures at night.[6]

In contrast, Orozco produced less controversial murals. While at Dartmouth College in Hanover, New Hampshire, where he was an artist-in-residence from 1932 to 1934, he painted the walls of Baker Library with a work entitled *Epic of American Civilization*. Limón saw the deeply moving images of the Dartmouth frescoes.[7] Humanist in outlook, Orozco made references to Native American, sixteenth-century, colonial, and modern sources when he created the mural's dramatic historical scenes: *The Human Sacrifices, The Appearance of Quetzalcóatl, The Culture of Maize, The Conquest and Evangelization, Industrialization, English America, Spanish America, Science, Human Sacrifice, Modern Sacrifice,* and *Christ Destroys His Cross.*

Although Mexican mural art was sufficiently dynamic to have captured the attention of anyone involved with the New York art scene, it probably had special significance for Limón. First, both the artists and their themes originated in the land of his birth. The first two dances he choreographed in the 1930s derived from Hispanic themes: *Danza de la Muerte* appeared in response to the Spanish Civil War, and *Danzas Mexicanas* dealt with themes of the Spanish Conquest and the Mexican Revolution.[8] Second, Limón had originally aspired to be a painter. He had studied art for a year at UCLA before coming to New York to pursue a career as an artist, only to find himself discouraged when he saw the paintings of El Greco, whose talent he could not hope to match. Fortunately, however, he was so struck by seeing a performance of the German expressionist dancers Harald Kreutzberg and Yvonne Georgi that he turned his artistic leanings toward dance instead.[9] The fact that he ultimately expressed his creativity in modern dance does not mean he lost interest in painting or painters.

Limón shared yet another interest with the muralists Rivera and Orozco. All three were intrigued by historical themes and sought to render them in art. Indeed, Limón often used historical and literary figures when he choreographed his dances. His most famous work, *The Moor's Pavane*, inspired by Shakespeare's *Othello*, was created in the same year, 1949, that Limón created *La Malinche*.[10] Rivera and Orozco also turned to history—often Mexican or U.S. history—for their inspiration.

While both Orozco and Rivera depicted figures from Mexico's past, they had different visions of that history. Rivera's murals at the National Palace in Mexico City, for example, narrate a literally historical process, with such figures as Montezuma, Malinche, and Cortés depicted during the Conquest war of 1519. By contrast, the mural Orozco painted at Dartmouth College symbolically depicts historical figures like the legendary Quetzalcóatl. Rather than the god-king from Mexico's golden past, Quetzalcóatl represents Orozco's hope for the future.[11]

Limón learned from both Rivera and Orozco. While the contributions of Rivera may be deduced from Limón's immersion in the New York cultural scene of the 1930s and 1940s, the influence of Orozco is clearly established. Well before Limón began working on *La Malinche* in the 1940s, he found a kindred spirit in Orozco. The dancer's unpublished choreographic notes reveal that Orozco's murals inspired the character of Conquistador in 1937 for *Danzas Mexicanas:* "Conquistador. The vision of Hernán Córtez, as seen by José Clemente Orozco. An Apocalyptic apparition, bringing doom and destruction, wielding the double edged symbol of redemption and death."[12]

The three characters in Limón's *La Malinche* reflect Orozco's use of historical as well as symbolic figures in the *Epic of American Civilization*.

Malinche represents not only the historical individual who translated for Cortés in the Conquest of Mexico, but also the *soldaderas* (Mexican women soldiers) who fought alongside their men during the Revolution. El Conquistador represents Cortés but also symbolizes all Spanish conquerors as well as Spanish control of Mexico. El Indio represents the defeated Aztecs of the sixteenth century as well as the rediscovery of Indian culture and the rekindling of Indian aspirations during the Revolution.[13]

In both the muralists' and Limón's artistic renderings, the time continuum begins in pre-Conquest Mexico and connects these figures from the Conquest with events of the Revolution. In the costuming and props for his characters, Limón followed the aesthetic initiative of the twentieth-century nationalists from his homeland rather than his own family's alienating experience with the same events.

Although the Mexican muralists of the 1930s provided visual stimulus for the dance, Limón did not choreograph his work until the late 1940s. At that time, he worked with Lawrence, who served as the dance company's business manager and costume designer, as well as with Doris Humphrey, its artistic director. Since the production of *La Malinche* was a collaborative effort, it is difficult to know who was actually responsible for the costumes and props in the performance. Limón's interest in painting ties him to the Mexican muralists, but Lawrence and Humphrey both lived and worked in New York City as well as near Dartmouth College in the summers of the 1930s. Hence either one or both may also have been stimulated by the Mexican muralists.

Lawrence worked as a receptionist and costume designer for the dance company of Humphrey and Charles Weidman during the time Limón studied with them. When arthritis severely compromised Humphrey's dancing career—a problem complicated by financial difficulties—she was forced to stop performing in 1948. That same year, however, she became artistic director of Limón's nascent company and held that position until her death ten years later. Although Lawrence gave up her position as business manager for Jose Limón and Company in the 1950s, she designed costumes for the company from its inception until she died in 1971. While it is clear that Limón choreographed *La Malinche* and certainly gave his ultimate approval to its costumes and props, the exact contributions of Humphrey and Lawrence remain problematical. Any subsequent reference to Limón's props and costumes in the dance should be read as likely including contributions from these two talented women dancers in his company.[14]

FIGURE 4.1 José Clemente Orozco, "The Appearance of Quetzalcoatl" from the *Epic of American Civilization.* Baker Library, Dartmouth College: Commissioned by the Trustees of Dartmouth College, Hanover, N.H.

From his exposure to Mexican cultural and artistic creativity in New York, Limón incorporated the muralists' sense of transcendent time and emphasis on Indian heritage into *La Malinche.* The dance expresses the eternal triangle of love and hate.[15] At the outset of the dance, the female character, Malinche, allies with the European male character, El Conquistador, who represents Cortés and the Spaniards who conquered and ruled Mexico. Together Malinche and El Conquistador defeat the Indian male character, El Indio. El Indio then rejects Malinche for her collaboration with El Conquistador, and she dies in sorrow. Her spirit rises, however, and as *La Malinche* ends it becomes the spirit of the *soldaderas.* El Indio, now the landless revolutionary peon, gains the strength he needs from Malinche to overthrow El Conquistador and reclaim his country.

In the dance, Malinche never acts alone; whichever male she supports, historically in 1519 or spiritually in 1910, becomes strong enough to attack and defeat the other. Rather than end with an idealized vision of the Indians' future, the dance ends as it began, with a Mexican children's song. The three players regroup, the song begins again, and they march off the stage. El Conquistador leads the group in the prologue, while El Indio leads it offstage in the epilogue. The change in the position of the male characters is matched by another change: at the end of the dance El Indio is carrying the flower that Malinche carried in the prologue and during the first part of the dance.

Three props in *La Malinche*—the stylized flower, the sword carried by El Conquistador, and the skirt worn by Malinche—seem to derive from the documents researched by Rivera. If Limón saw the New York retrospective of Rivera's work in the 1930s, it is reasonable to conclude that they inspired him to learn something about the painter's sources. The art historian Benjamin Keen writes, "Rivera's historical art in general displays a great, almost obsessive concern with factual accuracy." [16] An analysis of his murals at the Palacio de Cortés in Cuernavaca, for example, reveals that he used "such published and manuscript codices as the Lienzo de Tlaxcala, the Matrícula de Tributos, [Bernardino de] Sahagún's Florentine Codex and his Primeros Memoriales, [and] the Codex Mendoza." [17] Among these sources, the Lienzo de Tlaxcala, a mid-sixteenth-century pictorial history of the Conquest of Mexico by the Spaniards and their Tlaxcalan allies, seems to have inspired three of the props in *La Malinche*.

Whether Limón ever learned about the Lienzo de Tlaxcala either through an interest in Rivera's work or by other means cannot be established. Certainly individual illustrations from the Lienzo de Tlaxcala as well as copies of the entire work were available to him, if he sought them. Long before the Revolution promoted the cultural nationalism that focused on the Indian, the Lienzo de Tlaxcala was in the public domain. Alfredo Chavero published two versions of it. The first was a partial copy in black and white that appeared in the first volume of his *Historia Antigua de México*. Then he published a complete copy in color to celebrate the 400th anniversary of Columbus's first voyage.[18] While neither version was commonly available, the anniversary edition probably could be found in university libraries or special collections, presumably in Los Angeles or New York City, since Limón lived in those two places.[19] Also appearing in the nineteenth century, the Mexican edition of William H. Prescott's *History of Mexico* included seven small scenes and four details from the principal scene of the Lienzo de Tlaxcala. Then, in 1939, during the cultural florescence prompted by the Mexican Revolution, G. Echaniz produced another version of the Lienzo that originated in the nineteenth century when Colonel Próspero Cahuantzi governed Tlaxcala under President Porfirio Díaz.[20] Whether or not Limón saw any of these versions of the Lienzo de Tlaxcala or learned of the Lienzo by seeing Rivera's work is unknown. Yet three of the *La Malinche* props are striking in their visual similarities to the Lienzo, although they do not reflect its unique concept of the Spanish victory over the Aztec Empire in 1521.

The Lienzo presents a one-sided view of the Conquest war in detailing the quantities of food, supplies, and warriors that the Tlaxcalans provided to Cortés and his fellow Spaniards. The Tlaxcalan contributions are illustrated in this giant painting in a large central scene and numerous smaller scenes. Longtime enemies of the Aztecs, the Tlaxcalans resided in the highlands west of the Aztec capital. The Lienzo portrays the Tlaxcalans as allies of the Spaniards in the battles of the Conquest and thereby entitled to special privileges from the Spanish crown.[21] In support of the Tlaxcalans' claim for preferential treatment, the Lienzo idealizes the history of both sides: The Tlaxcalans welcome the Spaniards, and the Spaniards never attack them; the Tlaxcalans provide food and supplies to the Spaniards, and the Spaniards never demand tribute from them. Even in its portrayal of fierce combat, the Lienzo never depicts Tlaxcalans and Spaniards as being captured or killed by their enemies. No Tlaxcalan weeps or mourns for relatives lost in the war. The Lienzo is a paean to the conquerors that presents the Tlaxcalans as peers of the Spaniards. Only the Aztecs and their allies appear defeated, bloodied, dead, or dying, often naked and stripped of their dignity. In contrast, the Lienzo asserts the Tlaxcalans' high status through elaborate attire the equal of that of their Spanish allies. The richly costumed Lienzo scenes could have been an excellent source for the clothing and props in Limón's *La Malinche*.

Figure 4.4, below, in the Lienzo de Tlaxcala may have inspired three of Limón's four props—the flower, the sword, and the skirt.[22] The title of the scene, "Ye omo nahuateque Tlaxcallan," or "ic monahuateque Tlaxcallan," means "When they embraced in Tlaxcala." In the scene, a high-status Tlaxcalan lord embraces Cortés while a second lord of equal rank offers the Spanish captain a bouquet of flowers to honor his arrival. Besides the bouquet offered to Cortés in this scene, scenes in figures 4.2 and 4.3 depict Indians presenting Cortés with flowers. Cortés receives the bouquets, although other gifts are offered to the Spaniards, particularly food for the men and their horses. The stylized and almost architecturally arranged bouquets are specifically presented to Cortés in acknowledgment of his position as military leader. The flowers seem to have become distilled into the single flower Malinche offers El Conquistador in *La Malinche*. She holds her stylized, perfect flower upright, in a posture reminiscent of the Tlaxcalan lord carrying

FIGURES 4.2 & 4.3 "Atlivetsyan" and detail of "veyotlipan" or Hueyotipan. Chavero plates from *Homenaje a Cristobal Colon: antiguedades mexicanas,* 1892. Courtesy of the Nettie Lee Benson Latin American Collection, University of Texas Libraries, the University of Texas at Austin.

the bouquet in figure 4.4. Just as the Tlaxcalans honored Cortés with bouquets, Malinche honors El Conquistador with a flower. As he extends the sword in front of him as if it were a cross, Malinche attaches the flower to its center to symbolize her acceptance of him, his Spanish culture, and his Christian faith. Near the end of the dance, she takes the flower from the sword/cross of El Conquistador and gives it to El Indio in recognition of his military and cultural dominance of Mexico. The transfer of the flower from the female to the male Indian character and the repositioning of the male characters as they march off the stage are the visual distinctions between the prologue and the epilogue of the dance. In all other respects these two segments of the dance remain the same, which shows how the prop reinforces the choreography.

In the center of "When they embraced in Tlaxcala," a sword is suspended in midair, detached from Cortés. It is the most prominent sword pictured in the Lienzo, although fifteen swords appear in forty-eight separate Lienzo illustrations. The sword reminds the viewer of the large wooden cross behind Cortés. Limón achieves the same effect in the opening of *La Malinche,* when El Conquistador marches on stage with an oversized sword in front of him, holding it like a cross. In both *La Malinche* and the Lienzo scene in figure 4.4, the viewer knows that El Conquistador/Cortés is supposed to be wearing a sword, but no belt or holder attaches it to him. During the dance the sword simultaneously serves as a weapon, a religious symbol, and an emblem of the sexual relationship between Cortés, in the character of El Conquistador, and

FIGURE 4.4 "Ye omo nahuateque Tlaxcallan," or "When they embraced in Tlaxcala." Cauhuantzi plates from *Lienzo de Tlaxcala* (ca. 1890) courtesy of the Bancroft Library, University of California, Berkeley.

Malinche. Representing Cortés, El Conquistador lifts Malinche with the sword/cross; then he suspends it between his body and hers as he hovers over her. A new race and culture are born of this union, but they doom El Indio and his way of life. El Conquistador uses his sword to attack El Indio until nearly the end of the dance, when the spirit of Malinche inspires El Indio to become a revolutionary. Then the combined power of Malinche and El Indio defeats El Conquistador.

The third prop, a black skirt with a gold border, signifies the sexual relationship between El Conquistador and Malinche. Even before the dance begins, the audience sees the skirt located upstage in the left corner. During the dance, Malinche actually uses the skirt as a cape, which she attempts to wrap around El Indio.

The prop resembles the dark cape worn by Cortés in the Lienzo scene in figure 4.4. How is the skirt related to the Lienzo cape? In both

FIGURE 4.5 "Ye oyaque Atimpan oqui yipito in Narváez" or "When they went down to the banks of the water (coast), (when) they went to apprehend Narváez." Cauhuantzi plates from *Lienzo de Tlaxcala* (ca. 1890) courtesy of the Bancroft Library, University of California, Berkeley.

FIGURE 4.6 Detail of Cortés's cape from "Ye oyaque Atimpan oqui yipito in Narváez."

La Malinche and the Lienzo, the cape or skirt represents protection and status. Dark capes are identified with Cortés in numerous Lienzo scenes, although the style varies from one to another. A full-length dark cape is draped over Cortés's shoulders and falls below his throne chair in several other Lienzo illustrations. In the figures below, Cortés wears a dark cape as he rides his horse.[23]

When the Aztecs turn against Cortés and his Tlaxcalan allies, the Lienzo usually depicts Cortés in armor or other clothing suited to military combat. But Cortés wears luxurious capes in four towns depicted in the Lienzo: Tenochtitlán, Quauhximalpan, Aztaquemeca, and Tetzcohco.[24] The capes distinguish him from other Spaniards while they protect him from the highland cold. The cape in Lienzo (figure 4.4) seems the most likely inspiration for Limón's prop, which symbolized Malinche's relationship with Cortés.

During the dance, El Conquistador wraps the cape-turned-skirt around Malinche, who fastens it at the waist and wears it during the middle part of the performance. The black fabric of the skirt contrasts with Malinche's bright dress. As she dances, a slit appears in the front of the skirt because it is attached only at the waist. Flashes of the brightly colored dress against the black outer fabric dramatize the union of Malinche and El Conquistador. The black color of the cape/skirt represents death; the gold border signifies Spain's power. In Limón's vision, Malinche's relationship is born of innocence but marked by death during the Conquest war and Spanish colonial rule. The cape/skirt seals her sexual alliance with the conqueror and the dominance of his culture over Mexico. After El Conquistador attacks El Indio and he lies center stage in a heap, Malinche wraps the skirt around him as if she were covering him with a cape. El Indio immediately throws off the garment and rejects her protective gesture, which symbolizes Spanish rule. In despair at his antagonism, she leaves him in pain and sorrow. With each step the skirt becomes heavier as she is weighed down by Spanish colonial rule, European culture, and the death associated with any type of foreign dominance. Upstage left, she removes the cape/skirt and drops it back on the floor.

When El Conquistador wraps the cape/skirt around Malinche, he also hands her a scarf that she carries while wearing the skirt. The scarf seems purely European in origin, perhaps reminiscent of aristocratic Spanish women of the sixteenth century, who carried the same kinds of lace handkerchiefs and scarves that the leading ladies of the theater did.[25]

The scarf reinforces and extends Malinche's performance, both with El Conquistador and El Indio. The cape/skirt symbolizes European cul-

FIGURE 4.7 "Tetzcoco" or "Texcoco." Cauhuantzi plates from *Lienzo de Tlaxcala* (ca. 1890) courtesy of the Bancroft Library, University of California, Berkeley.

FIGURE 4.8 Detail of Cortés's cape from "Tetzcoco."

tural and sexual domination, while the scarf defines European femininity. When Malinche first receives the scarf from El Conquistador, she holds it extended from her body, almost the way that she held the flower at the beginning of the dance. She holds the scarf in this position while she dances in unison with El Conquistador. The scarf expresses her anguished appeal to him to refrain from attacking El Indio. She finally allows her arms to fall and the scarf to touch the floor as El Conquistador

FIGURE 4.9 Cortés on horseback in the midst of Tlaxcalan and Spanish infantry at "Aztatl-quemecan" or "Aztaquemeca." Cauhuantzi plates from *Lienzo de Tlaxcala* (ca. 1890) courtesy of the Bancroft Library, University of California, Berkeley.

ignores her and lunges with his sword at El Indio. Thereafter, Malinche sees the wounded El Indio, turns away and covers her mouth and cheeks with the scarf, as if stifling a scream and absorbing her tears. The scarf becomes one with the cape/skirt when she lifts it to cover and protect El Indio. When he rejects her, she extends her arms above her head and uses both hands to pull the scarf taut, signifying her anger and despair. She circles around in her grief, with outstretched arms and the scarf fluttering in the air. The scarf symbolizes vulnerability as she holds it as far away from her body as possible. The fluttering scarf contrasts with the heavy skirt, which she barely lifts as she turns since it is symbolically weighed down by the dual burdens of colonial power and sexual domination. When Malinche unfastens the cape/skirt after her dance with El Indio, she merely allows it to fall to the floor. With the scarf, however, in a much more deliberate gesture, she turns, extends her arm over the skirt, and drops the scarf to the floor. The act ends her association with

El Conquistador and the cultural repression he represents. The fallen scarf in the dance marks the end of her earthly life and frees her spirit to return to its Indian origins.

Nowhere is Limón's humanism more apparent than in the costume of El Conquistador. Limón drew from both the visual imagery of the Spanish colonial period and the Revolution of 1910 to clothe the character who symbolized the dominance of Spain and Europe over Mexico. Although the male costumes are made of simple cotton fabric, in the DVD presentation of the dance their texture and thus their simplicity are less obvious. Reflecting light masks the rough texture of the fabric and gives the costumes a sheen which suggests greater refinement than the costume designer intended. The sheen accentuates the more elaborate appearance of El Conquistador.

The costume of El Conquistador—wrapped white cotton pants and pleated shirt—appears more elaborate than that of the similarly clad Indio. His high-necked shirt has a "fluted insert to match the fabric and color of Malinche's handkerchief," but only the ruffle, not the fabric's color or quality, is discernible in the DVD performance.[26] El Conquistador's shirt, tucked into his pants, is decorated with black cuffs, black bands, and gold cord. A narrow, inset black band sewn into the shirt goes over the shoulders and around the neck.

In Renaissance Europe, high-ranking government officials often wore a royal emblem or seal of office on a chain or cord around the neck to identify the wearer with the monarchy.[27] El Conquistador's costume performs the same function in Limón's dance. The medallion could possibly represent the title of marquis that the Spanish crown awarded Cortés. Wearing the medallion, however, El Conquistador becomes not only Cortés but every imperial administrator that ruled the New World. Another circle of golden medallions linked by chains decorates the cape/skirt that El Conquistador wraps around Malinche during the dance. While the skirt symbolizes the imposition of Spanish culture and religion on Mexico, its medallion border reinforces the symbolism of Spain's political domination over Mexico.

While El Conquistador is dressed as the quintessential Spanish colonial administrator, his costume and the dark backdrop of the stage also take cues from the *desornamentado* (unadorned) style used in portraits by Spanish and colonial Mexican painters. In the "unadorned [desornamentado]" style, ordinarily used for architecture but also applied to portraiture, the subject, wearing dark clothes, appears in a bare space, with perhaps an object to create perspective. The stark external attributes

FIGURE 4.10 Mexican, unknown artist. Portrait of Sor Juana Inés de la Cruz. Courtesy of the Philadelphia Museum of Art: The Robert H. Lamborn Collection, 1903.

directed the viewer to the subject's inner personal character as an expression of Spanish concepts of dignity and status.[28] The absence of set decoration in *La Malinche*—the plain backdrop of the performance—recalls the same austere style of Spain and Hispanic America.[29]

The New World tradition of the plain style appears in portraits of another legendary woman in Mexican history, the extraordinarily gifted seventeenth-century poet, Sor Juana Inés de la Cruz. Her self-portrait depicts her in the unadorned manner. While the sixteenth-century Spanish painter Antonio Moro originally developed the ascetic style for King Philip II, Limón's costume for El Conquistador reflects a famous example of the unadorned style as used in a portrait of a later king. Diego Velázquez's *Philip IV, King of Spain* (1624), which hangs in New York's Metropolitan Museum of Art, where Limón could have seen it, contains some of the details of El Conquistador's costume. In *Philip IV* Velázquez depicts the king completely in black, with a light collar and cuffs. His chain of office hangs over one shoulder, and his dark stockings become one with his equally black shoes.

Limón reverses the colors but uses the same combination. El Conquistador appears completely in white, with a dark band around his neck and cuffs. His chain of office hangs around his neck, and his white pants meld into his bare feet, which at times in the DVD appear to be white shoes. In Velázquez's portrait Philip holds a piece of paper, perhaps signifying the written order that could change his far-flung empire. Limón's El Conquistador holds a sword, signifying the military order that created a frontier empire. The single difference between the two figures is that Philip wears a cape, while El Conquistador's cape/skirt waits on the floor upstage left. In the portrait, Philip's face conveys character, while in the dance Limón reveals El Conquistador's character through movement.

Although Indianist cultural nationalism may have inspired Limón, his creative designs employed multiple sources, including Iberian ones. Having successfully reconciled his own Hispanic and Native American heritage, Limón said he was at peace with himself.[30] The visual imagery of *La Malinche* bears witness to that reconciliation.

In contrast to the European and Spanish colonial sources for the costume of El Conquistador, the inspiration for the attire of the two Indian characters seems to be chiefly American and dating from the early twentieth century. Despite the story's origins in the sixteenth-century Spanish Conquest of Mexico, Limón utilized the dress of 1910 Mexican revolutionaries as a model for the Indians' costumes. Limón's choice of these costumes links him to the twentieth-century nationalist celebration of the Mexican Revolution and Indian culture.

As does El Conquistador, El Indio wears the simple white cotton pleated shirt and wrapped pants worn by the landless peasants who fought in the Revolution. In the political mythology of Mexico in the

FIGURE 4.11 Diego Rodríguez de Silva y Velázquez, "Philip IV (1605–1665), King of Spain." Courtesy of the Metropolitan Museum of Art, Bequest of Benjamin Altman, 1913 (14.40.639). Image © The Metropolitan Museum of Art.

1920s and 1930s, the peon revolutionaries became cultural heroes, their simple clothing adorning Mexico's murals and thus gaining worldwide exposure.

Limón may have found inspiration for the costume of El Indio in mural paintings of Mexican peasant revolutionaries in works such as

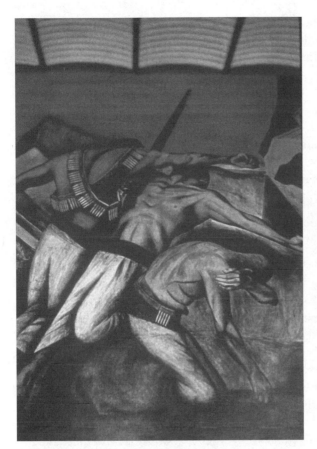

FIGURE 4.12 "The Trench" by José Clemente Orozco, 1921, fresco at the National Preparatory School, Mexico City. Courtesy of the Granger Collection.

FIGURE 4.13 Emiliano Zapata. Photographer unknown.

Orozco's *The Trench*.[31] The simple pants worn by the peasants in Orozco's painting are counterbalanced by the ammunition and weapons that revolutionaries carry. In Limón's dance, El Indio's simple costume contrasts with his use of the sword near the end of the dance to attack El Conquistador.

Another possible source for El Indio's pleated shirt is the one worn in a widely publicized newspaper photograph from the revolutionary era of Emiliano Zapata, the leader seeking land reform for countless tenant farmers trapped in a life of poverty.

Zapata's and El Indio's white cotton shirts button at the neck and have pleats in the front. Both wear the shirt over their pants—in Zapata's case even though he is wearing the suit of a caballero—so the pleats gently opened to provide ease of movement.

Also twentieth century in inspiration is Malinche's costume, which more likely would be worn by a *mestizo* woman than by an Amerindian. It differs dramatically from the historical tuniclike *huipils* that Malinche wears in the illustrations of the Lienzo de Tlaxcala. Dressing Malinche in patterned Indian *huipils* or El Indio as an Indian warrior in an *ichcahuipilli* (armor) and *ehuatl* (tunic) would have underscored their respective sorrow and defeat.[32] But the soft gathers and silhouette of Malinche's costume instead derive from the clothing of rural mestiza women and from that of the Revolution's female soldiers, the collarless, short-sleeved white cotton blouse tucked into a three-quarter-length, black gathered skirt.[33]

By clothing her as a mestiza, Limón perfectly symbolizes Malinche's position in the dance. Malinche is part of an eternal triangle of love and hate. Whichever male she supports becomes strong enough to attack the other, but Malinche never acts alone. As does a mestizo, she reverberates between two men, two cultures, and two periods in time.

The apparently red color of Malinche's costume in the DVD performance adds a layer of symbolic meaning distinct from the live performance, in which she wears bright pink. Red vibrates with symbolism. It represents the color of blood, which links Malinche to the bloodshed of the Conquest. Limón portrays her as both the victim and instrument of El Conquistador's killing of Indians. In the last part of the dance, Malinche dances with El Indio as together they attack El Conquistador. Since the Revolution also caused a great deal of bloodshed, Malinche's apparently red costume in the DVD also symbolizes the countless Mexicans who died in that uprising.

Although the shape of the costume is the same as that of the rural mestiza turned *soldadera* during the Revolution, its ruffles and bright color are unique. In contrast, the costumes of the male characters, El Conquistador and El Indio, reflect their various roles from the past into the present. El Conquistador is Cortés the conqueror, the Spanish colonial administrator, and the foreigner dominating Mexican culture. El Indio is the Indian destroyed by Cortés, the peon laboring on the haciendas, and the revolutionary calling for land reform.

The character of Malinche, unlike her costume, reflects two distinct historical eras. She is the sixteenth-century Indian woman who helped Cortés conquer Mexico, only to be reviled by her own people. Later, her spirit, the spirit of the *soldaderas*, infuses El Indio with the strength to become a revolutionary. Malinche's dress is not the *huipil* of an Indian woman or the gown of a Spanish woman, even with the addition of the cape/skirt and the scarf. Despite its silhouette, Malinche's costume does not look like that of a *soldadera*. In bright pink, Malinche is a little girl, and even though the seemingly red costume of the DVD conveys deeper symbolic meaning, it does not associate her with an historic time period.

Besides visually reinforcing the narrative of the ballet, the props and the costumes add to the story with symbolic nuances drawn both from Mexico's Conquest and from Spanish colonial, Christian, and European traditions.

The sword/cross and cape/skirt may have derived from the Lienzo de Tlaxcala. The sword defines the character of El Conquistador as religious zealot, military conqueror, and progenitor of a new race. El Conquistador marches on to the stage and holds the sword in front of him as a weapon and a cross. He uses it as a weapon to conquer Mexico by attacking and killing El Indio.

Limón's El Indio begins the dance as the conquered Indian of the sixteenth century and ends it triumphantly, after the spirit of Malinche motivates him to kill El Conquistador with the cross/sword. The symbolic transfer of power from El Conquistador to El Indio occurs when Malinche removes her flower from the cross/sword of the defeated El Conquistador and hands it to El Indio.

The flower is Malinche's prop. Its stylized form may have originated in the architecturally constructed bouquets of the Lienzo de Tlaxcala, where such an arrangement represented propitiation and honor. Carrying the flower, Malinche enters the stage. Then she gives it to El Conquistador, and after his death she hands it to El Indio. Carrying the flower, he leads the march off the stage. Again, the gesture of transferring the flower from one man to the other is consistent with the mediating character of Malinche.

Limón's Malinche, like Orozco's Quetzalcóatl, is legendary, but she represents the future as much as the past. She offers her flower to El Conquistador in innocence, propitiating and honoring the powerful foreigner. Malinche willingly accepts the cape/skirt offered to her by El Conquistador, which suggests her hopes for Mexico under Spanish colonial rule. Her failed defense of El Indio, as she implores El Conquistador to refrain from using brute force, reveals her expectation that the Spaniards would act humanely. Any effort to help El Indio fails, as much from his recalcitrance as from Spanish venality. When she uses her skirt as a cape to protect El Indio, he throws it off to reject it as well as

Malinche. Alone and disillusioned, she dies in pain and suffering, but her spirit lives on as the spirit of the *soldaderas*. Malinche's spirit inspires El Indio to attack El Conquistador and rid Mexico of foreign domination. In acknowledgment of El Indio's success, Malinche, as the *soldadera*, gives him the flower she removes from El Conquistador's sword/cross. But what happens to the flower? The dance ends almost as it began, with the three characters marching off the stage, led by El Indio carrying the flower. What will El Indio do with it? What is the future of Mexico? Limón ends *La Malinche* as the Mexican muralist José Clemente Orozco ended his *Epic of American Civilization*, with a visual message of hope for a better era in some unknown time.

ACKNOWLEDGMENTS

I wish to thank my late colleague Jayne Durnal and her husband, William, for their technical assistance with illustrations and the original layout. I am also grateful to Allen Ward of the University of Connecticut for his help in editing and proofreading the text.

NOTES

1. Jose Limón, "Composing a Dance," *Julliard Review* (Winter 1955): 18.
2. Michael C. Meyer and William L. Sherman, *The Course of Mexican History* (New York, 1979), 621.
3. Ibid., 574; Jean Charlot, *Mexican Mural Renaissance* (New York, 1979), 315.
4. José E. Limón, "Greater Mexico, Modernism, and New York: Miguel Covarrubias and José Limón," in Kurt Heinzelman, *The Covarrubias Circle: Nickolas Muray's Collection of Twentieth-Century Mexican Art*, Harry Ransom Humanities Research Center Imprint Series (Austin: University of Texas Press, 2004), 83–98.
5. National Palace, Mexico City, http://www.interamericaninstitute.org/View_from_Tlatelolco_before_conquest_Diego_Rivera.JPG 7-29-2005; "Edificio Principal y la Capilla," http://www.chapingo.mx/academicos/capilla/Nrev/NE.htm 7-29-2005; "Diego Rivera, Chapingo (Capilla Riveriana)," http://www.chapingo.mx/academicos/capilla/Mprin/ 7-29-2005.
6. "Diego Rivera Web Museum: Biography," http://www.diegorivera.com/bio/ 7-29-2005; "American Masters. Diego Rivera," http://www.pbs.org/wnet/americanmasters/database/rivera_d.html 7-28-2005; "Diego Rivera: Man at the Crossroads," http://www.fbuch.com/crossroa.htm, 7-28-2005; "Culture Shock: Flashpoints: Visual Arts: Diego Rivera's Man at the Crossroads," http://www.pbs.org/wgbh/cutureshock/flashpoints/visualarts/diegorivera_a.html, 7-29-2005.

7. Patty Delaney, in this book, refers to Limón's unpublished choreographic notes for *Danzas Mexicanas* (1937), the predecessor to *La Malinche*.

8. Delaney, in this book, notes that when creating *Danzas Mexicanas*, Limón first realized he was a choreographer.

9. "Dancer History Archives-José Limón," http://www.streetswing.com/histmai2/d2Limón1.htm 7-29-2005; "Limón (Jose) Photographs, BIOGRAPHY," http://digilib.nypl.org/dnyaweb/dhc/findaid/Limón http://people.smu.edu/zhammer 7-28-2005.

10. Norton Owen, ed. *Limón Journal* 3, no. 1 (Fall 1998).

11. Jacquelynn Baas, "Interpreting Orozco's Epic," *Dartmouth Alumni Magazine* (January/February 1984).

12. Delaney, in this book, transcription from Limón's unpublished choreographic notes for *Danzas Mexicanas*, 1937.

13. Patricia Seed, personal communication, 2004.

14. "Lawrence, Pauline. Pauline Lawrence Limón Collection," http://digilib.nypl.org/dynawre///doris-humphrey.bigraphy.ms/ 7-29-2005; Weidman (Charles) Papers, BIOGRAPHY," http://digilib.nypl.org/dynaweb/dhc/findaid/weidman/GenericBookTextView/136 7-29-2005.

15. George Ferguson, *Signs and Symbols in Christian Art* (New York, 1961), 152.

16. Benjamin Keen, *The Aztec Image in Western Thought* (New Brunswick, 1971), 329–330.

17. Ibid., 530.

18. Carlos Martínez-Marín, "History of the Lienzo de Tlaxcala: Originals, copies, and editions," *El Lienzo de Tlaxcala* (Mexico, D.F. 1983), 42; Charles Gibson, *Tlaxcala in the Sixteenth Century* (Stanford, 1967), 250.

19. Martínez-Marín, "History of the Lienzo," 43.

20. Ibid.

21. Gibson, *Tlaxcala in the Sixteenth Century,* 165–166.

22. Martínez-Marín, *El Lienzo de Tlaxcala*, 67. All titles of Lienzo images in this chapter, in Nahautl and English, unless otherwise noted, are from *El Lienzo de Tlaxcala* (Mexico, D.F. 1983).

23. Ibid., 74.

24. Ibid., 80–81, 83, 87, 104.

25. Douglas Gorsline, *What People Wore* (New York, 1951), 57.

26. Sarah Stackhouse, personal communication forwarded from Patricia Seed, 7-25-05.

27. Diego Velázquez, "Felipe IV." Henry Kamen, *Philip of Spain* (New Haven, 1997). In a portrait of the administrator of the Spanish Netherlands, the third duke of Alba, for example, William Key shows him wearing an elaborate chain holding the Hapsburg royal emblem (Figure 4.11 in this book). The emblem visually identifies Alba as a servant of the king.

28. Linda Bantel and Marcus B. Burke, *Spain and New Spain, Mexican Colonial Arts in Their European Context* (Corpus Christi, 1979), 40–41.

29. Patricia Seed, personal communication, 2006.

30. Shelley Berg, "Historical Context," *La Malinche*, CD-ROM.

31. Bradley Smith, *Mexico, A History in Art* (Garden City, 1968), 366.

32. Patricia Reiff Anawalt, *Indian Clothing Before Cortés* (Norman, 1981), 46–51.

33. Frances Toor, *A Treasury of Mexican Folkways* (New York, 1947), photograph #44.

5. MARINA, MALINCHE, MALINTZIN

Nahua Women and the Spanish Conquest

Susan Kellogg

The variously named woman doña Marina, Malinche, Malintzin, who lived a brief and violent life, has gone down in history as one of the most important yet enigmatic participants in the Spanish Conquest of the Mexica and other Nahuatl-speaking peoples of the central region of Mexico. No document exists in which she narrates or interprets her life, even though Spanish sources refer to her, somewhat ironically, as *la lengua* ("the tongue"). The circumstances and events of her life—at least those which we can be reasonably certain about given the paucity of sources discussing her—can be used to illustrate some of the ways in which sexuality and gender figured into the process of European conquest, foreshadowing the changing status of indigenous women in the early colonial period. In this essay I also argue that a discussion of Marina/Malinche/Malintzin's life can shed light as well on the gendered patterns of Nahua culture and society that shaped women's lives during the pre-Hispanic period. These gendered patterns reflected a degree of male dominance tied to the emphasis on warfare among many late pre-Hispanic central Mexican peoples, but also allowed women roles of authority in the economic, political, and religious realms.

THE LIFE AND TIMES OF MALINTZIN

Even the name of the young slave woman who labored among the Gulf Coast Chontal Maya in the town of Potonchan is in doubt. While many writers, past and present, assert that the Spanish gave her the name Marina because it closely matched her indigenous name, Malinalli ("twisted grass"), Malina (or Malintzin, an honorific form used in indigenous-authored texts) more likely reflected a native pronunciation of the name Marina, given to her by a priest in 1519.[1] Whatever her birth name, that she would become known by the Nahuatlized version of her name, Malintzin, is appropriate because she was not Maya in origin but had been born among Gulf Coast Nahuatl speakers. Thought by Bernal Díaz del

Castillo, a participant in the Cortés expedition and the author of the most informative source about her, to have been born into a noble family, Malintzin was given away after her father died and her mother remarried. Eventually she ended up among Maya speakers whose culture, given her young age, may have also influenced her and who in turn gave her to Cortés in 1519.[2] Malintzin's life was thus marked by loss of family, loss of social status, and geographic displacement, a not uncommon experience for indigenous women before, during, and after the arrival of the Spanish. For Cortés and his group, her Nahuatl-Maya bilingualism (later trilingualism when she added Spanish to the mix) became useful. Before she learned Spanish and some Spaniards learned Nahuatl, Cortés was forced to rely on a chain of translators. It included Malintzin, who translated from Nahuatl to Maya, and Gerónimo de Aguilar, a Spaniard who had been enslaved by Yucatec Maya after a shipwreck in 1511, who translated from Maya to Spanish. Malintzin soon became fluent enough in Spanish to translate directly, though by then some Spaniards were also comfortable enough speaking Nahuatl to translate. She served as Cortés's primary translator throughout the conquest of the Mexica and even after, including on his ill-fated Honduran expedition. As both Spanish and indigenous sources make clear, Malintzin's importance lay not only in her translation work but in her loyalty to the Spanish cause.

Whatever else is or is not known about her, that she was loyal to the Spanish cannot be doubted. While she continually aided them by translating, her role in the very bloody Spanish massacre of Cholulans (after she reported to Cortés about Cholulan plans to aid a Mexica attack on the Spanish) is the event that forms the basis of the popularly held modern Mexican view of Malintzin as the very definition of both informer and traitor. But her role in the execution of Cuauhtémoc, the last Mexica supreme ruler, may even better illustrate her deep loyalty to the Spanish since she was not only present for his execution, but also aided two Franciscan friars in ministering to him before his execution.[3]

Was the source of this loyalty love, a concept whose use here is perhaps an anachronism but is nonetheless of interest? Malintzin first had relationships with two Spaniards: Alonso Hernández de Puertocarrero, to whom she was given and with whom she stayed for only a short time in 1519, and then Cortés himself, with whom she had a son. Cortés then married her to a third Spaniard, Juan Jaramillo, in what Cortés's secretary-chaplain-biographer, Francisco López de Gómara, viewed as an inappropriate wedding during which the groom was intoxicated. She later had two children with Jaramillo. Did love play a role in these relationships? Was Malintzin driven by a very pragmatic will to survive? or was she driven, at least in part, by an anti-Mexica desire to overthrow imperial domination, perhaps born out of bitterness over the several displacements she had suffered in her life?[4] Her actions, not inconsistent with an anti-Mexica sentiment, are those of a woman making choices among a limited and unsatisfactory set of options presented by others— Nahua, Maya, Spanish—to her. And she could hardly be a traitor to the Mexican nation when no such nation existed.[5] Her role as a translator was unusual for women in the Conquest and post-Conquest eras and was rooted partly (though not completely, as argued below) in the multicultural circumstances thrust upon her from the time she was a young child and her own exceptional linguistic abilities. The pathos of her existence as object to be used and passed around is undeniable and exemplifies the pragmatic, even uncaring, nature of most relations between Spanish conquerors and indigenous women in the Conquest and post-Conquest periods. Before taking a look at how Malintzin's life illustrates several important aspects of women's lives and roles in the post-Conquest period, I want to consider how her life illustrates some aspects of the roles of pre-Hispanic Nahua, particularly Mexica, women.

WOMEN'S ROLES IN MEXICA SOCIETY

Most descriptions of Nahua history and cultural patterns emphasize how warlike many Nahua ethnic groups were as they sought to expand their spheres of influence and create alliances such as the Triple Alliance, also known popularly as the Aztecs, a conglomeration of three cities and ethnic groups—the Mexica of Tenochtitlán, the Acolhua of Texcoco, and the Tepaneca of Tlacopan—who built a conquest state organized primarily around war, tribute, and trade. Over time (here I am referring to the late Postclassic period from roughly 1300 to 1519, a period of accelerated warfare and expansion by the Triple Alliance powers), the role of war expanded and increasingly resulted in the celebration of maleness and masculine values through a gendered discourse that described victory as masculine and defeat as feminine. Yet paradoxically the increased militarization of Mexica society opened up social space for women to play important, often parallel and complementary, social roles. This form of social organization and the discourse associated with it were rooted in the patterns of warfare and empire building of this period, but also in ancient Mesoamerican notions of the complementarity of maleness and femaleness.[6]

One area in which such complementarity and parallel roles are particularly evident is in the world of work. Unquestionably, Mexica women worked hard, and this observation applies whether women came from the noble or commoner stratum. We have already seen how Malintzin's life may have crossed this class divide. Both girls and boys began to receive training in future work tasks between the ages of five and six. While men were responsible for farming and fighting along with hunting, fishing, production of many craft items, and the long-distance trading of those items, women performed vital household functions, including cooking, cleaning, spinning and weaving as well as rearing and socializing the much-prized Mexica infants and children. They also participated in household-based crafts production. Outside the home, commoner women especially provided labor in market exchange, worked as healers, midwives, and marriage brokers, and served as teachers and priestesses in temples and song houses. Sometimes portrayed as laboring drudges whose productive efforts were socially necessary but not valued, Mexica women, the weight of evidence shows, had some control over the conditions and fruits of their labor and, through work, even when household-based, achieved authority, even prestige.[7]

Every Mexica home, or *calli*, contained multiple rooms in which related families lived, centered around a patio and hearth area. In this society, the *calli* made up the female space par excellence where labor, often under female control, took place. Mothers, especially the "good mother" as described in the *Florentine Codex*, were thought to be energetic, careful, and thrifty workers who would serve and teach others.[8] This source, consisting of texts set down in the mid-sixteenth century by Nahua elders in response to questions from the Franciscan friar Bernardino de Sahagún, often depicts what these male elders viewed as ideal social types. Among female kin, good grandmothers and great-grandmothers received special praise from the elders, who observed how they bore the responsibility of correcting others. In a discussion of the roles of family and kin group members, the elders stated that the Mexica valued great-grandmothers as founders of kin groups as well. As Sahagún's Nahua informants themselves said of the role of the great-grandmother, "She is the founder, the beginner [of her lineage]."[9]

Why did the Mexica view women as the founders of kin groups? The notion of women as, ultimately, the originators of kinship relations (either by themselves or with their husbands) was rooted in two features of Mexica life, one mythical and historic, the other reflecting the way the kinship system operated. Mexica nobility flowed from female as well as male sources. The first Mexica *tlatoani*, or supreme leader, Acamapichtli, for example, became ennobled through his marriage to Ilancueitl, daughter of a Culhuacan king. More generally, the birthplace and status of a nobleman's mother or wife could enhance or weaken his status in the hierarchy of status among the nobility. In the mythical realm, a female priest named Chimalma helped lead the Mexica to their eventual settling place, thereby acting as a founding ancestor of the Mexica as a people.[10]

Likewise, in the realm of kinship as conceptualized in everyday life, a child was seen as being connected to ancestors by his or her mother's blood and father's semen.[11] This bilateral conceptualization of kinship provided the basis for the Mexica kinship system, one in which household members and members of larger descent units could use ties through mothers or fathers, or other female or male kin, to claim ties and activate rights. However, their cognatic kinship system was neither completely bilateral nor egalitarian in practice. Early colonial legal and genealogical evidence shows that men gained greater access to rights over land and that ties through men were mentioned more often when genealogies were recounted. The Mexica also gave more individualizing and varied names to boys than to girls, who frequently bore names referring to birth order. But genealogies frequently included women as links through whom kin connections could be traced and as ancestors, especially as one member of a founding couple, from whom kinship and property flowed.[12]

Women's authority, based in both their work and the cognatic kinship system, extended beyond the household as well. In the markets, for example, women were not only buyers but also vendors. In addition, they could serve as marketplace judges or administrators called *tianquizpan tlayacanque*, a position held by both men and women. Supervisory positions within guilds associated with craft production were also held by women, though whether they oversaw women's guilds within or parallel to those of men is not known. References to a ceremony involving "the most important *joyera*" (female jewelry maker) and "the most important merchant woman" suggest that female crafts producers might have been hierarchically ranked.[13]

In the realm of religion, an arena of great importance in Mexica life because of both the complexity of their beliefs and the time they devoted to religious activities, women also held positions of religious and political authority. In the song houses, or *cuicacalli*, that young adolescent girls and boys attended to learn the songs, dances, and moral codes part of the Mexica belief system, male officials called *tiachcahuan* and *telpochtlatoque* (terms which mean "older brothers" and "leaders of [male] youths," respectively) judged young men who misbehaved. Parallel female officials, *cihuatetiachcahuan* (a term which could be translated literally as "female older brothers," the prefix *cihua* coming from the Nahuatl word for woman, *cihuatl*), judged young women. Like their male counterparts they could expel those who misbehaved, and the female officials were similarly referred to in hierarchical fashion either as *cihuatetiachcahuan* or as *ichpochtlayacanque* ("administrators" or "directors of young women"). In temples (sometimes, though not always, for female deities), priestesses known as *cihuatlamacazque* (lower-level priestesses) and *cihuacuacuiltin* (higher-level priestesses) helped care for buildings, carry out calendrical and other ceremonies, and train other priestesses.[14]

In the neighborhoods and local subdivisions of Tenochtitlán and other cities and towns, women, like men, served as neighborhood leaders who had responsibilities for seeing to daily affairs within these lower-level political units. Males holding these positions were referred to as *tepixque* and *tlaxilacaleque* (guards, leaders, and/or elders of local neighborhoods), and women holding these positions were called either *cihuatepixque* or *cihuatlaxilacaleque*.[15] At higher levels of governance, Nahua women rarely served as rulers, though on occasion they did so briefly, generally when there was no male successor to a throne. Yet there are also clues that high officials and their wives shared responsibilities. The *tlatocacihuatl* ("female supreme ruler") was a "woman ruler, governor, leader—a provider, an administrator." The *cihuatecutli* (high-ranking noblewoman) "governs, leads, provides for one, arranges well, administers peacefully." [16]

Nahua women thus held positions of authority, positions which were hierarchically organized and parallel to those of men and which afforded women prestige based on their own activities and achievements. This shadowy hierarchy, difficult to tease out of early colonial Nahuatl and Spanish sources, is clearly there, yet it does not appear to have been as highly elaborated as male politico-military hierarchies were. But in addition to holding these positions, women gained both respect and access to material goods through their activities in homes, markets, neighborhoods, song houses, and temples. These material items and the property rights attached to or expressed through them, by bequeathal, gifting, or investment, afforded Mexica women a degree of independence.

While there are few statements that clarify how rights of inheritance were passed along in early colonial chronicles, there are several reasons to think that women customarily bequeathed and inherited property. First, the early colonial Nahua wills from a number of communities illustrate women's ownership of houses, land, and a variety of other items, clothing, cooking implements, jewelry, and religious artifacts among them.[17] Such testaments suggest that female control over property was not a colonial modification. Second, women's property, gained through dowry and inheritance, was kept separate from men's at marriage, and the Mexica made distinctions between household goods belonging to women and those belonging to men.[18] Furthermore, if women managed their resources skillfully, others saw them as being successful. The woman who was not as skillful risked falling into poverty. A talented woman merchant, if born under a fortunate day sign as described in the *Florentine Codex*, could become "quite rich, she would be a good provider, she would be well-born. She would look to and guard the services and the property of our lord. She would be a guardian and administrator. Much would she gather, collect, save, and justly distribute among her children." [19] But another kind of woman worker, the embroiderer, who did not properly perform her religious obligations would be punished with "complete poverty and misery." [20]

Just as Mexica women could be responsible for their own economic successes and failures, they were also responsible for their own behavior. Mexica women, particularly the daughters of the nobility, were taught to be chaste, circumspect, and dutiful in fulfilling their wifely and maternal obligations. Those women who transgressed social and legal responsibilities could be punished for their misbehavior or crimes. Willful female children, prostitutes, female adulterers, and women who had abortions were subject to strong social sanctions and punishments, including death. Nahuas might punish adulterers and adulteresses, for example, with death by stoning or strangulation, indicating the importance they attached to marriage, a significance to be upheld by both male and female partners.[21]

Male sexuality and expressions of violence were given somewhat freer rein, though such behavior could be seen as socially controlled in that sexuality outside of marriage and violent action most often took place in war or through institutions associated with war. Yet women were also known on occasion to engage in violent, aggressive, or assertive behavior. Marketwomen's fighting, for example, was said to have worsened relations between Tenochtitlán and Tlatelolco prior to the war they fought in 1473.[22] Women who were too aggressive verbally or physically were not admired, as the day sign discussion for One Eagle illustrates.

Women born on this day were fated to be "of evil tongue, vile-mouthed, inhuman in speech," and physically aggressive as well.[23] Women's words, especially taunting and freely spoken words (so very different from the seemingly measured, often highly ritualistic speech of men, especially those holding high governing positions), could mock men and even provoke warfare.[24] But Nahuas also believed that women could speak well. Women born on the day One Flint Knife, *ce tecpatl*, for example, could be courageous and have a gift for speaking and leadership, paralleling men born on this day, who would be brave and successful in war. Such a woman would be not only successful in providing sustenance, becoming wealthy as a result of her labor, but also "courageous, strong, reckoned as a man, and hardy. She would give honor as a man. And, [among] all her gifts, she would speak well, be eloquent, give good counsel, and arrange her conversation and manner of speaking well in her home."[25] Thus Malintzin's verbal skills were not at all culturally inappropriate—though she may have been particularly talented in that area even if the uses to which she ultimately put them undermined Mexica and Nahua sovereignty.

Women wielded both formal and informal political influence and, while their sexuality was under tighter social control than men's (especially true of the daughters of the nobility), sexuality was associated with pleasure for both sexes and not viewed as inherently sinful. The Mexica thought of sex as a natural and healthy part of daily life, though they believed too much sex could be harmful and might lead to chaos, a state they feared. Sex carried with it the obligation for men and women to please each other and behave responsibly both toward one another and toward the children they created.[26]

Thus, in addition to the compelling evidence of parallelism in the sociopolitical hierarchy and of the mutual enjoyment and responsibilities of sexual relations, both commoner and elite Mexica women held property rights and produced socially valued goods and services. They held positions of authority across a variety of realms of daily life and were held liable for their transgressions of rules and laws. Were women then under the patriarchal authority of fathers and husbands, as some have argued?[27] Before I answer this question, another realm of Mexica life needs to be considered. This is the realm of religion, especially as it is revealed through the texts and images concerning female deities.

The Mexica pantheon was complex in structure because the deities cannot simply be understood as representing a single (or simple) idea, substance, or social group, nor do they relate neatly to each other through family or kin relations. The gendering of deities also presents a challenge to the deconstruction of their meanings because many deities have both female and male versions or identities (with the female aspect sometimes labeled as a sister or wife), some are androgynous, and some are either solely male or female. But even those deities who are clearly female have complicated images and associations that are both life giving and life enhancing yet also are powerfully warlike, with negative images and associations.[28] Sometimes these powerful, warlike female images are, to modern eyes, demeaning.

The most important deities of sustenance were all female. The deities associated with maize (Xilonen, Iztac Cinteotl, and Chicomecoatl), maguey (Mayahuel), and salt (Uixtocihuatl) were joined by Chalchiuhtlicue, the water goddess and wife of Tlaloc. Important earth deities with both fertility and military associations whose images and ceremonies were common included Toci (Our Grandmother), Cihuacoatl (Snake Woman), Xochiquetzal (Flowery Feather or Plume), and Tlazolteotl (Deity of Filth). The rituals for these goddesses expressed the way that central Mexican peoples prized and conceptually linked agricultural and human fertility.[29] The particularly fierce Cihuacoatl had a lusty appetite for both human hearts and blood. Tlazolteotl was a goddess of sexuality to whom peoples' sins could be confessed in her guise as Tlaelcuani, or "Eater of foul things."[30] While these earth, fertility, and warrior goddesses were perhaps the most prominent of female deities, no single female figure stood as supreme (as was also true for male deities). Instead, these goddesses express the multiple complementary oppositions which shaped and formed Nahua worldviews, of which the central ideas and oppositions were male/female, earth/moon, sun/moon, and war (death)/sustenance (life). Such oppositions, with their inherent ambiguities, can be seen even in the famous Coyolxauhqui image, often cited as strong evidence for women's subordination among the Mexica.[31]

Coyolxauhqui (Bells on Cheek or Face) was the sister and adversary of the Mexica patron and war deity Huitzilopochtli. Having led her four hundred brothers, the Centzonhuitznahua, in an attempted matricide (against their mother Coatlicue, Snake Skirt, because she had impregnated herself by placing on her body a ball of feathers that fell onto her waist), she was attacked, defeated, and killed by her brother. Should this myth and Coyolxauhqui's famous bas-relief sculpture—located at the foot of Huitzilopochtli's temple in Tenochtitlán's ceremonial precinct that shows her as a dead, decapitated figure—be interpreted solely as evidence of the negation of a female power and authority, perhaps portrayed and perceived by male leaders as threatening "the power and legitimacy of the state itself"?[32]

Because the control of women can be both a means through which the state controls households and a metaphor for that control, one could readily conclude that Coyolxauhqui's image tells only the story of increasing Mexica male power rooted partly in violence against women.[33] Did Mexica men use images of female subordination to bolster a growing state's imperial governing apparatus and ideology? Yes, they did, but Mexica women were not the subordinated, passive, and silent beings dominated by patriarchal fathers and husbands that have been inferred from stone and paper portrayals. Their reality was far more varied, and the gender parallelism of Mexica thought and social institutions formed, expressed, and reinforced the integration of complementary oppositions. For the Mexica, these oppositions, so often symbolized through gender, constituted that fleeting wholeness, the fragile balancing of celestial and human forces, that laying at the root of the philosophy, worldview, and conceptual and social patterns that constituted basic parts of their everyday life. And Malintzin's life, that portion of it lived prior to the arrival of Cortés and the Spanish, reflected the complexities, even paradoxes, of Nahua cultural patterns.

Malintzin's early life, her passage from noble to slave, shows that women could at times be treated as objects, passed from a ruling or noble family to other families as marriage partners or gifts to create or cement the constantly shifting political alliances of the late pre-Hispanic period. Yet women had a degree of independence and autonomy, and some filled roles of authority. The art historian Jeanette Peterson has pointed out how colonial indigenous images and writings depict Malintzin as a central figure in the Conquest period. These texts show that "responsibility and direct action are attributed to Malinche/Malintzin alone, whereas in the Spanish translations Cortés is generally speaking through Marina, thereby reducing her to a more passive and secondary player."[34]

MALINTZIN AND WOMEN AFTER THE CONQUEST

Malintzin's life during and after the chaotic events of the Spanish invasion also foreshadowed many of the processes of change that transformed Nahua women's roles and lives. The actions of Cortés toward Malintzin and other indigenous women epitomize the nature of the relationships between native women and the invading Spanish forces. In addition to fathering four children with his Spanish wife and another out of wedlock with another Spanish woman, Cortés was reported to have four *mestizo* children, each by a different mother. One of the women was Malintzin, another was Tecuichpochtzin, a daughter of Moteuczoma.[35] Such transitory relations were perhaps a variant of other, still more exploitative, even violent, relationships between European conquerors and indigenous women caught up in the tumultuous events from the late fifteenth century on.

Relations between Spanish men and native women took several forms. One, already mentioned, is the informal relationship that, while variable in length and depth of affection, often resulted in a child or children who may have been legitimated by their Spanish fathers and remembered with property in their wills. Such was the case with several of Cortés's mestizo children. Those children legitimated by their conqueror fathers usually did not live for very long with their native mothers. Malintzin's son, don Martín, was separated from his parents by the march to Honduras and was later taken by Cortés to Spain, where he lived for most of the rest of his life.[36]

Other relationships resulted in marriages, marriages that were as stable as others of the same time period. However much affection may have motivated these marriages, status, wealth, and security probably played a greater role, as most involved native women born to noble families, especially those families that held landed estates.[37] Sometimes native fathers presented their daughters to the Spanish conquerors, continuing a preexisting way of creating and maintaining political ties, in the hopes of solidifying alliances. In other cases, powerful Spaniards arranged marriages between indigenous women and some of their men, as Cortés did with Malintzin. An extreme example of such a marriage took place in sixteenth-century Peru. In 1566, a wealthy Spanish resident of Cuzco, Arias Maldonado, promoted a marriage between his brother Cristóbal and his eight-year-old Inka stepdaughter, doña Beatriz Clara Coya, granddaughter of Manco Inka, ally and later rebel against the Spanish during the conquest of Peru. A formal betrothal and intercourse took place. While the Maldonados were arrested, doña Beatriz went on to marry another Spaniard, don Martín García de Loyola, in a marriage arranged by the viceroy, don Francisco Toledo. In this instance, the use of coercive sex in the interest of fortune hunting seems clear.[38] Whatever the differences in culture, wealth, and power between partners, some of these relationships endured, in sharp contrast to the third type of relationship, which was brief and violent and used sex neither as a sign of affection nor a tool of acculturation but as a weapon of war.

Descriptions of violent incidents suggest that European men treated coercion as a normal part of the range of sexual relations, and everywhere Spaniards went, from the Caribbean and Mexico to California and Peru, sexual violations occurred.[39] Although *rape* is a difficult term to define cross-culturally, Iberian chronicles, both Spanish and Portuguese, contain many descriptions of what can only be viewed as coercive relations in which various kinds of pressure—psychological, social, physical—were brought to bear on sex acts.[40] The famous passage by Diego de Landa in which he describes Maya women's pride in their modesty and chastity and then narrates a chilling incident of attempted sexual abuse illustrates the point:

> Captain Alonso López de Ávila, brother-in-law of the *Adelantado* Montejo, had captured a young Indian woman, who was both beautiful and pleasing, when he was engaged in the war of Bacalar. She had promised her husband, who feared that he would be killed in the war, not to have relations with another than he; and so no persuasion was sufficient to prevent her giving up her life so as not to be defiled by another man, on which account they caused her to be put to death by dogs.[41]

Some Europeans, such as Bartolomé de las Casas, criticized such behavior. But while it might be going too far to say that rape was a consciously used strategic tool in conquest and colonial rule, it is undeniable that sexual coercion was part of the process of Iberian exploration and conquest. Yet the frequency of sexual violence and the willingness of military leaders like Cortés to distribute indigenous women among their close lieutenants suggest that conquerors indeed used "the phallus as an extension of the sword," which may help explain some aspects of Malintzin's behavior and relationship with the Spanish.[42] Nonetheless, Malintzin, like other indigenous women, demonstrated an admirable capacity to survive and adjust to a myriad of changes that affected Nahuas and other native peoples of central Mexico and across Mesoamerica. While women lost political and economic power during the colonial period, through their labor, their roles as wives and mothers, and their positions as community elders and protectors, women found a variety of means to support and defend themselves, their families, and their communities.

NOTES

1. This essay is based on parts of chapters 2 and 3 of my book *Weaving the Past: A History of Latin America's Indigenous Women from the Prehispanic Period to the Present.* For a discussion of the Marina/Malinalli argument, see Cypess 1991:2, 33. For another and very plausible explanation of how she received the name Marina, see Karttunen 1994:506. But as Jeanette Peterson has pointed out, the association of *Marina* with *Malinalli* may not have been entirely accidental, but *not* because Marina was picked to closely match the indigenous name. The "twisted grass" meaning has powerful associations with the skin, hair, and brooms of the important Mexica earth goddesses (1994:195–196). Furthermore, Malintzin may have been subtly imaged as a warrior goddess, at least in the mid-sixteenth-century images of the Lienzo de Tlaxcala (ibid., 196–199).

2. Díaz del Castillo 1955 [1568]:I:121; Karttunen 1994:5.

3. For a description of incidents in which she helped the Spanish, including her presence at the execution of Cuauhtémoc, see Karttunen 1994:7–8, 19. Townsend's recent book (2006) discusses these and other events in her life. Her loyalty, combined with the fact that she bore Cortés a child, serves as the basis for the highly negative Mexican view that emerged in the post-Independence and, especially, postrevolutionary periods. Cypess 1991 and Núñez Becerra 1996 trace how this view has been expressed in Mexican literature. Several Mexican American feminist scholars have sought to portray Malintzin in a more sympathetic light. See, for example, Cotera 1976:31–36; De Castillo 1977; Alarcón 1989; and Hurtado 1999. Also see the sympathetic, popular biography by Lanyon 1999 along with a collection of essays analyzing her as a historical and literary figure in Glantz 1994. Hassig 1998 provides an in-depth analysis of the events surrounding the Cholula massacre. He raises doubts about whether it happened in the way Cortés and others describe and questions the importance of Malintzin's role.

4. López de Gómara 1943 [1552]:II:132–133; Karttunen 1997:312. See Seed 1988 (ch. 3) for a discussion of early modern Spanish conceptions of love. Indigenous conceptions of love are even more difficult to discern because of a lack of written sources that speak to this concept.

5. Somonte 1969:131.

6. While Todorov has stated that "the worst insult . . . that can be addressed to a man is to treat him as a woman" (1984:91), Burkhart argues that such comments could be interpreted less as demeaning to women than as insulting to men by pointing out that they were unfit (1997:347n79). Note also that I discuss at greater length the evidence for ancient Mesoamerican conceptions of gender complementarity and the relationship of such conceptions to political and religious power (2005:chaps.1, 2).

7. *Codex Mendoza* 1992 [1542]:III:fs.57v–58r. The women who served as priest-

esses were primarily of the noble stratum. For women's work, in addition to primary sources such as the *Florentine Codex* and the *Codex Mendoza*, summarized in Hellbom (1967:126–145), also see Rodríguez-Shadow 1997, esp. chaps. 3, 4; Brumfiel 1991; Kellogg 1995a; 1997; Anderson 1997; Sousa 1998:175–199; and Goldsmith Connelly 1999.

8. *Florentine Codex* (cited hereafter as FC) 1950–1982 [1569]:X:2.

9. FC 1950–1982 [1569]:X:5.

10. Carrasco 1984:43–44; Gillespie 1989:19–21; Schroeder 1992:70; and Klein 1993:46–50.

11. FC 1950–1982 [1569]:130, 132.

12. For gendered naming patterns, see Cline 1986:117–122; Lockhart 1992: 117–130; and Horn 1997:107–108. On kinship, see Kellogg 1986a; 1995a: ch. 5; and Cline 1986:ch. 5.

13. On marketplace judges, see FC 1950–1982 [1569]:VIII:67–69. For female crafts producers, see Durán 1967 [1581]:I:130.

14. For female officials in the *cuicacalli*, see FC 1950–1982 [1569]:II:97. Eloise Quiñones Keber shows that the inventors of the *tonalpohualli* (or 260-day count) were the deities Cipactonal, male, and Oxomoco, female (2002: 253–255). On priestesses, see FC 1950–1982 [1569]:II:215–216; Durán 1967 [1581]:II:544; Clavijero 1976 [1781]:206; Nicholson 1971:436–437; Brown 1983; and Alberti Manzanares 1993:ch. 3.

15. For definitions and discussions of the terms, see Durán 1967 [1581]:I:189; Cline 1986:54; and Lockhart 1992:44.

16. FC 1950–1982 [1569]:X:46. Also see Schroeder 1992:81–82; and Bell 1992: ch. 5.

17. Motolinía 1971 [1591]:134–135; Cline 1986; Kellogg 1986b; 1995a; 1997; and Horn 1997.

18. Durán 1967 [1581]:57; FC 1950–1982 [1569]:VII:31.

19. FC 1950–1982 [1569]:IV:59.

20. Ibid., 25.

21. "Estas son las leyes" 1941 [1543]:281; Pomar 1891 [1582]:32–33; Alva Ixtlilxochitl 1975–1977 [ca.1600–1640]:I:385; and Motolinía 1971 [1541]:355–356. On Aztec crime and punishment, see Offner 1983:ch. 6; on punishment and gender, see Rodríguez-Shadow 1997:218–219. On the punishment of younger men, see Hassig 1988:34–37, 110–111.

22. See the discussion of instances of rape and violence against women in pre-Hispanic central Mexico in Lipsett-Rivera 1997:561–567. For marketwomen's fighting, see Durán 1967 [1581]:II:255; Clendinnen 1991:159.

23. FC 1950–1982 [1569]:108–109.

24. Ibid., II:61–62.

25. Ibid., IV:79.

26. Burkhart 1989:131–133. Several of the *huehuetlatolli* ("elders' words"; ancient words of knowledge) collected by Sahagún, especially those for a young man

or woman before marriage, depict sexuality as potentially pleasurable for both sexes. But each partner was also obligated to wait until marriage and to carry out his or her social responsibilities, maintaining the Mexica ideal of moderate behavior (FC 1950–1982:VI:chaps. 18–22). Also see Clendinnen 1991:163–168, 180–182. On sexuality, also see Evans 1998 and 2001:255–264. Sousa's discussion of Nahua sexuality as pleasurable yet potentially polluting, especially if indulged in excessively, is also relevant (1998:356–360). López Austin (1982:160–163), Quezada (1977), and Rodríguez-Shadow (1997:184–185) emphasize the negative, even polluting, connotations of sexual activity and argue that women's virginity was highly valued.

27. Those contending that Mexica culture, or that of the Nahuas generally, was marked by gender asymmetry (with some arguing that extreme forms of male dominance existed) include Delgado 1964; MacLachlan 1976; Blanco 1977; Nash 1978; Klein 1988; 1993; 1994; Brumfiel 1996; 2001; Rodríguez-Shadow 1997; and McCaa 1996; n.d. Others who argue either that forms of male dominance were tempered by complementary and parallel forms of ideology and social organization or that complementarity is more fundamental than asymmetry include Hellbom 1967; Ladd 1979; Kellogg 1988; 1995a; 1995b; 1997; McCafferty and McCafferty 1988; Garza Tarazona 1991; Burkhart 1997; Evans 1991; and Joyce 2000:ch. 5.

28. Complicating the Mexica pantheon was its character as assimilative rather than proselytizing (Berdan 1982:125). Insightful general discussions of Aztec religion can be found in Caso 1958 and Nicholson 1971. For the complex images of female deities, see Carrera 1979 and Alberti Manzanares 1993.

29. Sullivan 1982:7; Lewis 1997; González Torres 1979; and McCafferty and McCafferty 1999.

30. For Cihuacoatl, see Klein 1988:237; for Tlazolteotl, see Burkhart 1989:92.

31. On the Mexica cosmos as composed of male and female elements, see López Austin 1998. See Rodríguez-Shadow (1997:ch. 7) for a discussion of Mexica goddesses as subordinated and reinforcing of a patriarchal gender hierarchy. On the Coyolxauhqui image in particular, see Klein 1994:225–227 and Brumfiel 1996:156–160.

32. The quote is from Klein 1994:225. For the story of Coyolxauhqui, see the FC 1950–1982 [1569]:III:1–5.

33. Brumfiel 1996:146.

34. Peterson 1994:194. The extent to which her life may also reflect Maya gender roles in unknowable, but for a discussion of those roles, see Kellogg 2005:35–41.

35. For Cortés's amorous history, see Karttunen 1997:306. Tecuichpotzin had her own complex marital history. Possibly married to Cuitlahuac (who ruled briefly after Moteuczoma), she married Cuauhtémoc, the last Mexica *tlatoani*, who was executed in 1525. Soon thereafter, she married a Spaniard, Alonso de Grado. At the age of fifteen (if the year of her birth was 1510, as

López de Meneses speculates), she then joined the growing line of Cortés's partners and gave birth to his daughter, doña Leonor Cortés. She subsequently married twice more, both times to Spaniards, bearing one child with Pedro Gallego de Andrade and five children with Juan Cano de Saavedra (López de Meneses 1948; Pérez-Rocha 1998).

36. Karttunen 1994:305–307.
37. Carrasco 1997:102; Stern 1993:170–173.
38. Muñoz Camargo 1986 [ca. late sixteenth-century]:195–197; Hemming 1970:180–269.
39. While both Herren 1991 and Wood 1998 discuss sexual violence in colonial Latin America broadly, on California, specifically, see Castañeda 1990: ch. 2; Hurtado 1999:ch. 1; and Bouvier 2001:chs. 1, 6.
40. In her classic work *Against Our Will*, Susan Brownmiller offers a legally oriented "female definition" of rape: "If a woman chooses not to have intercourse with a specific man and the man chooses to proceed against her will, that is a criminal act of rape" (1975:18). Other attempts to define rape are discussed by Linda Brookover Bourque (1989); also see Wood 1998:10–18. Castañeda cites other literature on male violence toward women (1993:32n61). While medieval and early Spanish law did not clearly define rape, it recognized coercive sex in a variety of contexts, using the terms *rapto, violación,* or *estupro* (Lipsett-Rivera 1997:567–568).
41. Tozzer[Landa] 1941 [1566]:127.
42. 1994:93. Wood argues that European men not only saw the sexual coercion of women as part of conquest but as key to a "new, multilayered power structure" (1998:10).

6. MALINCHE IN CROSS-BORDER HISTORICAL MEMORY

Sonia Hernández

The opening lines of a recent song by the popular *norteño* band Los Tigres del Norte exemplify the constant juggling of two cultures by Mexican immigrants and Mexican Americans in the United States:

> For those who say I am a *malinchista* and that I betray my flag and my nation, so that boundaries can be broken with my song, I will open my heart to you. I left the tombs of my parents and grandparents. I arrived crying to the land of the anglosaxon . . . don't call me a traitor because I love my two nations. In the morning I left the dead, here my children were born, for defending my rights I cannot be called a traitor.

—*Mis Dos Patrias* (My Two Homelands)[1]

For the writers of this song, as for many Mexican Americans who inhabit the border between the two countries, the term *malinchista* means a traitor, someone who has betrayed their Mexican heritage by participating in the culture of the United States. Yet the songwriter pleads with his fellow *fronterizos* (the people residing along the border) not to call him a traitor because he loves both countries, the United States and Mexico.[2]

The popular border term *malinchista* makes an adjective out of the name Malinche, the indigenous woman given to Hernán Cortés by Mayans. But this song does not refer to her crucial role in the Spanish victory in Mexico. Rather it is the political perception that she betrayed her people by translating for Cortés and helping the invaders.

This interpretation emerged in the wake of the Mexican Revolution, whose leaders were hostile to the privileges accorded foreign investors during the dictatorship of Porfirio Díaz. Stressing nationalism, twentieth-century political leaders rewrote Mexican history schoolbooks, identifying Spaniards as foreign intruders. In these newly rewritten history texts, Malinche became a turncoat because she had aided the invading Spaniards.

Once the international boundary was crossed Malinche no longer fit within the confines of the Mexican political understanding. However, the association between Malinche and betrayal remained. In South Texas a *malinchista* became someone who contravened the local Mexican community's cultural norms. A Texas *malinchista* might be a woman who married a North American man or a man whose friends were English speakers.

Yet, having grown up along this border, I knew there were far more perspectives on Malinche than this simple political one, or even on the well-known epithet *malinchista*.[3] Cultural scholars argue for the "possibility of multiple identities and contradictory positions."[4] Historians who focus on the concept of historical memory remind us that recollection evokes the past. "We consciously reconstruct images of the past in the selective way that suits the needs of our present situation," writes Patrick Hutton.[5] Mexican American culture both converges and diverges from the cultures in which it originates.

When the Mexican immigrant-turned-artist José Limón crossed the border with his family into the United States as a child, his formal schooling in his Mexican heritage ceased. But that brief exposure did not stop Limón from remembering that history any more than it has stopped generations of Mexican Americans from recalling their earliest memories of Mexico's past. Most Mexican Americans, however, do not translate that past into great artistic works, as Limón did in *La Malinche*, *Danzas Mexicanas*, *La Piñata*, and *Carlota*.

Unlike the murals of José Clemente Orozco and Diego Rivera, which directly reflected Mexican cultural practice, Limón's vision of Mexico's past stems from what the Tigres del Norte band describes as the experience of two homelands: the lived experience of Mexican Americans is rooted in two cultures, Mexican and American. Limón's *La Malinche* embodied both American and Mexican attitudes toward this controversial woman, and his choreography reflected some of the contradictory attitudes toward Malinche that I heard growing up on the Texas–Mexican border. No longer simply the traitor of conventional twentieth-century Mexican history or its American avatar, the traitor to her culture, she was a half-remembered shadow, but a shadow of a woman whose life was wholly singular.

What follows is a border perspective of Malinche, one that derives from the diverse bicultural, binational experiences of two dozen residents along the Texas-Mexican border whom I interviewed for this essay.

For one *fronteriza* who came to the United States in her early twenties, Malinche evoked issues of race and pride. During the 1950s, Eustolia (Tola) Hernández attended a ranch school in the outskirts of Río Bravo, Tamaulipas (Mexico), where she received only a third-grade education. Tola learned about the heroes of Mexican Independence and the revolutionaries of 1910 and participated in school contests to determine who was the best reciter of national poems. She commented, "They only spoke to us about the history of Benito Juárez, Miguel Hidalgo, Venustiano Carranza, Belisario Domínguez, and all those other presidents . . . and the Niños Heroes."[6] When I asked her, "And the Aztecs, they did not talk to you about them? . . . indigenous people, the Indians?" she began recounting the story of Cuauhtémoc and how he was tortured by the Spanish. As we conversed in my car she reached for a book in the back seat. It had a picture of Malinche. Ignoring my followup question about Cuauhtémoc's honor, she opened the book and then asked me, "This book, isn't it the one where you have a picture of La Malinche? The Spanish is descendant of us?" Tola continued her query: "That is where we come from?" "From whom?" I asked. "La Malinche," Tola answered. "Not only from La Malinche," I retorted. Tola added, "And the Spanish, right?"[7]

I continued questioning Tola: "Why, you did not like that?" She responded, "Well, I didn't like it [laughter]." I then asked her, "Where did you think we came from?" Tola responded, "I thought we came from *alcurnia*." We continued conversing and, surprised that I did not know what *alcurnia* meant, she continued, "You don't know what *alcurnia* means?" I said no. She explained, "Like the ones from Alcalá [a province in Spain] . . . like the ones from, from the important people." I immediately reacted by asking her if she thought an Indian woman was unimportant. Tola answered, "Well, for me it's not like very important, an Indian woman . . ." "Why not?" I asked. "Well," Tola continued, "no, well, I say that because one comes from over here, like third generation [or] second generation or whatever, and you consider yourself like, like you don't want to be a child of an Indian woman and [keep in mind] that I did see that soap opera of the Indian woman." "But what did you say, what Indian woman?" I asked. Tola's comments were final: "Que no me gustaba la idea de que viniéramos de La Malinche" (I do not like the idea that we come from La Malinche).[8]

Such a dialogue can evoke questions about racism and anti-indigenous sentiments. However, Tola's comments should be considered within the context of our conversation and, more important, within a borderlands context. Tola's status as a resident of the border (on both sides), far removed from her mother country's center, influenced the way she perceived her origins. Born in Los Ramones, Nuevo León, a *pueblo* about one hour north of the industrialized city of Monterrey, Tola left the small town with her family as a toddler. Growing up on a ranch on the Mexican side of the Río Grande, Tola had little contact with people from south and central Mexico. Leaving school after third grade, she led a life during childhood and adolescence that consisted of working alongside her siblings and interacting with nearby residents of other ranches in the region.

What can one make of Tola's perception of Malinche? Tola's memory is informed by the dualities in her life that resulted from her passage from northern Mexico to the United States. Her sense of origin, of having been born in "el norte" (northern Mexico), distanced her from central Mexico, where Malinche's drama had unfolded. Her family's relocation to the Mexican side of the border created an even greater distance. Finally, when she married, her husband brought her to Pharr, Texas, only minutes from Mexico. In light of her history, her rejection of the label "India" is not surprising. We need to consider her position as a woman from two worlds who had children on both sides of the border. She resembles Malinche and Limón, two people who had to juggle two cultures and often assume multiple identities. Tola's status as *fronteriza*, as a mother of Mexicans and Americans, and as a seamstress working for both Mexicans and Americans testifies to the bicultural, binational nature of the life she has led. In fact, Tola identifies more with American values than those originating from indigenous tradition.

Tola's younger brother and former classmate at the ranch school, Artemio Véliz, touched on a critical aspect of the Conquest. Artemio could not tell me much about Malinche's life, but his recollection of the historical events surrounding Malinche focused on racial mixing. Artemio claimed, "I don't remember what role Malinche played with the . . . but there were other characters, Mayos . . . and the Criollo and I don't know which other one . . . then they mixed and we have descendants of the Malinche and the Criollo and I don't know what other things . . . the Mexican is made."[9] Artemio struggled to recall the events and insisted that I consult a book one of his children had brought home from school. I encouraged him to continue and told him that it was his perspective on Malinche that mattered. He continued, "That is why when one is angry . . . you do things . . . the criollo enters you [your body]." I asked, "The criollo enters your body?" Artemio assured me that this happened because "we have Indian blood, Indian and Spanish." Although, unlike Tola, Artemio seemed undisturbed by his Indian heritage, he justified the Mexicans' rage at the mixture of Indian and Spanish blood. While Artemio's "history" of Malinche is not representative of academic discourses, it illustrates the complexities surrounding Malinche's life. Malinche, for Artemio, evoked an intimate relationship between temper and *mestizaje*.[10]

Ten years old in 1991, Mario González, currently a university student, remembers his sister calling him a *malinchista* when he "snitched" on her about her "hanging out with boys."[11] Mario, who grew up in the Ejido Soledad de los Pérez, which forms part of Cruillas, Tamaulipas, vividly recalled Malinche's history: "She was the one who betrayed . . . one of the principal ones, who betrayed the Indians. She was also Hernán Cortés's mistress." Mario continued, "If you ask me if Malinche was a bad woman, based on what I have learned in school, I say yes, but based on the comments made by the community, she was not. *She had her reasons for doing what she did.*" Here is yet another dimension to historical memory. In this case, Mario has two memories of Malinche. One involves his school curriculum and the other is based on his community's view on Malinche. While one might very well inform the other, Mario separated the two and ended his commentary by stating that Malinche "had her reasons for doing what she did."[12]

If *malinchista* meant "snitch" or "traitor" to Mario, to another border resident, Felipe López, *malinchista* or *malinchismo* was simply a "modismo," an adage.[13] Felipe, a twenty-five-year-old Río Bravo resident who crosses the river everyday to perform odd jobs in South Texas, argued that these terms have been transformed throughout time and do not have anything to do with Malinche. "People just use words differently as time passes," Felipe argued. According to Felipe, Malinche acted as translator for Cortés because "she knew the language, Maya." He continued, "Malinche had nothing to do with our [Mexican] origins . . . we are just Spanish and Indian." I then asked, "But is it true that she had a child with Cortés?" Felipe replied, "Yes, but she has nothing to do with us." Much like Tola, Felipe's comments, in which he uses a present tense verb, demonstrate the overwhelming importance his present situation and his feelings about his origins have on his sense of the past. While he agreed that Malinche had a child with Cortés, he rejected the idea that she played a role in the creation or origins of what is thought of today as Mexican. While his comments may not reflect the documentary evidence presented by scholars from various disciplines about Malinche's relevance to present-day Mexicans, they constitute an attempt to reconstruct a history through adaptation and modification. Felipe adapts that part of history with which he is comfortable while modifying that with which he is not. Finally, when I asked Felipe if he thought Malinche was a bad woman, he answered, "No, Malinche was simply an Indian who knew . . . the language."[14]

As I continued conducting interviews with various people, the stories of Malinche changed. In answer to my questions, the respondents not only emphasized Malinche's language skills, but also entered into conversations about gender and culpability with regard to her sexual relationship with Cortés. For instance, Oscar Chávez, a Houston resident originally from Vallehermoso, Tamaulipas (about thirty minutes southwest of Matamoros), highlighted the gendered dimension of the story of Malinche. After staring at a drawing of Malinche and Hernán Cortés, Oscar reacted by commenting, "So [then] this one was the one who was with Hernán Cortés, this one, La Malinche? . . . Hernán Cortés . . . he took over everything and everybody."[15]

Oscar's perspective on Malinche leaned toward a more positive interpretation than those of the others. When asked if Malinche was a *mujer mala* [bad woman], he responded by saying that her betrayal of her "own people" was bad, but then he hesitated and argued that, "She did not want to go 'around' with him, he was going 'around' with her, he forced her, or something like that?" He continued, "He forced her *que anduviera con él [to go around with him* because] he was like a big shot . . . he took over, he was a big shot . . . so I'm pretty sure he got with her . . . to [either] help him out or . . . just to be with him."[16] Switching from English to Spanish, he continued rationalizing Malinche's justification for helping Cortés and his justification for "getting with her." Recognizing the possibility of the coercive nature of the relationship, he pointed out that Cortés might have done what he did because "he want[ed] [Malinche] to be his girl . . . whenever [he] wanted a girl." He continued, "It's like whenever you want some . . . *o que le hiciera todo . . . todos los mandados* [demanding that all chores be completed]."[17] In other words, Cortés might have "gotten with her" for motives other than sexual ones. Nonetheless, Oscar's remark "whenever you want some," pointed to the insistence on using a recent present, in this case, engaging in intimate relations, to recreate the history of two people who engaged in a similar (sexual) act five hundred years ago.

My conversation with Oscar was brief. He could not remember more. In fact, he lamented the fact that once he crossed the border he no longer heard stories about "Hispanics." He said, "They won't talk to you about that [in U.S. schools]."[18] The act of crossing the border, which was so close to Oscar's hometown, colored his perspective on life and history. Like Limón, Oscar came to the United States as a young boy and quickly became exposed to American culture, especially through music and schooling. In spite of the lack of "Hispanic" history on "this" side and his distance from central Mexico, Oscar recalled Malinche and his Mexican heritage in the confines of his home in Houston, Texas.[19]

Like Oscar, Manuel Véliz, a middle-aged man from Río Bravo now living in Houston, deplored the absence of Hispanics in the history taught in the United States. Manuel's inability to remember Malinche did not prevent him from sharing comments with me. In fact, Manuel blamed the Mexican, not the U.S. government for failing to emphasize an Indian past. He asserted, "If the government gave a different importance to the Indians it would be different, but the government, the Indians it was like one thing, without knowing that the Indians were the ones who built [structures] . . . and good Indians." He added, "I am proud . . . I mean, my mother is Indian and a good Indian, from the good ones, because, there are [Indians] in Oklahoma, we have Indians, but those American Indians built their homes with grass, and these Mexican Indians built structures that still can be seen, then, well you have to be proud of that."[20] Although my questions regarding Malinche remained unanswered, the inquiries sparked memories of Manuel's indigenous past. Manuel spoke of an indigenous pride based only on comparison with a different indigenous history, one rooted in the land which he now lives in, the United States.

Offering a different, more positive perspective, a middle-aged hairdresser in San Juan, Texas, Rosita Hinojosa, originally from Monterrey, eagerly shared comments about Malinche. For Rosita, Malinche's participation as mistress and mediator should not be critiqued. In her beauty salon Rosita recounted the following story: "When Hernán Cortés arrived, right, he is the one who goes out to supposedly conquer the world, to see if the world was round or square . . . then he arrived in Mexico City . . . and they liked the Indian because she was a very beautiful Indian woman."[21] She then recalled Cuauhtémoc's torture and embarked on praising Malinche's virtues: "She was a woman who believed in purity, she believed in decency . . . despite all their ignorance, [Indians] were people who were loyal . . . very honorable . . . Malinche and Cuauhtémoc, they adored them . . . still, they did not know a real God existed . . ." It is apparent that Rosita's present views influenced the way she recalled the history of the Conquest: "They did not know a real god existed." She felt compelled to rationalize the situation and argued that Cortés and the Spaniards brought the real truth to the Indians, the real God.[22]

Rosita's remarks point to a striking aspect of Mexican and Mexican American life. While it is difficult to measure how much of a Mexican or how Spanish Rosita is, one can begin to understand the complexities behind her dual or multiple identities. By asserting that the Spanish brought the "real truth" to Mexico and defending the Indians at the same time, Rosita finds a middle ground. This struggle between recognizing an indigenous past and a Spanish one continues playing a vital role in the way in which Mexicans and Mexican Americans deal with their past. Even Limón, we know from his memoir, struggled with his Mexican past. He wrote, "After all, Spain is also the mother country. She gave us *nuestro Señor Jesucristo* and his crucifix." He then described, contradictorily, the Spanish and Cortés as the "destroy[ers] and despoil[ers] of ancient native cultures."[23] Here, Limón's words, like Rosita's, remind us of the often ambiguous approach of Mexican immigrants and Mexican Americans to their history. It should come as no surprise, then, to hear Mexican nationals calling Mexican immigrants or Mexican Americans *malinchistas*. They are considered traitors not only to their mother country but also to the idea of being Mexican. Ironically a Mexican is also constructed of two or more cultural traditions.

Rosita's description of Malinche and subsequent explanation of her behavior also point to the weight of the present in her recollection of the past. Her response, "They did not know a real god existed," is significant because Rosita's belief in a god in the twenty-first century immediately becomes the "real god" that the Spanish brought over to Mexico in the sixteenth century. Therefore, Malinche, Cuauhtémoc, and the entire native population simply did not know the truth, a truth that transcends time, and this lack of knowledge led to their destruction. More important, it justified Malinche's relationship with Cortés. Because she was unaware of the real god, to Malinche Cortés represented one of many gods from the Indian world.

The last question I posed to Rosita dealt with whether or not Malinche's aid to the Spanish as a translator made her a *mujer mala*, or bad woman. Rosita responded,

> She helped them translate the language, but then she realized that she had done wrong, she was not a bad woman, what happens is that they [Spanish] entered Mexico as friendly visitors . . . and then they pulled a fast one. Then they [Indians] helped them and finally the

Spanish were the ones who betrayed the trust when they [Spanish] began to see Mexico's riches. They [Indians] offered them [Spanish] good hospitality because . . . when the Spanish arrived . . . Malinche and Cuauhtémoc saw them as gods. Because they were already dressed differently . . . she [Malinche] was only partially clothed and they were fully clothed.[24]

Clearly, for Rosita the situation in which Malinche found herself justified her actions.

Malinche, with all her "virtues" and "ignorance" or "innocence," did what she could. In the end, according to Rosita, she committed suicide:

She stabbed herself with a knife so that they would not know where to find the real secrets of Mexico. They saw her as a traitor because they thought she liked the Spanish but . . . she always told them [Indians] not to tell [the real secrets of Mexico] . . . so that's why they [people] call you *malinchista* because when they [Spanish] arrived, they were white and they [Indians] were *morenos* (dark)—she saw a white people with colored beards . . . something very different to what was in Mexico, so for them [Indians] they were like gods.[25]

To Rosita, a *malinchista* or *el malinchismo* refers not to a traitor but to discrimination. She explained it as follows: "If I tell you, oh, you don't like dark skin, oh, I like this one more because [she] is white, that is *malinchismo* . . . because the Indians saw Malinche adoring Cortés." According to Rosita, Malinche "adored" Cortés because in her mind "she adored him as a god . . . she felt obliged to serve him." "She was amazed" by Cortés. Colored by her religious and political beliefs, Rosita's historical memory of Malinche and *malinchismo* is unique in that it defines *malinchismo* as discrimination based on preference over a certain skin color and does not apply to traitors.

Antonio Solís, also from Monterrey, echoed Rosita's comments about Malinche. Only for Antonio, a full-time insurance salesman and part-time poet, it was his understanding of today's gender relations that provided the context for his perception of Malinche. After correcting me about Malinche's real name, "Malintzin," he explained, "Malinztin was a woman given to Cortés by Moctezuma along with other twenty women."[26] Antonio continued,

Malintzin was very astute, intelligent, and beautiful. She knew Nahuatl, Maya, and learned Spanish. You can just imagine the value of such a woman. She was not a bad woman, it was just that back then, women were not given their place, like we give them today. Women were treated as objects, they were instruments.[27]

I asked Antonio if it was true that Malinche was a traitor, and he responded immediately by explaining that men simply treated women as objects: "Malintzin did not betray, she only responded the best way she could. After all, she was given away by her people." Antonio reiterated his position: "She was not a bad woman." That the individuals who gave Malinche away treated her as an object is hard to deny, but it should be pointed out that Antonio mentioned nothing about Cortés's use of Malinche with regard to her translating abilities. Moreover, Antonio did not comment on Cortés's role in marrying Malinche to his fellow Spaniard Gerónimo de Aguilar.[28] Just as Oscar made sense of Cortés's and Malinche's relationship as one of utility, and not based entirely on sex, Antonio assured me that women such as Malinche "were instruments." Oscar and Antonio justified Cortés's use of Malinche in terms of utility—Oscar by saying, "que le hiciera todos los mandados" (that is, he made her perform chores) and Antonio by referring to Malinche as an object or "instrument."[29]

Contrary to Rosita's and Antonio's historical memory, Asención Melchor, a native of La Estanzuela, Nuevo León, twenty minutes south of Monterrey, explained, "La Malinche was given away by her parents to the Spanish conquistadors."[30] Asención continued, "Because she was given away by her parents, La Malinche developed much hatred toward the Indians." Asención's emphasis on Malinche's hatred and her anger toward her own people for giving her away was missing from Rosita's interpretation. Asención continued, "She eventually married a Spaniard, and she began to see the beautiful possessions of the Spanish, which she wanted, too. La Malinche was confronted by the Spanish to spy on the Indians and bring back information, in exchange for material possessions and power." While Asención granted Malinche an important position in the encounter between the Spanish and Indians, he underscored Malinche's decision to act in favor of the Spaniards: "Essentially, the Spaniards wanted to overthrow Moctezuma and once he was out of power, La Malinche was promised by the Spanish to have a position of power. In the end the Spaniards killed Moctezuma, and they never found the gold they were looking for. Despite La Malinche's efforts, she was killed by the Spaniards."[31]

Asención further argued that Malinche was a bad woman, and he "felt like she betrayed her own people . . . it was a lose-lose situation for everyone in the end." As it turned out, despite Malinche's hatred and marriage to a Spaniard, the result did not favor anyone. While the historical record has proven the devastating effects the Conquest had on the indigenous peoples, Asención's recollection remains part of the popular discourse on Malinche. His reminiscence also included the term *malinchista:* "I have never heard this term used, but I take it to mean a 'traitor.'" The recurrent theme of traitor among Mexican and Mexican Americans along the border and its extended borderlands, which include Houston and Monterrey, is a daily reminder of the complexities surrounding the history of ethnic Mexicans.

The idea of "the treacherous woman" and *malinchista* name calling demonstrates the enormous weight of Malinche in people's historical memory. Juan Ramón Chávez, Oscar's brother, echoed Asención's comments regarding a treacherous Malinche. Juan Ramón, who also grew up in northern Mexico, asserted, "She [Malinche] betrayed the Aztecs. She was the one who translated the Aztec tongue, to the Spanish." He continued, "She sold herself, it's clear . . . that you betray your country." Juan Ramón's perspective on Malinche as well as Asención's resemble the interpretations of the noted Mexican writer Octavio Paz.[32] While their perspectives do not go so far as to blame Malinche for Mexico's contemporary problems, they do not paint a picture of Malinche as empowering. In fact, Asención's rationale, if juxtaposed with recent scholarly works, points to at least one possible justification for Malinche's behavior. For example, the issue of revenge is among the motives described by scholars writing on Malinche. The historian Mary Louise Pratt has identified what Asención narrates above as one of the four rationales for Malinche's behavior in contemporary debates. Pratt argues that one possibility for Malinche's actions described by scholars includes her "revenge on the society that devalued and objectified her," hence the "political strategy linked to her own lust for power." These explanations emerge in both popular and academic discourses.[33]

Furthermore, Chicana scholars and poets have developed a distinct explanation and meaning for Malinche. Poems like Carmen Tafolla's "La Malinche" (1978) evoke emotions of Chicana/o nationalism and portray a strong Malinche. Her opening and closing lines read, "Yo soy la Malinche" and "But *Chingada* I was not. Not tricked, not screwed, not traitor. For I was not traitor to myself . . . another world . . . *la raza* . . ."[34] Of the interviews I conducted, Rosita's is by far the most positive in its assessment of Malinche. Her view of Malinche falls somewhere between the empowering renditions of such writers as Tafolla and the Texas border native Gloria Anzaldúa.[35] However, Rosita has never heard about or read such positive academic portrayals of Malinche. It is popular discourse, the way in which ordinary people like Rosita make sense of their past and how they express this past, that paints a vivid and variant picture of what history is and means. It is the invocation of the present to recall the past that makes historical figures and events meaningful to people. Consider, for example, Rosita's closing remarks: "Malinche's life was very short . . . she was not an ordinary Indian, she was almost like an empress . . . she was Cuauhtémoc's wife . . . let's just say she was like today's Hillary Clinton."[36] For Rosita, the wife of an ex-president, Hillary Clinton, is comparable to Malinche. Clinton's successes and popular appeal helped Rosita make sense of Malinche's life and role in the Conquest. Rosita made use of a current American female figure to describe an indigenous person from the past.

Still, the construal of Malinche as an empowering symbol has not entirely crossed the academic boundary. Norma Alarcón writes that Chicanas such as Tafolla "would simply like to see Malintzin recognized as a visionary and founder of a people, yet . . . the realities that this figure encompasses are much too complex to simply replace them with the notion of a matriarch."[37] However, Alarcón argues that the fact that Malinche figures prominently in Chicana/o poetry "emphasizes the pervasive preoccupation and influence of the myth and women's need to demythify." While there is much more to Malinche than the simple bad woman/good woman dichotomy, the reification of Malinche as a cultural symbol for Chicana pride and Chicana feminism is yet another piece of the historical memory puzzle. Anzaldúa's historical memory as reflected in such works as "Borderlands" in her book *Borderlands/La Frontera: The New Mestiza* is highly informed by her experiences growing up along the U.S.-Mexican border. In ways that are analogous to Limón's artistic works, Anzaldúa's writings point to yet another historical memory of Malinche—one that has led to a growing body of literature that embraces the indigenous woman as a bicultural feminist icon.[38]

The academic historical memory represented in the works of Anzaldúa has not entirely crossed the academic boundary. However, the comments made by two of my interviewees, one Mexican and one Mexican American and both in college, echo some of the positive interpretations of Malinche. Monica Cantú, a young *Mexicana* in graduate school who grew up in Control, Tamaulipas, a small town about one hour west of the Matamoros/Brownsville border, spoke of Malinche in terms of her positive qualities. Cantú, who immigrated to Houston several years ago, commented on the intelligence of Malinche: "Malinche was a knowledgeable woman since she learned the language, Spanish, and [she] was able to translate." However, she later commented,

> Malinche was seen as a traitor by the natives because she translated for Cortés and was his mistress. They met because she ended up as Cortés's slave. I cannot tell if she was truly a traitor or not since I don't know the details, so I cannot make a reliable comment without the knowledge, right? Anyway, I still think she had an extraordinary linguistic competency since she learned Spanish and Maya, I'm not so sure about this one [Maya], besides her native Nahuatl, and was able to translate. Maybe she helped the Conquest to be not so bloodish (*sic*). After all, Cortés wanted to conquer no matter what but was able to negotiate for a while thanks to Malinche.[39]

Even if Monica's recollection was not entirely one of an empowering Malinche, she acknowledged Malinche's role as a mediator. Unlike Oscar, Monica did not mention Malinche's more intimate relationship with Cortés. Similarly, the brief comments by a history graduate student, Alice Garza, underscore the continuing disparity between academic and popular interpretations of Malinche. The Brownsville native now residing in Houston said,

> I recognize Marina (La Malinche) as pioneer of the feminist movement and an intellectual of the Spanish Colonial period. She was the first woman to serve as a translator, negotiator, and *conquistadora* in the Aztec and Spanish culture. Although she led the war of the Spanish, she will be branded in history as a traitor of her culture, language, and religion. Marina will be remembered as the mother of a new culture and language.[40]

Clearly, Alice described Malinche as an active agent in the encounter between the Spanish and the people of present-day Mexico, not simply a passive woman. While Alice placed Malinche at the forefront of Mexican life, "as the mother of a new culture and language," she argued, "she [Malinche] will be branded in history as a traitor." This ambiguous way of making sense of Malinche's actions once again demonstrates the idea of "the treacherous woman" as a recurring theme in Mexican culture.

The interpretation of Malinche as traitor and the concept of *malinchismo* are not entirely unique to the Texas-Mexico border. Mexicans and Mexican Americans in California, for instance, have used Malinche and her supposed betrayal to describe or explain dramatic moments in their lives. The comments made by several Chicana college women demonstrate the way in which the history of Malinche shapes their sense of the present. Discussing her incestuous relationship, one woman argued, "I knew I was a Malinche, I knew it was my fault, how could a father, a brother, hurt a child this way. I had to be doing something to provoke them."[41] As the clinical psychologist Yvette G. Flóres-Ortiz writes, "The theme of treachery and the association with *la madre de los chingados* [the raped woman and her offspring] is a 'particularity of the Chicano experience.'"[42] Similarly, a twenty-one-year-old Chicana, emphasizing a peaceful pre-Conquest period, argued,

> We need to go back to how things were before the Spaniards came, before the colonizer brought us sickness to the body, mind, and spirit. We need to remember our place as *mujeres*, alongside our men, supporting them, taking care of them. All we have to do is go back to how things were.[43]

Flóres-Ortiz points out that as well as evoking the theme of the treacherous woman represented by Malinche, Mexican American women often perpetuate the notion of the woman as the nurturer. The comments made by these women point to their understanding of Malinche as a woman whose actions still shape their own lives. The historical memory of these California women regarding Malinche resonates with some of the interpretations circulating along the Texas-Mexico border region.

Women and men from various parts of Mexico made similar comments about Malinche. In a 1999 documentary by Daniel Banda on Malinche, people throughout Mexico shared their views on Malinche. The historical memories of Malinche included the common "treacherous" woman, "intelligent," and "very kind woman."[44] Banda uses his own search for an identity as a launching point for Malinche's story. As Banda narrates the story, he reminds the audience that he too lives in a bicultural world. While these stories resemble some of the interpretations in this essay, they differ in that Malinche, for many border residents, is associated not only with the Conquest in Mexico and *mestizaje*, but with U.S. culture. The way in which border residents such as Rosita and Manuel developed perspectives on Malinche, combining American and Mexican culture, differs from the interviews conducted by Banda. Rosita compared Malinche to Hillary Clinton, and Manuel made comparisons between indigenous groups in the present-day United States and those in central Mexico regarding architectural contributions. Thus, the historical memory of border residents has much to do with geographic place as well as culture. Furthermore, one border resident argued that Malinche was La Llorona, another woman whose story has received attention from scholars.[45] According to local legend and Mexican American folklore, La Llorona, or the Weeping Woman, refers to the ghost of a woman who lost her children and wept for them. La Llorona is also known as the "bloody Mary."

Sharing the same last name but having no family connections, Marc and Beth González related personal comments regarding Malinche. A mortician from Edinburg, Texas, Marc began recounting childhood stories of Malinche. For Marc, Malinche is not the traitor, mistress, or *India* described by the other *fronterizos*. "Growing up [and] going to elementary school in Edinburg," he said, "the perception that I have on Malinche was that she was the bloody Mary . . . whether in reference to the Virgin Mary, I don't know." He continued, "I had a picture of what the bloody Mary was, even though . . . *no la mirabamos* . . . we didn't see her or anything it was just a girl in white, all white, dressed in white with blood stains with black hair." Marc continued, "That was my perception of La Malinche, she was the bloody Mary." I asked Marc if his parents or anyone used Malinche as a disciplinary tool. "It was mostly done in school," he answered, ". . . being that you know most of the students would not say Malinche in Spanish, but bloody Mary, in English." When I asked Marc if he really thought this person existed he said she did "in her own time."[46] Despite the fact that the remainder of the interview dealt with legends, Marc's comments shed light on the way historical stories and myths merge and develop on the border. Marc received no schooling in Mexico, yet he was well aware of something or someone called Malinche. Whether in legend or history, Malinche formed part of Marc's childhood memory. The fact that South Texas and northern Mexico are far from the original site/s where Malinche appeared points to the way in which time and place shape the way people remember historical events.

Beth González, on the other hand, described Malinche as a woman whose actions had serious consequences for Mexicans: "For me it's like a reference to the Virgin . . . I think it's because of the immaculate conception, so Mary is the immaculate conception and La Malinche . . ." She continued, ". . . you know us Mexicans . . . I've heard that we're referred to as [Malinches] because we're all from the same father . . . because at the beginning when the Europeans came and the war with Mexico, they raped a lot of the women, they raped a lot of the natives . . . and from those rapes were children and then the kids—they would ask them who's your father?" Beth explained, ". . . but they would refer to the mother as, *tu madre es La Malinche* and that was an insult." The concept of insult was for Beth the most salient issue when she discussed Malinche. I asked, "Why was it an insult?" Beth responded, "They're claiming a rape; it's like a hypocrisy . . . like the Virgin . . . many people did not believe that there was an immaculate conception. . . . it's blasphemy," Beth responded. "It's coming from the low class . . ." "The people who believed this?" I asked. "Yes . . . low class, no education . . . and they use it as . . . like *te va a pescar la Malinche!*" [Malinche is going to get you!] "It's referring to the dirty deed." It is likely that Beth, a young woman who holds a bachelor's degree, might have been influenced by literary interpretations of Malinche's role in the Conquest. However, compared to other commentators with little or no formal education, Beth's commentary is not complimentary toward feminist cultural critics who hail Malinche as empowering for women of Mexican descent.[47]

Rosario Herrera, another South Texas resident, knew nothing about Malinche's role in the Conquest, nothing about her involvement with Cortés, and even less about Malinche as a traitor.[48] Yet, she was acquainted with the term. In fact, for Rosario, Malinche is not a historical person; Malinche refers to a "malías." A *malías* is a bully. Rosario recalled students' frequent use of the term in her high school days in Pharr, Texas. A Malinche referred only to girls, especially those who participated in gang-related fights. These Malinches usually bullied other girls and hung out together. Although Rosario attended an American high school, located only twenty minutes from Reynosa, Tamaulipas, in the 1980s, she never heard the "official" story of Malinche, but only a modified version of Malinche, the person or the term developed along the border.

Similarly, Yamel Melchor, originally from San Luís Potosí and now a resident of Houston, Texas, recalled "people being called Malinche." Yamel explained that "being Malinche is someone who is mean," as in *"la muchacha es muy malinche con la mamá"* (the girl is very *malinche* with her mother). Whether a girl misbehaved or treated someone badly, the connotation probably comes from the term *mala* (bad). Rosario's and Yamel's perspective illustrates the many transformations and forms Malinche has assumed throughout time and place. These historical memories represent what historians call "cultural hybridity." They underscore the obvious duality of the border and demonstrate the ambiguities that arise in explanations of Malinche. In short, the memories of Mexicans and Mexican Americans point to their continuous juggling of two cultures, their constant picking and choosing from the two sides.[49]

My conversation with an insurance salesman from McAllen, Texas, Fred García, further demonstrates the multiplicity of histories of Malinche.[50] Our dialogue began with Fred's acknowledgment of Malinche's role as translator and mistress: "She was the mistress of Cortés . . . and isn't she also the origin . . . or where the original expression of *la chingada madre*[51] comes from?" Fred asked. He continued, "The *chingada madre*, she represents a sort of mother figure and betrayal . . . she's like Mexico's fallen Eve . . . she had one or two children with him, with Cortés . . . Cortés wanted to return to Spain and take his children with him, but he did not want to take Malinche." "So what kind of a woman was she?" I asked. Fred answered, "With respect to her children, she's foul." He continued,

> She's a bad woman because she murdered her own children. But I don't even know if I even believe that . . . I don't even know if that is factual. From a historical political perspective I don't see her helping the Spanish necessarily bad, she was just facilitating a situation.[52]

Malinche's pragmatic role counterbalanced her unmotherly behavior. It is notable that such a negative portrayal of Malinche has resurfaced, resembling what the novelist Margaret Shed wrote in the early 1970s regarding Malinche's role in the conquest: "Malinche was a whore, but since everything this woman did was on a grand scale, so too was her whoring."[53] Informed by the *chingada* epithet that has been given to Malinche by many and while recognizing her limited options, Fred attempted to make some sense of Malinche. It was not her contribution to the Spanish cause through her language skills, according to Fred, but the "murdering of her own children" that makes Malinche a "foul" or bad woman. Here again, present gender ideas and society's expectations of women emerge as central factors in understanding the past.

A broad range of histories has developed among *fronterizos*, demonstrating the disparity between academic discourse and popular discourse. While many Mexican immigrants like Rosita Hinojosa (and, indeed, like José Limón) recalled Malinche's life during the Conquest and showed sympathy toward her, Tola Hernández and Asención Melchor offered different perspectives. Others, like Yamel, Rosario, and Marc, discussed Malinche not so much as a person but as an action or description. Still other ways of making sense of Malinche exist, as is exemplified by two final histories. The first is informed by stories of *curan-deras* (healers or medicine women [and men]) and luck along the border.

When asked what they knew about La Malinche, Juan Ayala and his wife, Senovia, began telling me a story about an incident that occurred many years ago. With some excitement and a peculiar expression on his face, Juan, a *norteño* by birth, recalled an incident that occurred during the first years of his married life. "The Indian Malinche," he reported, "the face of the Indian Malinche appeared on [a] coin . . . and what luck she brought to that woman healer."[54] Senovia, better known to her friends as Chobita, proudly added, "I was with him when we found the coin."

In the patio of my parents' home in San Juan, Juan recalled that strange afternoon in Reynosa, Tamaulipas, when he was a "*recién casado*" (recently married). The Ayalas, both from Linares, located in south-central Nuevo León, married and headed north to the border town of Reynosa. Together with Juan's family they worked a *parcela* where they cultivated cotton and tended to chickens and other animals. At their ranch it was normal to see animals running around, especially chickens. However, that afternoon one chicken along with her chicks began to wander around and disappeared. Juan's father told him that the chicken had gone toward some thick brush and ordered a search for the animals. Juan agreed but decided to wait until morning.

At the crack of dawn, Juan and Senovia headed to the place where the chicken was last seen. Following his father's orders, they began to dig near the brush because, according to his father, the site was probably haunted. They dug a hole about four feet deep. At the bottom of the hole lay many shiny rocks. The couple retrieved the rocks and placed them inside an old pail. The thought that the rocks might have some value crossed Juan's mind, but another more valuable discovery was yet to come. An old *moneda*, or coin, with the image of Malinche lay under-neath the rocks. "La India Malinche," to use Juan's words, appeared on the *moneda*.

The Ayalas used the *moneda* some time after they discovered it to pay for services rendered by a friend who was a *curandera*. According to the Ayalas, the *curandera* achieved remarkable financial success or what they called *suerte* (luck) owing to the fact that she possessed the coin.

Although the Ayalas' memory of Malinche did not reflect the "of-ficial" history of the indigenous woman, their emphasis on the impor-tance of the coin is quite telling. Juan insisted that the coin was valuable because of the image it bore. He asserted that the *curandera* "in all prob-ability" sold the coin, which explained her sudden popularity and subsequent financial success. The importance of Juan's and Chobita's story rests on their perception of the historical significance of Malinche as one tied to a local experience. Their response, based on one experience, points to the way in which national histories are interpreted and constructed at the local level. The Ayalas' historical memory of Malinche becomes yet another competing interpretation.

At a ranch about ten miles from the town of Río Bravo, in a *tiendita*, or little store, decorated with pictures of the revolutionary leaders Francisco ("Pancho") Villa and Emiliano Zapata and several old horse saddles, the owner, Martín Morado, excitedly began reciting lengthy poems about General Alvaro Obregón and Villa when I asked him if we could talk about history.[55] We discussed dates and names of figures involved in the Mexican Revolution, and then I asked him about Malinche. He explained, "I know little about La Malinche, about the life of the Indians. I want to know more . . . I went to chat with the teacher of the *escuela*, Lucio Blanco, about a mile from the ranch, so that he could tell me about those things, but he did not know much, he is not like the old teachers." Martín continued, "La Malinche was given to Cortés. She was very beautiful and that *malinchismo*, well, it comes from her." Martín spoke of his younger daughter and how she reminded him of Malinche. "There she was, brown-skinned, with her *trencitas* [braids] beautiful, just like Malinche. We always called her La Malinche." While Martín could not explain why *malinchismo* came from Malinche, his description of his daughter's beauty in terms of the "beautiful" Malinche and her "brown skin" points to his unique way of remembering Malinche. Martín asked me if I wanted to know more about the Mexican Revolution—I gladly said yes. Despite his limited schooling, Martín, like other residents along the border, has his own way of understanding history. His description of beauty in reference to a past historical figure, Malinche, is yet another example of Texas-Mexican historical memory.[56]

If these interviews with *fronterizos* can demonstrate anything, it is that Malinche as historical figure, modified or not, is highly informed by a person's geographic location, local experiences, and racial and gender biases. Indeed, the present plays a dramatic role in shaping people's perception of history. Obvious examples include Rosita's comparison of Malinche to Hillary Clinton and Rosario's definition of a Malinche as a bullying gang member in her high school in the 1980s. While this essay reflects the way in which a limited number of people from the border remember Malinche, it provides a reference point for understanding how people who live within two cultures recall history. It also suggests the multiplicity of histories in the population at large. The "official" history might not be the same for some as for others. Even the *fronterizos'* concepts of history, which inform the ideas of this essay, are diverse. But diverse as they may be, these interpretations of Malinche develop as historical memories that are rooted in two languages, two nations, two economies, in short, two cultures. Border people who have adapted to two worlds, as Malinche and José Limón did, possess a distinctive perspective on history. If we can be sure of one thing, it is that the figure, image, and recollection of Malinche are still very much alive in the minds of the *fronterizos*, whether intact, modified, or enigmatic.

NOTES

1. "Mis Dos Patrias," Tigres del Norte, Fonavisa, released in 1997. The original lyrics in Spanish are the following: "Para quien dice que yo soy un *malinchista*, y que traiciono a mi bandera y mi nación, para que rompa con mi canto las fronteras les voy a abrir de par en par mi corazón. Dejé las tumbas de mis padres, mis abuelos. Llegué llorando a tierra de anglosajón . . . no me llamen traicionero, que a mis dos patrias las quiero—En la mañana dejé mis muertos, aquí, aquí mis hijos nacieron. Por defender mis derechos no puedo ser traicionero." I would like to thank Diego Montalvo and Hernan Hernández Jr., of TN Ediciones (California), for allowing me to use the lyrics from "Mis Dos Patrias." All translations are my own. *Norteño* refers to people from northern Mexico.

2. On the meaning of *malinchista*, see Norma Alarcón, "Chicana's Feminist Literature: A Re-vision Through Malintzin or Malintzin: Putting Flesh Back on the Object," in Cherríe L. Moraga and Gloria E. Anzaldúa, *This Bridge Called My Back: Writings by Radical Women of Color* (Berkeley: Third Woman Press, 2002), 279: "Among people of Mexican descent . . . anyone who has transgressed the boundaries of perceived group interests and values often has been called a Malinche or *malinchista*." For an interesting discussion of *malinchismo* along the border from a cinematographic perspective, see Glenn A. Martínez, "Mojados, Malinches, and the Dismantling of the United States/Mexico Border in Contemporary Mexican Cinema," *Latin American Issues* (14) 2:http://webpub.allegheny.edu/group/LAS/LatinAmIssues/Articles/Vol14/LAI_vol_14_section_II.html.

3. The people interviewed for this essay are from northern Mexico and migrated to the United States (all live along the border or within the extended borderlands) or are Mexican Americans (defined as individuals born in the United States of Mexican descent). The extended borderlands concept is based on Mary Louise Pratt's "contact zone" approach to the study of cultures. A contact zone is a social space in which "disparate cultures" coexist.

Mary Louise Pratt, *Imperial Eyes: Travel Writing and Transculturation* (New York: Routledge, 1992).

4. George Sánchez, *Becoming Mexican American: Ethnicity, Culture, and Identity in Chicano Los Angeles, 1900–1945* (New York: Oxford University, 1993). For a discussion of culture within an anthropological (and ethnographic) framework, see George Marcus and Michael M. Fischer, *Anthropology as Cultural Critique: An Experimental Moment in the Human Sciences* (Chicago: University of Chicago Press, 1986).

5. Historical memory as a concept and methodology for this essay is based on Patrick Hutton, *History as an Art of Memory* (Hanover: University of New England Press, 1993). It is Hutton's contention that history is an art of memory: "it mediates the encounter between two moments of memory: repetition and recollection. Repetition concerns the presence of the past. It is the moment through which we bear forward images of the past that continue to shape our present understanding in unreflective ways," x.

6. Interview with Eustolia Hernández, June 7, 2003, San Juan, Texas.

7. Ibid.

8. Ibid.

9. Interview with Artemio Véliz, June 7, 2003, Río Bravo (Rancho Santa Ana), Tamaulipas.

10. On *mestizaje*, see Jaime E. Rodríguez and Colin MacLachlan, *The Cosmic Race: A Reinterpretation of Colonial Mexico* (Berkeley: University of California Press, 1980); Eric Wolf, *Sons of the Shaking Earth* (Chicago: University of Chicago, 1959). For a gendered interpretation of *mestizaje*, see Gloria Anzaldúa, *Borderlands/La Frontera: The New Mestiza* (San Francisco: Aunt Lute Books, 1999).

11. Interview with Mario González, September 16, 2003, Houston, Texas. The interview was conducted in English. Name has been changed at the request of the interviewee. An *ejido* or *ejidal* lands refer to communal landholdings, particularly those created as a result of the agrarian reforms brought about by the 1910 Mexican Revolution; see John Mason Hart's article on agrarianism and agrarian reform in William Beezley and W. Dirk Raat, eds., *Twentieth-Century Mexico* (Lincoln: University of Nebraska Press, 1986).

12. Interview with Mario González.

13. Interview with Felipe López, May 19, 2003, Río Bravo, Tamaulipas. Felipe, a recently married mechanic and carpenter, is one of many Río Bravo residents who travel to South Texas towns on a daily basis to work. Name has been changed at the request of the interviewee.

14. Ibid.

15. Interview with Oscar Chávez, June 18, 2003, Houston, Texas. The interview was conducted in Spanish and English. Oscar was born in Vallehermoso, Tamaulipas, and left to go to Houston at age seven. His father was born in Alice, Texas. The picture shown to Oscar was obtained from the Internet.

The original is housed in the Bancroft Library. http://www.mexconnect .com/mex_/history/malinche.html. "So [entonces] ésta era la que andaba con Hernán Cortés, ésta la Malinche?"

16. This sentence was not translated to illustrate the switching back from English to Spanish. "He forced her to be with him, [because] he was like a big shot. . . ."

17. Ibid. Oscar made reference to how perhaps Cortés used Malinche as a servant.

18. Ibid.

19. José Limón, like Oscar, came to the United States at a young age. José Limón, *An Unfinished Memoir* (Hanover: University Press of New England, 1998).

20. Interview with Manuel Véliz, June 6, 2003, Río Bravo, Tamaulipas.

21. Interview with Rosita Hinojosa, July 29, 2003, San Juan, Texas.

22. Ibid.

23. Limón, *An Unfinished Memoir*, 5.

24. Interview with Rosita Hinojosa.

25. Ibid.

26. Interview with Antonio Solís, Monterrey, Nuevo León, June 13, 2004. Antonio is originally from General Treviño, Nuevo León. Name has been changed at the request of the interviewee.

27. Ibid.

28. On Gerónimo Aguilar and Malinche, see Tzevtan Todorov, *The Question of the Other* (New York: Harper-Perennial, 1992); Bernal Díaz del Castillo, translated and introduced by J. M. Cohen, *The Conquest of New Spain* (London: Folio Society, 1974).

29. Interview with Oscar Chávez; see note 15.

30. Interview with Asención Melchor, September 16, 2003, via email, Houston, Texas.

31. Ibid.

32. Interview with Juan Ramón Chávez, September 21, 2003, Houston, Texas. Juan Ramón was born in Vallehermoso, Tamaulipas, and moved to Houston as an adult.

33. Mary Louise Pratt, "Yo Soy La Malinche: Chicana Writers and the Poetics of Ethnonationalism," *Callaloo* 16:4 (*On Post-Colonial Discourse: A Special Issue* [Autumn 1993]). The four rationales identified by Pratt include "passion-driven acts of women in love; as the inevitable playing out of female subordination; as revenge on the society that devalued and objectified her; as political strategy linked to her own lust for power; as an archetypal manifestation of female treachery and woman's inconstancy," 860.

34. Carmen Tafolla, "La Malinche," in Tey Diana Rebolledo and Eliana Rivera, eds., *Infinite Divisions: An Anthology of Chicana Literature* (Tucson: University of Arizona, 1993), first published in *Canto al Pueblo: Anthology of Experiences* (Texas: Penca Books, 1978).

35. Anzaldúa, *Borderlands/La Frontera*s; see the various works by Carmen Tafolla; see also Sandra Messinger Cypess, *La Malinche in Mexican Literature: From History to Myth* (Austin: University of Texas, 1991); Frances Karttunen, "Rethinking Malinche," in *Indian Women of Early Mexico*, ed. Susan Schroeder, S. Wood, and R. Haskett (University of Oklahoma Press, 1997); Adelaida Del Castillo, "Malintzin Tenépal: A Preliminary Look into a New Perspective," in Antoinette Sedillo López, ed. *Latina Issues: Fragments of Historia (Ella) (Herstory)* (New York: Garland, 1995). For a discussion on how scholars such as Anzaldúa have redefined Malinche and have used her as a Chicana symbol, see Naomi Helena Quiñonez, "Hijas de la Malinche (Malinche's Daughters): The Development of Social Agency Among Mexican American Women and the Emergence of First Wave Chicana Cultural Production" (Ph.D. diss., Claremont Graduate School, 1997).

36. Interview with Rosita Hinojosa.

37. Alarcón, "Chicana's Feminist Literature," 208–209.

38. Anzaldúa, *Borderlands/La Frontera*, 216.

39. Interview with Monica Cantú, January 2004, Houston, Texas. Name has been changed at the request of the interviewee.

40. Interview with Alice Garza, February 22, 2004, Houston, Texas. Name has been changed at the request of the interviewee.

41. Yvette G. Flores-Ortiz, "Theorizing Justice in Chicano Families," JSRI Occasional Paper #43, The Julian Samora Research Institute, Michigan State University, East Lansing, Michigan, 1999, 5. Flóres-Ortiz interviewed Chicano/Latino college students on "the impact of exposure to family and social violence." The work of Flóres-Ortiz is based on a three-year interview project in California.

42. Ibid., 4.

43. Ibid., 7.

44. "Indigenous Always," documentary by Daniel Banda, filmed at the "U.S. Latina/Latino Perspectives on La Malinche" conference, August 26–28, 1999. The conference was part of the Latina/Latino Studies Program in conjunction with the Spanish, Italian, and Portuguese Department, the Illinois Program for Research in the Humanities, and the Women's Studies Program.

45. Ibid.

46. Interview with Marc González, June 15, 2003, Edinburg, Texas.

47. Interview with Beth González, June 12, 2003, Pharr, Texas. Name has been changed at the request of the interviewee.

48. Interview with Rosario Herrera, July 30, 2003, Pharr, Texas. Name has been changed at the request of the interviewee.

49. Interview with Yamel Melchor, September 16, 2003, via email, Houston, Texas. The term "cultural hybridity" is borrowed from a number of scholars working on culture as a nonstatic concept. See Néstor García Canclini, *Culturas Híbridas: Estrategias para entrar y salir de la modernidad* (Mexico

City: Grijalbo, 2001); Todorov, *The Question of the Other;* Matt García, *A World of Their Own: Race, Labor, and Citrus in the Making of Greater Los Angeles, 1900–1970* (Chapel Hill: University of North Carolina Press, 2001).

50. Interview with Fred García, May 18, 2004, McAllen, Texas.

51. The term *chingada* comes from the verb *chingar* (lit. "to fuck" or to do violence to another through rape). There are many variations of *chingar*, i.e., *chingada, chinga*, etc. Malinche's association with the term is due to the writings of several authors who referred to Malinche as "chingada," or "the raped one," which has a negative connotation. The raped woman and her offspring are referred to as *chingados*. See Octavio Paz, *Labyrinths of Solitude*, and Margaret Shed, *Malinche and Cortéz* (New York: Doubleday, 1971). Such derogatory views still exist but have been critiqued and reevaluated by Chicana feminists and other scholars. See Adelaida Castillo, "Malintzin Tenépal," 18–19, for a discussion of Shed's derogatory comments about Malinche.

52. Ibid. Malinche and La Llorona are often treated as the same person. See Daniel Houston-Dávila, *Malinche's Children* (Jackson: University of Mississippi Press, 2001).

53. Shed, *Malinche and Cortéz*, vi.

54. Interview with Juan Ayala and Senovia Ayala, June 6, 2003, San Juan, Texas.

55. Interview with Martín Morado, Río Bravo, June 4, 2004. Name has been changed at the request of the interviewee.

56. Martín Morado completed the third grade in Río Bravo, Tamaulipas.

7. JOSÉ LIMÓN AND *LA MALINCHE* IN MEXICO
A Chicano Artist Returns Home

Margarita Tortajada Quiroz

Mexican artists began to embrace modern dance in 1939, following the arrival of two North American women: Waldeen (known only by her first name; 1913–1993) and Anna Sokolow (1919–2000).[1] Waldeen, whose performances had been coolly received by New York dance critics, found Mexico's ethnic variety entrancing. She soon began composing ethnically inspired dances, and she made the nation's capital her home for the remainder of her life. Sokolow, initially a Martha Graham dancer, also embraced Mexico and began to travel there regularly to perform.

In 1947, a government fine arts initiative united followers of both artists in a single national group, creating the Academy of Mexican Dance. Guillermina Bravo, a Waldeen enthusiast who became one of the pillars of Mexican dance during the second half of the twentieth century, became director. Ana Mérida, the daughter of the painter Carlos Mérida and a supporter of Sokolow, became subdirector.

The two parts of this first company coexisted uneasily. While some members of the nascent company created abstract pieces, others looked to the nation's indigenous peoples for inspiration. Waldeen's followers, headed by Bravo, supported socially and politically committed dance, whereas Sokolow's supporter Mérida favored a more formalist approach. In 1947, the socially oriented academy members started researching ethnic themes in Oaxaca's Yalaltec sierra and along the Tehuantepec Isthmus coast. The first choreographic work created by this group enjoyed the support of numerous prominent artists; Diego Rivera introduced the ethnic-inspired choreographed dances to the press in November, and a month later the academy's inaugural season began in the country's most important venue, the Palace of Fine Arts (Palacio de Bellas Artes). The debut performances represented a combination of abstract dance and Mexican themes.[2]

The initial fragile compromise between formalist and ethnically conscious dance did not survive the year. Director Bravo also became unhappy with the imposition of an artistic agenda from the director of the National Institute of Fine Arts. She resigned, and in 1948 she and a majority of members of the Academy of Mexican Dance founded the National Ballet of Mexico.

To overcome the negative fallout from Bravo's defection, Mérida invited Sokolow to join the academy as director and bring along with her her original disciples and various other ballet dancers. Even this solution proved unsatisfactory. When Sokolow left Mexico to return to the United States, the internal fighting continued, and Mérida started her own group within the academy.

A new Dance Department was created in January 1949, with the sculptor Germán Cueto as director. But the department was not to remain autonomous for long. A few months later it merged with the Department of Theatre and Literature under the direction of the writer and prominent Mexican intellectual Salvador Novo. Only a few months later, in May 1949, it separated from literature and became a separate Department of Theatre and Dance under the theatrical director Fernando Wagner.[3]

MEXICAN DANCE UP TO 1950

In December 1946, Mexico's first postrevolutionary civilian college-educated president, Miguel Alemán Valdés, came to power. Alemán represented a new generation of politicians who supported economic growth and embraced a comprehensive modernization program, including the arts. In order to legitimize his regime as a continuation of the Mexican Revolution's political tradition, however, Alemán had to retain traditional nationalist political discourse, only partially modifying it through the rhetoric of modernization and the then-popular rhetoric of anti-Communism.

Nationalism had fueled Mexican painting, music, and literature during the first half of the twentieth century, giving rise to some of Mexico's best-known international achievements: the nationalist murals of Rivera and José Clemente Orozco. At the time of Alemán's election, however, the government-supported arts lagged behind. Official cultural representations commemorated rather than innovated and typically glorified national culture as the expression of "the sum of [the brilliant] personalities" of the country.[4]

In 1946 Alemán founded the National Institute for Fine Arts and Literature (Instituto Nacional de Bellas Artes) to serve a nationalist agenda. According to the government decree creating the institute, art is "the most sincere and vigorous expression of the national spirit, . . . artistic personality provides the country's physiognomy, . . . and . . . the state must support the various forms of art that help to consolidate 'Mexicanness.'"[5] This institution served nationalist cultural politics until the end of the twentieth century, at which time a new institution, CONACULTA, took over that role. But it also embraced a new and sophisticated conception of official art and culture. Alemán placed the distinguished composer Carlos Chávez, who had considerable experience within the cultural bureaucracy, in charge of this new project.

Chávez's appointment as the first director of the National Institute for Arts was a boon for dance. He had worked directly with the Mexican dance companies and also had a special interest in the art form as a promoter, researcher, and composer. Chávez was also the first musician to incorporate pre-Hispanic motifs into his musical creations.

When the National Institute for Fine Arts was founded, Chávez did not appoint a separate head of the Dance Department but instead took personal charge of the position, financing and commissioning works himself.[6] In February 1947 Chávez founded the Academy of Mexican Dance, a professional company devoted to the creation, research, and diffusion of dance. The academy was also directed to provide a space for dance creation and experimentation intended to reflect national identity within a modern language of universal reach.

Fortunately for supporters of modern dance, such a nationalist agenda had to employ a modern language. The other official school (National School of Dance) could not take the lead in this new nationalist artistic expression, as its goal was to present classic ballet (considered old, dead, and unoriginal). An expressive, complete, humane, intense, and committed language capable of revolutionizing the form and content was needed. And this need opened up an opportunity for the "second Mexican art fine-tuning of the 20th century," modern dance.[7]

In 1931, during the conversations to establish the National School of Dance, Chávez suggested appointing a painter as director. He thought that "a non-dancer but one with esthetic abilities and the general notions of art needed to choreograph for the company"[8] should be appointed. Chávez's choice turned out to be Carlos Mérida. Chávez ultimately dropped Mérida but continued to look for another painter, and in June 1950 he selected Miguel Covarrubias (1904–1957) as chief of the new Department of Dance.

Covarrubias was a renowned artist who worked as a painter, cartoonist, researcher, anthropologist, and dance stage designer, among other things; the press reacted to his appointment by saying he was "like Terence's character," since nothing was foreign to him, and predicted that his tenure would be "clearly laudable."[9]

Covarrubias organized the department with the aim of setting solid foundations for a profound and authentic national art. He immediately saw the urgency for a "renewal in the concept of modern dance," teaching of "a broader and advanced technique," a stricter and more effective discipline of the dancers, their economic welfare, and, above all, "the elimination of antagonistic groups and incorporation of all the valuable elements in a single body of dance."[10]

In this respect, Novo observed, Covarrubias's lack of ties to either of the dance factions enabled him to integrate all the dancers successfully.[11] Covarrubias appointed the painter Santos Balmori as director of the academy and hired Xavier Francis (1928–2000), an American dancer from the New Dance Group of New York, also unconnected to the internal quarrels, who began to improve the discipline and professionalization of the Mexican modern dancers.

Beginning with Wagner's tenure as head of the dance section in 1949, members of Mexico's artistic community began to discuss a visit by José Limón.[12] Raquel Gutiérrez, a ballerina who, through her sister Carmen, also a dancer, had heard about the success of *The Moor's Pavane* in 1949, first suggested to Wagner that he contact Limón and invite him and his company to come to Mexico to teach and perform.[13]

When this suggestion was eventually forwarded to Covarrubias, he recognized that Limón could be the channel through which both professional dancers and the Mexican audience "could acquire closer contact with the great personalities of modern dance." He envisioned this happening through performances in local theaters, and also through the teaching of dance theory and choreography. According to Covarrubias's later assessment, "The performance of Limón and his company was a revelation to our dancers and had great success with the audience."[14]

THE IMPACT OF LIMÓN'S WORK IN MEXICO

Before 1950, few foreign modern dance companies had visited Mexico: in the thirties Michio Ito's groups (with Waldeen), Waldeen as soloist, and Anna Sokolow's Dance Unit had performed, and in the forties Katherine Dunham. There was scant awareness of international modern dance choreographers. A Mexico City newspaper, however, had published a note in 1949 mentioning Limón's company's performance in New York and quoted the critic John Martin's assessment of Limón as "the most extraordinary [dancer] in his class."[15]

At the beginning of September 1950, Limón arrived in Mexico at the invitation of the Department of Dance (the company members arrived later in the month). He met numerous artists, visited several culturally important places, gave interviews to the press, and rehearsed at the academy. The Spanish composer Rodolfo Halffter, in Mexico City at the time, said,

> After seeing José Limón rehearsing, now we understand why he is considered the first "modern" dancer in the world. His expression is comparable to that of a mime like Louis Barrault or an "academic" actor like Laurence Olivier. His contractions and distensions, typical of a modern technique, are performed with remarkable efficiency. He is the absolute ruler of his own movements, agile and elastic; but what is most impressive about him is the steadiness of his balance.[16]

After admiring Limón, whom he too regarded as one of the great masters of this form of artistic expression, Novo defined modern dance as a liberating new form:

> The "civilized world" has been able to rectify its idea of art in some respects by turning its gaze, questions, and demands to primitive communities, to their paintings, sculptures, and purity. It has returned, contrite, to cultivate and examine the origins of dance as [artistic] expression. This is the dialectic point in which the Mexican dances can be of interest. It is not about the circus anymore, or the incredible jump, or dancing on tiptoes. It is about the ordinary human body, launched to express the soul incited by the music: prisoner of the rhythm and dynamics of the universe, and of life, in terms of the pain and happiness of the human being; its sense of death and aspiration to immortality.[17]

Numerous newspaper columnists advertised the performances of Limón and his company. All of them emphasized the dancer's Mexican origin. The dance and music critic Wanderer said not only that Limón's having been born in Culiacán defined him as Mexican, but also that the "unavoidable power of his ancestry" could be observed in the careful selection of his themes and the music of his works. When he danced, "his temper, his nerve, his passion have an unmistakably Mexican flavor." He insisted that the Limón Company's performances in Mexico would be "a revelation," "as perfect as Graham's," and that with his performers "the dance acquired its maximum expressive power[,] and great technical grandeur became pure dramatic intensity, and pure elastic and eurhythmic power." [18]

In the weeks before his performance, the journalist Gabriel del Río wrote that he was one of the central figures of the dance scene. Throughout his life Limón had accumulated "profoundly human" knowledge and experiences that had taken him to an "incomparable summit of plasticity, filled with great artistic enthusiasm and an enormous expressive strength." Limón lived "consciously the psychological challenges of our times," which he tried to solve through artistic means. Limon's art balanced the human side of art with the spiritual side, and this contribution could be expected in his performances. Del Río noted Limón's Mexican expressiveness and said that his ambition was to bring to life, through dance, "the magnificent concept of José Clemente Orozco, an ideal that has attained superlative status in the aesthetic realization of a pure Mexican sentiment in body and soul." Limón considered that such Mexican art could be achieved by "being simply Mexican" in the spirit, without having to fall into an "irrational nationalism." [19]

Another columnist used Limón as an excuse for highlighting the importance of the ballet academy's work, and conversely to attack the modern dance academy. He said that perhaps Limón's presence would make it possible for the modern Mexican dance to "find the necessary support" and achieve the level of the National School of Dance. Foreigners had been behind all the previous attempts, but Limón's Mexican identity could allow him to assume leadership.

During an interview, Limón appeared "equamenable" about the superiority of modern over classic dance (which had widespread support in Mexico). According to him, modern had the advantage of enabling the "expression of dramatic contents" and the creation of "descriptive dances"; in addition, it was the only one that could evolve. Nevertheless, he acknowledged that the works of George Balanchine, David Lichine, Léonide Massine, and Antony Tudor "widened the potential of classic style, often taking advantage of the progress of modern dance."

In an interview in the Mexican journal *Tiempo* in September 1950, Limón said that "ideological ballets" that attempted to express extra-artistic problems were absurd, because the dance should not sacrifice "its emotional and formal values in exchange for a whimsical desire to express purely intellectual contents." About his dancing, he said it was "perfectly intelligible" because "true art tends, in my view, not to mystify or darken, but to enlighten." Even though he was interested in traditional dance, he did not believe it should be emulated: "If an artist pays too much attention to the typical, he might sink into the details and lose what is most pure and substantial." He trusted that the works of a Mexican are always Mexican "in their own nature; the most important thing was for the artist to try, above all, to be human, profoundly human."[20] Throughout his interviews, Limón repeated that modern dance could not limit itself to the traditional and that "it could be Mexican because of the essence of its creation."[21]

The rest of Limón's group arrived in Mexico on September 13. Wanderer declared that all the dancers were "perfect," especially Pauline Koner.[22] The debut was at the Palace of Fine Arts on September 19, and performances continued until October 1. The original performers were Limón, Koner, host dancer Leticia Ide, Lucas Hoving, Betty Jones, and Ruth Currier. Doris Humphrey was in charge of the artistic direction, Simon Sadoff was the musical director, and Pauline Lawrence was in charge of costume design. The National Symphony played with Sadoff as guest director.[23]

The repertoire, divided in three parts, included works by Humphrey and Limón. Of Humphrey's works, the group performed *Invention* (music by Norman Lloyd); *Lament for Ignacio Sánchez Mejías* (music by Lloyd, scenery by Michael Czaja, verses by Federico García Lorca, host actress Beatriz Aguirre); *The History of Humanity* (music by Novak, scenery by Czaja); and *A Day in the Earth* (music by Aaron Copland, actress Cibeles Henestrosa). From Limón's choreography they performed *Chacona en Re Menor* (music by Johann Sebastian Bach, violinist Fortino Velázquez); *The Exiles* (music by Arnold Schoenberg); *Concerto Grosso* (music by Antonio Vivaldi and Bach); *Danzas Mexicanas* (music by Novak); *The Moor's Pavane* (music by Henry Purcell, script based on Shakespeare's *Othello*); and *La Malinche* (music by Lloyd, trumpet Mario Martínez, drums Carlos Luyando, piano Sadoff, soprano Betty Jones).[24]

The journalist Igor Moreno described Limón's first moments on stage in his native land. Just before the show began, "the audience looked restless," the theater was filled with a selective and "strange public" (artists and intellectuals). "Limón appeared onstage with no costumes or decorations, only a few properly placed, spare, and attractive objects.

When he was about to start, an initial burst of applause forced him to respond to a display of affection for his extraordinary personality as a dancer." The salute created a strong bond between the audience and the dancers, and the performance began with the first part (*Invention, The Moor's Pavane, Lament*, and *La Malinche*).[25] The response to the program was largely positive and enthusiastic.

Critics hailed Limón as "the greatest male dancer of our time" and the best choreographer in his field. His company was considered the most talented that had ever performed on Mexican soil. Details of Limón's biography were published, highlighting his achievements, prizes, and repertory; the great quality of his dancers; and ovations they had received. One of the reviews described the Palace of Fine Arts as "shaken to its farthest corners" by the applause and also listed the personalities who had attended the presentation: "All of Mexican society; our most accomplished artistic figures; middle-class aficionados, journalists, etc.," in addition to "the cream of the crop of specialized critics of the capital." Among the audience were the composers Carlos Chávez and Julián Carrillo, the poets Carlos Pellicer and León Felipe, the painters Juan Soriano and Adolfo Best Maugard, the cinema director Julio Bracho, the theater director Seki Sano, many dancers, and, of course, Covarrubias "in the center of the room."[26]

The reviewer José Morales Esteves said that Limón performed "at the level of a dancer with steady technique, impeccable, strong, and masculine, a choreographer of great imagination and talent."[27] Another reviewer said that Limón had shown "new horizons in ballet techniques for the professionals, and a marvelous and especially provocative performance for the eyes of his fans."[28] Novo wrote that the entire season's program had been magnificent and that from the first presentation "the performances finally reconciled lovers of classical ballet with the bare feet and the anti-circus naturalism of modern dance." He said Covarrubias had feared that Limón might fail because his work was different from the dance other ballet companies had presented in Mexico and because the small number of dancers could make the company look "so refined and select, like the most delicate music chamber, that it would not be able to attract the crowd needed to fill an auditorium as big as the one at the Palace of Fine Arts." Covarrubias was wrong, Novo wrote, because "from the moment the curtain was lifted and the strong, vigorous, and vibrant silhouette of the colossal José Limón was offered to an energetic and engaged audience the public felt it was in the presence of an electric motor."[29]

The dance critic Horacio Sánchez Flores spoke about the amazing impact produced: "The audience [was] grabbed by the ten fingers of the hands and shaken without being able to take a breath. They remained under the spell of [these] great artists and received one of the most incredible experiences of their lives." They had met an authentic form of art, one that employed a direct, incisive language; it was the first time they had seen modern dance "in its most abundant and powerful expression, and the reaction to his novel and genuine artistry was truly overwhelming."[30]

The composer Rodolfo Halffter said that Limón had convinced even the fans of classical ballet, who "felt compelled to join the standing ovation." He thought that Limón's performances constituted Covarrubias's victory; he compared Limón's mime to that of Massine and said that the Mexican was a "remarkable actor of the dance and a dancer of wonderful plasticity"; as a choreographer, he was comparable to Tudor and Balanchine.[31]

To the journalist Manuel Lerín, writing in the newspaper *El Nacional*, Limón's art revealed its "Mexican guts," because his dances showed the presence of "his non-Latin, Mexican temper; the passion; the giving; the torrent, the poetic smoothness when necessary, the blazing push in any performance, and the veiled modesty that is a distinguished prudence."[32]

Manlio S. Fuentes wrote in *Impacto* that Limón, in addition to being "a great dancer, was also a great dramatic actor"; and that he was also a "brilliant creator." Citing Jean Dufresne, he included Limón among the artists who could "capture the new ethical tendencies, the new feelings" of their surroundings: Limón was an artist who showed the "most sensitive expressions of the social whole." Limón and his company had succeeded remarkably "because of the sublimity and exquisiteness of their performance; [their] authentic art, without mystifications, without theatrical tricks; inspiration, mimetic dramatic expression, [but with] plasticity in attitudes and movements that responded to states of mind and not to stereotypes of Greek statues." The performance included a "message of choreographic modern art" and an inspiration for other Mexican dancers "to create a new form of expression of our artistic personality, taking advantage of the musical folkloric themes and modes of indigenous dances, as painters have done." Fuentes continued, Limón was the "most beautiful and eloquent example" of that expression, and for Mexican art "the time for emancipation from the artificial and the necessity to return to nature have arrived, transforming [dance] into an art form through our racially mixed Creole temperament." To Fuentes, Limón's art was unique, with "the seal of the Latin temper, cast into an indigenous Mexican mold."[33]

Jorge J. Crespo de la Serna, the well-known art critic, regarded Limón as brilliant for having "assimilated and refined" the best heritage of modern dancing (formal basis, directives, and new concepts) adapting it to "his idiosyncrasy, to his temper" and elaborating his own style. Crespo spoke of the "admirable homogeneity and artistic refinements" of the lights, décor, and costumes "of exquisite taste." The importance of Limón's dances was "the way in which the profound biology of dancing was imprinted on diverse artistic variations." The dance emerged from the "inside out, spreading itself and grabbing the bodies"; it would give voice to them using all of its resources, "and makes the spectator feel the emotion of its vital rhythm." Limón had managed to "merge the purity of old dancing with the most beloved popular symbols and forms, combining it in a stylized modern expression."[34]

Critics and columnists highlighted Limón's authority as a dancer and as a choreographer, but they also applauded Humphrey's works and made positive comments about the work of Sadoff, the dancers, and other participants. Each of the productions garnered comment, generally very positive. As one might expect, *The Moor's Pavane* was considered the masterpiece of the program because of Limón's successful artistic interpretation of *Othello*; his expression, emotion, and dramatic content; his "robust psychological penetration"; and his originality of movement and gestures, in addition to the characters, music, costumes, and lights. The compliments were countless. But not everyone was pleased.

Even though the majority of the comments praised Limón's creativity, the Mexican stamp of his work, and the perfection of the dancers, a few discordant voices appeared. One bitterly criticized representatives of the National Institute of Fine Arts for scheduling a modern dance season, regarding it as suitable for the enjoyment of only a few.[35] Even though they admitted that modern dance had a technique, as Limón's dancers had shown, one anonymous critic ("S. H.") said the technique was "limited, one-dimensional, monotonous, and disrespectful."[36] In addition, he added that the company had been unsuccessful in attracting the interest of the public, as only the opening night at the Palace of Fine Arts had been fully attended.

Nevertheless, even the most ferocious critic, G. González y Contreras, recognized Limón's virtuosity as a choreographer for his role in *The Moor's Pavane*, although he thought the work was affected by "stereotypical and Taylorized" gestures.[37] In 1952, a harsh critique of Covarrubias and his role as head of the Dance Department appeared in *El Tiempo,* stating that since 1950 Limón had been saddled with "great expectations," but that his success was limited "almost exclusively" to *The Moor's Pavane* because "some of his performances had been rejected" by audiences.[38]

Defending Limón against critics who voiced the Mexican public's preference for ballet, Moreno wrote that although the "fanatics" of classical dance had resisted Limón's work, Limón had been able to capture the interest of a group of spectators who liked ballet and allowed themselves the privilege of "enjoying the beauty of a new artistic dance that had found its path" and was already "of legal age." He compared the opponents of modern dance with those who had once underestimated Serge Diaghilev's Russian ballets and Igor Stravinsky's music. He asserted that in spite of the disagreements and conflicts in the field of dance, "Tyrians and Trojans" had recognized the quality of Limón, and his presence had "brought comfort to the faith" of specialists in modern dance.[39]

LA MALINCHE AND THE MEXICAN CRITICS

Almost every single columnist and critic remarked on *La Malinche* and the *Lament.* In many cases they were divided in their opinions.

When Limón's 1950 season in Mexico was announced, *La Malinche* was advertised as a "strong piece with primitive pride, a danced legend of a traitor who, after her death, offered her purified and militant soul to those whom she had betrayed."[40] The program notes for the performance read as follows:

The story of La Malinche, interpreted through José Limón's childhood memories in Mexico. The dance represents a naive and simple concept of a Mexican Indian, of the popular legend based on an important chapter in Mexican history. Doña Marina, an Indian princess, betrayed her people when she became partner, lover, translator, and adviser of Hernán Cortés. According to popular belief, her bedeviled spirit came back to earth to suffer for her betrayal, and it will not find peace until her people are liberated. During the battles for Independence and during the [Mexican] Revolution the tortured spirit of La Malinche returned to be purged for her betrayal. The dance is, as a result, a simple story of love, infidelity, and repentance.[41]

The program notes may have led one columnist to say that the dance was conceived by a childish mind, one in which "popular legends are simplified to reach a deeply poetic and strong symbolism, of an immense

FIGURE 7.1 The original cast that performed *La Malinche* in Mexico. Left to right: José Limón, Pauline Koner, and Lucas Hoving. Photograph by Walter Strate. Courtesy of the José Limón Dance Foundation.

plainness." The Indian that Limón personified was like that, "almost timeless, distant from the story . . . set on a musical background strewn with themes played by the revolutionary trumpets that Norman Lloyd, the piece's composer, imagined hearing."[42]

Novo wrote that *La Malinche* "offered live and dynamic paintings of Orozco at different moments." He thought it was odd to hear opinions about the inadequacy of the costumes because nobody expected them to be "realistic or documented." He also said that this "delicate summary of childhood reminiscences"[43] could be the "source of inspiration" for local choreographers to build their own dances on their own themes.

Sánchez Flores considered *La Malinche* an unfinished experiment, whose "spirit is admirably interpreted and synthesized (Limón's ability to synthesize is truly amazing), and it obviously shows a deep knowledge of Mexico through its contemporary painters." This skill made the "brief historical interpretation" look authentic (except for Cortés's wardrobe), but the writer also recommended that Limón "reevaluate" and transform the piece into "something better structured."

The three main dancers of *La Malinche* were Limón as El Indio, Pauline Koner as La Malinche, and Lucas Hoving as El Conquistador. In the opinion of Sánchez Flores, Koner managed to play her character "with all the versatility of its symbolism," Limón had portrayed an Indian "almost truthful to the incarnation of the Mexican people," and Hoving had played a conquistador who "required the public's fantasy as the choreographer's character demanded." Lloyd's music was "very well written" and had an "original combination of piano, percussions, trumpet, and voice."[44]

To the music critic Gerónimo Baqueiro Fóster, the works of Limón, including *La Malinche*, revealed him as a "cautious artist, with an active and creative imagination." Limón did not need décor, Baqueiro Fóster wrote, because "everything is dealt with on a plain stage with a sense of modernity that stands out as solemn." His characters were "purely symbolic representations, and such symbolism played a key role in the costume as well as in the gestures and attitudes."[45]

The music critic Julio Sapietsa said that *La Malinche* was yet another "expressive summary," like *The Moor's Pavane*, that with only three characters portrayed a historical passage. Limón created "the whole Mexican flavor that becomes deeper with the repetitive percussion beats accompanied by sad chants, that take us to a kinetic intoxication."[46] Manlio S. Fuentes declared that *La Malinche*'s music was well structured and superbly performed by the symphony and the Mexican soloists; from a choreographical standpoint, it was a work of "modern architecture" that revolved around "the agitated and enamored lover of Hernán Cortés."[47]

Lloyd's score received harsher criticism. Wanderer stressed that *La Malinche* was an "action ballet," choreographically excellent, but that the music had taken away its "flavor, temperament, and importance." He criticized the music as being of poor quality, showing "questionable taste, with strange instrumental resources inappropriate for the Mexican setting of *La Malinche* or the Spanish setting of *Llanto*."[48]

Halffter added that *La Malinche* "was damaged by the vulgar music," which had a "commercial and tasteless flavor." He said that the scores of Bach, Purcell, and Copland showed artistic quality, but not those of either Lloyd or Novak.[49] The music critic Junius referred to the music as being a "very curious evocation." In addition, he lamented the use of the "symbol of our sacred religion [the cross used during the dance], that is even used to raise *La Malinche* from the ground!"[50]

To Lerín, the dance showed "a plain depiction of the capricious Malinche mating with Hernán Cortés, betraying her people. During Cortés's bewitchment—sword and cross confounded—the Indio Limón, hieratic and on his knees, accepted the material conversion of the female; but then both [El Indio and La Malinche] repudiate the conqueror." That part of the piece had not reached him "in the complete Mexican sense that could be expected," and even though one could feel the presence of "the distinctive short steps of our Indians as they walked," these were not enough to "make an impression on our psychological roots"; there was a need for "more of the plaintive attitude, the involuntary submission, the deepest acceptance of destiny." But the dancers had kept their art "at a high level."[51]

The music critic Esperanza Pulido considered that in both *Llanto* and *La Malinche* one could not "look for a Mexican or Spanish atmosphere," but what the spectator was presented with was a "real impression of the motive that inspired the choreography, with the assistance, in the case of the first ballet, of García Lorca's verses, and of the symbolic cross" in the second.[52] To another columnist, *La Malinche*, which "should be Mexican, does not have anything that could be positively considered ours, but in any case some of its parts are appealing."[53]

The theater critic J. N. Huerta affirmed that none of the dances "appealed to us because, in spite of the good intentions, these were mere musical mimes; *La Malinche* without more music than *teponaxtle* and the *chirimía*" [wooden drum and flute] and *Llanto*, which was "gray and inexpressive."[54]

González y Contreras said, in almost unintelligible language, that the intervention of the soprano Betty Jones and the two Mexican soloists in *La Malinche* were a pleasant surprise to him, but "neither showed any indigenous or Spanish roots from a musical and choreographic standpoint." He continued,

> In that piece, Limón completely responds to the angular, slow, and mechanical aesthetic present in his choreographic style; which follows the same directives as his previous creations and *The Moor's Pavane*, which follows: this [Malinche] is an adequate treatment of a harmonious substance of mechanical quality, exclusively concerned about the concrete choreographic fact, within a form that corresponds to the modernization of the archaic and in proportion with a slow and mechanic idea of the pieces.[55]

By contrast, Moreno wrote that Limón had been able to perform the "historic scene of La Malinche through a symbolic representation of hallucinatory artistic effects." He highlighted the "sweet voice" of Jones, used "not as an instrument, because her vocalizations are no more than the meaning of a timbre," next to the piano, trumpet, and drums.[56]

Covarrubias defended Limón, noting that he had migrated to the United States as a child and had kept "his affection for Mexico, to the extent of taking Spanish lessons to avoid losing the language." He said that Limón's Mexican gift was revealed in *La Malinche*, which was "a kind of pastoral about the Conquest seen through the naive eyes of a Mexican boy from the other side of the Río Bravo; in other words, José Limón's blurred memories of Mexico." In addition, his admiration for the Mexican arts was obvious, as the dance was "unmistakably inspired by Orozco's paintings."[57]

LA MALINCHE THROUGH THE EYES OF DANCERS

Limón's presence in Mexico left a mark on many Mexican dancers; it had a clear impact on their work and their idea of modern dance. The 1950 performances, especially *The Moor's Pavane*, are still remembered by those who witnessed them. Many Mexican artists who later became famous as actors, dancers, and choreographers were spectators at the Limón Company's first performance. Many worked with him when he returned to participate in the two seasons of Mexican dance in 1951 and regarded the opportunity as a privilege and a stimulus to their artistic development and growth. Among the dancers whom I interviewed who witnessed those performances were the principal dancer Colombia Moya, a practitioner of Mexican nationalist modern dance; Guillermo Arriaga, principal dancer and choreographer in Mexican nationalist modern dance, who created one of the most important pieces of the Mexican repertory, *Zapata*; Rosa Reyna, a dancer, choreographer, and teacher in the first Mexican nationalist modern dance movement, who choreographed one of the important early works, *La Manda*; Rocío Sagaón, the film actress, one of the best-known dancers in the nationalist tendency of Mexican modern dance and the companion of Covarrubias;[58] Nellie Happee, a well-known Mexican classical and modern dance choreographer and performer, one of the pioneers of Mexican modern dance in the 1950s; Josefina Lavalle, a dancer, teacher, researcher, choreographer, and director of the first generation of Mexican nationalist modern dance, who choreographed one of the most important early Mexican modern dance pieces, *Juan Calavera*, and continues to play an important role in contemporary modern dance; Farnesio de Bernal, an actor who decided to become a dancer when he saw Limón perform in 1950, a dancer in the Mexican modern dance tradition, and choreographer of *Los Gallos*, one of the most important early Mexican modern dances.

Moya has a vivid memory of Orozco's presence in *La Malinche*.[59] Arriaga says the piece was of "first-rate quality," achieved a historic synopsis with only three characters, and was superbly danced; the music, he thought, was adequate.[60]

Reyna was very much aware of the clash between two races and two cultures (the indigenous and the Spanish) in *La Malinche*.[61] Happee vividly remembers Koner dressed up with her hair braided but thinks the dance portrays Limón's personal view of the Conquest, which did not correspond to history.[62]

Sagaón recalls the company's amazing strength and dynamism; building its works from concrete ideas and never doing free moves. During the company's rehearsals, she admired Koner above everyone else and identified with her, as they were both petite. In spite of her size, Koner was able to project in gigantic fashion. Observing her led Sagaón to realize that lack of height was not a disadvantage, and she committed herself to dance like the American.

To Sagaón, *La Malinche* presented a transparent choreography, the dancers were perfect, and their characters were well performed and able to achieve a "surprising unity." With strength and clarity, they expressed "the core of the Mexican dilemma, of the woman who is caught between the Spanish and the Indigene. I have never seen anything so perfect and stylized that goes straight to your heart. One does not need flags or uniforms to say, 'This is Mexican,' and José was able to capture the Mexican spirit in spite of his North American education." She identified with "that woman's character, which was very complex, and which also, in the case of the Spaniard and the native, could encapsulate the central idea."

According to Sagaón, Koner had sufficient skills to bring complexity to her character: "her strength was like dynamite, she moved internally, and at the same time was very reserved, very delicate in her movements. She showed La Malinche exactly as one might imagine her, smart, multifaceted, like Pauline herself." She had enough skills to give complexity to her character; she was "subtle and overwhelming," "sweet and strong" at the same time, with both men; La Malinche was her "bridge" and it was "politically perfect (she was, indeed, the diplomat of her times)." Even though she showed sweetness, "suddenly her demons came out" or expressed pain; she was the strong character of the play, "the dominant part."[63]

Lavalle remembers Limón's choreographic works in general, as she has examined the way in which he handled his characters from a theatrical and conceptual standpoint; she felt connected to his concern in rescuing Mexico's history: "The symbolic summary that Limón achieved in *The Pavane* was already present in *La Malinche* (as it was in the sword/cross) and in just a few minutes it said many things. That conflation of symbols affects me, and it matters a lot to me."

She thought that the music did not fit the dance and that Limón should have searched for a more suitable score from Mexican composers. She considers the choreography to be "very elaborated" and embodying the topic, characters, and wardrobe without ruining its symbolism; "he did not need anything more." The treatment of the female character was "exactly as it is treated in our official history: a woman who followed Cortés for love, betraying her own people." It did not show a "battling or conscious woman, neither did it show a docile woman who walks behind Cortés. She was a real woman." To Lavalle, Koner had the capacity for giving duality to this character, "sweet, but a traitor," and points out that it evolved at a "secondary level," as the action was led by the two males.[64]

De Bernal talked about Koner as a great dancer and a "superb actress."

He remembers her beautiful dress ("stylized, nonauthentic"), her artificial braids, her small size, the strength she projected in the theater, and her curt moves. "Limón's Malinche was not sweet," he said. "She was a very strong woman, decisive, tough," like Koner; she assumed an "active position" and mediated between the two men who struggled for power. He remembered her with more clarity and declared that "her character was created with a terrible force, internal, the force that emerges from the creativity that great artists have."

De Bernal thought the presence of Limón and his company "had a smashing impact." He was particularly taken aback by the fact that, unlike classical ballet, Limón's dances showed a contrast between the soft and the staccato; but above all, Bernal was most impressed by Limón's theatricality, which made him ask himself, "How can anybody express so much, so many ranges of feelings without speaking, such gentleness, with pure movement?" The impact of the performance was so strong that Bernal decided to become a dancer.[65]

A dancer of nationalist modern dance and an activist in contemporary Mexican dance, Valentina Castro, who saw La Malinche in 1950, also had vivid memories of the piece, including the design and the action, the intentions of gestures and movements, the sword/cross, the wardrobe. She declared that the three dancers entered the stage as if they were a child's little Mexican dolls and then transformed themselves into the characters. La Malinche was the mediator in a struggle between two cultures; she looked like "the mother, the sister, the Mexican woman who suffers for the Indian" or "like the virgin, the land that offers to help." To Castro, that character was not the woman who "betrayed the indigenous peoples," but the woman who made possible the fusion of two races when she became "the land that simply accepted the masculine to be fertilized." During the play, La Malinche "never took sides" with one of the men; she was only the "pacifying element."

Because Koner "does not belong to our culture and does not know the natives," she could not assume the "manners of her character," but in her version of "a village woman (of any village)" sometimes she appeared as a "statue of high energy" attacking each move, or made her way with softness and sweetness, "as if she were floating."

Castro noted that Limón held women in high esteem and treated them with care and tenderness. She saw that care in the character of La Malinche and in the difference between the "masculine movements" of the male dancers and the "feminine movements" of the female dancers in his works. Castro considers this to be of great value in Limón's work "because the woman can be very strong, but is not a man."

About the music score of *La Malinche*, Castro says that "it wanted to be Mexican," but it sounded more "childish" and "light." The work in general she depicts as being "innocent, naïve, idealized, graceful," and it did not affect her: "It was something that amused me, perhaps because I was a child and that is what I took from it."

Nevertheless, Castro harshly criticized what she perceived to be Limón's "desire to be Mexican." She explained that in spite of his origins, Limón experienced what happens to those who emigrate or who are born out of the country: "They keep their roots and feel part of a culture that supports them, but it becomes a ghost, a childish ghost" that does not allow them to discern and express it accurately; they are strangers, and their creations are hybrids, products of a "third culture, valid and valuable, but non-Mexican."

Castro says that the conventional wisdom about La Malinche is false, as it represents submission not to the external, but to its culture. She "was not an ordinary woman, but a very intelligent one, the daughter of an influential gentleman; she was given away to Cortés and was loyal to him because her moral principles demanded that she act in that way" (nowadays, even during this new century, "it is still expected that we Mexican women be loyal to our partners"). La Malinche "did not betray her culture, she obeyed it," and we, the Mexicans, "are not inferior to any culture."[66]

The character of La Malinche was present in Mexican popular culture in 1950. *The Labyrinth of Solitude* by Octavio Paz was published around that time, when the pejorative adjective *malinchismo* had already emerged to denote the attraction and seduction of the foreign, contempt for one's own culture, or the acceptance of colonialism.

Limón chose a topic with a strong referent within the national culture, one that has been defined even as the raison d'être of the psychology of Mexican identity. Malinche is a real character in Mexican history, but often she became indistinguishable from the poetry and the epic. Her name was Malintzin (Malin with the Nahuatl suffix *tzin*, which means "reverence"); she was born between 1498 and 1505; her father, a Nahuatl chief whose home territory was on the Gulf Coast, sold her into slavery. In 1519, when Cortés arrived in Tabasco, he received her as a present along with nineteen other young women, as indigenous custom stipulated. Cortés distributed the women among his captains, and when Malintzin's master returned to Spain, Cortés retrieved her and used her as a translator. They became an inseparable couple, to the extent that Cortés became known as "Señor Malinche." Even though they had a son together, Cortés made her marry Juan Jaramillo, and thus she bore the name of doña Marina until her death in Mexico City in 1531.[67]

According to Carlos Fuentes's 1979 interpretation, the name Malintzin came from the priestess of the dawn, tamer of beasts and men, who ruled until the males imposed their power. She was the "midwife" of the history of the Spanish Conquest: the "goddess who imagined it, then the lover who received its seed, and finally the mother who gave birth to it. Goddess, Malintzin; whore, Marina; mother, Malinche,"[68] the name and meaning that Limón took for his play.

Although she has been regarded as a traitor, in my view she never turned against her people, but rather against the bloody power that dominated the region. She led the drive for revenge on behalf of those oppressed by the Aztec empire and together with Cortés became feared and respected. The construct that emerged around her persona made her one of the "imaginary entities, remains of the past or ghosts begotten" by the Mexicans.[69] For Paz, she is the mother of all Mexicans, defenseless and passive (*chingada*) in the face of the conqueror; she is a "reincarnation of the female condition."[70] Her story is, above all, a representation of the tragedy that produced the annihilation of a culture whose mission of saving the world ended up blending with another one, giving way to a third, the Mexican, with its own symbols and destiny. That is the historic setting of La Malinche, but it represents something more. In every culture, women have been depicted as two-faced. La Malinche is the Mexican Eve, who, paired with the Virgin of Guadalupe, forms a unit: they are the potential sources of good and evil, the two poles of Woman.[71]

LIMÓN'S CONTRIBUTION TO MEXICAN MODERN DANCE

As Covarrubias and others have pointed out, Limón arrived in Mexico during a crucial moment for modern dance, which had been following its own dynamic but still needed a push in order to become professionalized. Covarrubias was essential, to the extent that his short tenure as head of the Department of Dance (1950–1952) is known as the golden age of modern dance.

Limón's longest lasting impact on modern dance occurred when he returned to Mexico in 1951 to work with the Academy of Mexican Dance. That year the company adopted the name Mexican Ballet and named Limón as its choreographer, artistic director, and performer during the first season (30 March to 22 April). Limón also served as ballet master (along with Humphrey and Hoving).

Limón performed *The Moor's Pavane* with his own company and then opened three productions with the Mexican Ballet. The first was *Los cuatro soles* (music by Carlos Chávez, written by Chávez and Covarrubias, scenery and costumes by Covarrubias). It turned out to be "premature," according to Covarrubias, because it had been conceived as a "great spectacle, disregarding the philosophical theme of the legend, and unable to fuse with the essentially rhythmic spirit of pre-Hispanic dance and music."[72] This failed piece, however, had a wonderful cast made up of a vast contingent of dancers from several other companies and the School of Physical Education.

Limón also debuted *Tonantzintla* (music by Fray Antonio Soler, orchestral version by Halffter, scenery and costumes by Covarrubias), which "reunited the primitive splendor and the bucolic ingenuity of baroque art, and was a patent success."

The third new dance was *Diálogos* (music by Lloyd, scenery and costumes by Julio Prieto), which once again took up the predicament portrayed in *La Malinche*. Indigenous and Spanish characters (Montezuma and Cortés) appeared, but their opposition was projected forward to another moment in the country's history through the depiction of Benito Juárez (reappearance of the indigenous) and Maximilian of Habsburg (the reincarnated conqueror). According to Covarrubias, *Diálogos* was an "interesting experiment" that the public did not understand. The "symbolic sense of the dance . . . was not attempting to reproduce historic individual characters, but to reflect the dramatic subjugation of the indigenous race." Once again, Lloyd's music "did not contribute to the success of the ballet."

Limón imparted two important lessons, as De Bernal recalls. He encouraged Mexican dancers to create new choreography, saying, "Do not be afraid, do mediocre things; because after one hundred mediocrities comes something worthwhile. I have done lots of mediocre things."[73] The other lesson De Bernal recalls was Limón's insistence that nationalist dance could not be something external, but must be the product of an expressive need:

One needs to go to the true source of Mexicanness: the one that we all carry inside. The choreography should be based on personal experiences, on the most intimate part of the artist. Himself. This is why my choreographical work, like my style, my rhythm, my movements and gesture, comes from the depths of my inner self, as atavisms. . . . If an artist responds to the call from the blood, from his spirit, his work will catch the spirit, the contour of his country. And it will be universally valid. But this is contrary to the search for the national in the externals of art. The indigenism, the professionally exploited Mexicanism will fail. Nevertheless, the emergence of a purely Mexican dance is imminent; dancers and choreographers will find it within themselves.[74]

With support from Covarrubias and Limón, and with the knowledge and accumulated experiences of Mexican artists, some important works of nationalist modern dance debuted in 1951. The most important ones were *La manda* by Rosa Reyna (music by Blas Galindo, script by José Durand based on "Talpa" by Juan Rulfo, design by José Chávez Morado); *Imaginerías* by Xavier Francis (music by Béla Bartók, design by Julio Prieto); and *Recuerdo a Zapata* by Guillermina Bravo (based on *Raíz y razón de Zapata* of Jesús Sotelo Inclán, music by Jiménez Mabarak, design by Leopoldo Méndez).[75]

According to the dramatist and modern dance supporter Emilio Carballido, the presence of Limón during this and the following season of the Mexican Ballet gave the performances "an international presence, and to the team of dancers and resident choreographers, an important contact with the universal life of the dance, a consciousness of level and direction."[76] In fact, that season was covered by both the local and the North American press (such as *Dance Magazine*[77] and *Dance Observer*);[78] the Mexicans traveled to the Fourth American Dance Festival and in 1952 to the Jacob's Pillow Dance Festival, in addition to Connecticut College.

During the second season of the Mexican ballet (24 November to 16 December 1951) Limón performed again as a dancer and, with Humphrey, guest choreographer. She showed *Pasacalle* (music by Bach, costumes by Antonio López Mancera), "a masterpiece of modern dance" which demonstrated "the technical achievement of the young dancers." Limón opened *Antígona* (music by Chávez, prologue by Novo, design by Covarrubias), "impressively danced by Rosa Reyna and Limón"; and *Redes* (music by Silvestre Revueltas, script by José Revueltas), which, according to Covarrubias, was "perhaps the best of what [Limón] composed in Mexico," reaffirming Limón's gifts both as a choreographer and as a dancer.[79]

Other openings that made a splash were *El chueco* by Guillermo Keys (music by Miguel Bernal Jiménez, scenery by López Mancera); *El sueño y la presencia* by Guillermo Arriaga (music by Blas Galindo, design by Chávez Morado); and *Tierra* by Elena Noriega (music by Francisco Domínguez, scenery by José Morales Noriega, costumes by Arnold Belkin).

The Academy of Mexican Dance had other seasons in 1952 without Limón, and even though they too were successful the company disappeared soon after Covarrubias and Chávez left the National Institute of Fine Arts (it was customary for officials to resign following the election of a new president). Still, a climax in the development of nationalist Mexican dance had been reached.

Limón and his company performed in Mexico for the last time in 1960, presenting several productions in the Palace of Fine Arts. Among these were *Ritmo hondo* and *Hechizo nocturno* by Humphrey and *Para todo hay un tiempo*, *Emperor Jones*, *The Traitor*, and *Missa Brevis* by Limón. Limón restaged *Missa Brevis* with the Ballet de Bellas Artes during a season in which Sokolow participated with *Ofrenda musical* and *Opus 1960*, and the choreographers Lavalle, Mérida, De Bernal, Arriaga, and Reyna presented their work.[80]

THE MASCULINE DANCE OF LIMÓN

Limón's artistic contribution to Mexican modern dance includes his performance and teaching as well as his mere presence, which revitalized male dancers and their masculine image. Limón's presence helped convince numerous men to become dancers; some of them, like Luis Fandiño and De Bernal (who later became important figures in Mexican modern dance), have acknowledged that what made them identify with Limón were his expressiveness and force on the stage as well as his masculine presence.[81]

During the fifties (and even today), most male dancers clashed with the predominant image of masculinity in Western cultures; dancing is perceived as a feminine activity because women and theatrical dancing are identified with the body, silence, the emotions, and the irrational, all foreign to the concept of hegemonic masculinity.

The "legitimate uses" of the male body (which establishes a "relationship between the phallus and the *logos*")[82] do not include showing oneself to others. Men's rationality and desiring gaze confine women to the physical level, preserving the "non-corporeal and disincarnated status" that men enjoy.[83] In addition, in Mexico dance is an activity that does not bring fame and fortune, which are vital to the image of the so-called real man.

Limón tried to redeem masculine dance and bring it back to its original grandeur. He supported "learning to dance in a dignifying manner for a man, and in a myriad of ways,"[84] and he achieved his goal of giving "a totally new meaning and a higher level to male dancing."[85] Limón said,

> There were only a few men willing to commit themselves to formal dancing, and to make its resurgence a manly purpose. Precisely because the danger of extinction is imminent, there is a need for dedicated men of high quality, who can reaffirm masculine good sense and dance it. No other art offers such a challenge. In a society that is in desperate need of all its art and artists, dancing gives a rare opportunity to talk again about it with those who are conscious of its ancient greatness.[86]

Limón made reference to the identification that men in the audience could establish with male dancers. Spectators could

> value more a man's performance than a woman's performance, because in order to make it possible the man had to struggle against a series of disadvantages and limitations. A woman is allowed to handle a large variety of issues and feelings; but a man can handle only a few decently and with good taste. I have seen numerous male dancers sinning against good taste in many ways.[87]

Limón found "decency and good taste" by using the logic of defensive strategies: showing domination, power, and aggressiveness in the dance.[88] We can observe this in the metaphors and masculine images of his dances, which attempt to perpetuate male power. He makes men look like heterosexuals, protecting their bodies and reinforcing the notion of a monolithic masculinity. When his body becomes a "spectacle" the dancer should look powerful and employ violence, mechanisms that prevent the gaze of desire from reaching him and transforming him into an object.[89]

Clear examples are the works in which Limón shows a confrontation between two men. The first one was in 1949 in *La Malinche* (a year after the appearance of his essay "La danza viril" [Virile dance]), and this was followed by *The Moor's Pavane* (1949), *The Exiles* (1951), *The Traitor* (1954), and *The Emperor Jones* (1956). One of the central elements of these works is the virility of their characters and the inclusion of dancers as warriors (his company could be regarded as a dance company "for men")[90], elements which repeated those developed within modern dance ever since Ted Shawn's productions.

The power and virility Limón exhibited gave an incentive to other Mexican men to become involved in the dance scene during the fifties. Xavier Francis was one so attracted, with his strength and precision and style that was so unlike classical ballet. This was a time in which male dancers struggled with familial and social obstacles that emerged because of their career choice. Women were the main figures (almost exclusively) of modern dance as performers, teachers, choreographers, and directors. They created feminine works and exhibited feminine bodies, which hampered the opportunities for men to "experiment with a genuine physical recognition of their movements"[91] and of the representations of "official" masculinity.

The latter, within modern nationalist dance, involved "the patriotic man,"[92] who was closely related to the "Mexican macho" (as in the movies), to identity, and to the history of the Mexican state, especially since the Revolution.[93] The Revolution had brought a "messianic spirit that transformed men into super-men and shaped a discourse that associated masculinity with social transformation."[94] "The figure of the macho mythical hero"[95] emerged as a result, sustaining an image of masculinity that was congruent with that of the nation: "The macho is Mexico incarnated."[96] And on the dance scene, the male dancer was its representative.

The idea of nationalist modern dance attempted to reproduce the images and ethos of that *machismo*, and that required a masculine dancer. This is why Limón's performance (and that of other dancers as well) was acclaimed by audiences and by the experts.

LA MALINCHE IN MEXICO THREE DECADES LATER

Thirty-one years after its opening in Mexico, *La Malinche* returned, to be danced this time by one of the most important companies in the country, the Ballet Teatro del Espacio, which was established in 1966 and was codirected by Gladiola Orozco and Michel Descombey.

According to Orozco, the dance arrived in the repertoire through Paul Lepercq, a French patron who also supported modern dance companies, including those of Graham, Sokolow, and Limón. Lepercq thought the Ballet Teatro del Espacio could perform a work by the Mexican choreographer, and Descombey traveled from Mexico to Canada in

1980, where Limón's company was performing at the time. Descombey chose *La Malinche* without even seeing it, simply because he thought the topic would be interesting to a Mexican audience.

The work began with the arrival of Carla Maxwell, the director of Limón's company in 1981, who came to negotiate the terms of an agreement. Soon thereafter, Risa Steinberg began to prepare the piece and taught the company lessons in technique in order to make it possible for the dancers to achieve the proper style. The company aspired to recreate all the elements exactly as in the original version, so no effort was spared. For example, Orozco traveled all over Mexico City in search of the appropriate material for La Malinche's dress.

When Steinberg concluded her task, Maxwell returned to supervise the work of the two selected casts: Mario Rodríguez and Lino Perea as El Indio, Jorge Gale and Tonio Torres as El Conquistador, and Laura Alvear and Alicia Andreo as La Malinche. Later on, Lucas Hoving, the "star supervisor," according to Gladiola Orozco, arrived. He was considered a prize for the Ballet Teatro del Espacio because during his lessons "an encounter with knowledge, sweetness, and love" took place.

To Orozco, this work experience was a labor of love by all of those who participated, starting with Lepercq, who provided the funds to make it happen, and including the dancers and the supervisors. Regrettably, the piece did not have the expected impact, "perhaps," according to Orozco, "because La Malinche has much more significance than the choreography and its characters."

While holding the utmost respect for this and other works by Limón, Orozco said that "the passage of time did not play in favor of" *La Malinche* because even though it was a good work, well composed, and well danced, it did not connect with the public that the Ballet Teatro del Espacio targeted. It looked very "naïve, very cute, tender and sweet, with characters like little Mexican toys."

As it happened, the male dancers' costumes were very plain, of cloth. La Malinche's dress was "very thin," pleated, of a Mexican pink color; her hair was braided. The three actors were barefoot. The sword/cross was of painted wood. According to Orozco, "The core of the play was the fight between the two men because of the woman. They fight for power, and this is, apparently, represented by La Malinche; having her means controlling the nation, and by getting her Cortés got Mexico. I think that Mexico was better represented by La Malinche than by the Indian." Unfortunately, the work did not depict a grand conflict; it was simple, and Limón did not pretend more than just taking "the more appealing part of the country."

The two dancers who played the role of La Malinche, Alvear (who is Ecuadorian) and Andreo (North American), were dark skinned like the character, who stood out because of her beauty and her intelligence. They and the rest of the dancers who participated approached the play with respect and a sense of responsibility. This and the quality of the Ballet Teatro del Espacio are most likely what made Steinberg ask to participate again, but the two could not agree on terms.[97]

The newspapers widely covered the Ballet Teatro del Espacio, and a columnist said the play was among the most representative of "our universal heritage."[98] José Enrique Gorlero pointed out that the company was interested in *La Malinche* because of its value as a dance "nourished by the Mexican past and by the need, in turn, to be universal." The significance of Limón in 1981 was "more than an organized myth or nostalgia," as history was still alive in his dances.[99] A month earlier, Limón's company had performed *The Moor's Pavane* at the Festival Internacional Cervantino, and everyone expected *La Malinche* to have the same quality and "tenderness."[100]

In addition to rescuing a piece that was "integrated in our artistic reality today,"[101] the Ballet Teatro del Espacio paid homage to its creator with an exhibition entitled "José Limón en México," which opened on 19 November 1981 at the company's headquarters, the Independent Space. The opening served as the occasion for a reunion of Hoving and many of the Mexican dancers with whom he had worked during the fifties.

In order to remake *La Malinche*, Steinberg did more than simply revive it; she researched the motivations of the author in Mexico. To her, Ballet Teatro del Espacio's version was very good because the dancers had "the same drive, the same expressive strength that all works of Limón require." In her view *La Malinche* had regained life in Mexico "because she belongs here." She searched throughout the country for "the woman who had attracted José during his Mexican childhood. I discovered, for example, that the story was not a love triangle. The conqueror has a personal role, in love with La Malinche, and the Indian takes the role of all his people. She was a very capable woman, a true princess." Steinberg said that La Malinche's relationship with the Spaniard was "very painful," because by loving him she betrayed her people. "All this subtleness in the creation of such important characters is very difficult to find outside Mexican borders. This is why I am very enthusiastic about this version, as it is a way of getting closer to José's creative spirit."[102]

To Raquel García Peguero, the greatest artistic event of the year was the opening of *La Malinche* by the Ballet Teatro del Espacio. She said that Hoving was very excited because the play had returned to the country, and, as he had said, "José's source and roots were absolutely in Mexico." In addition, he said he was "happy and amazed" because the dancers had learned the piece quickly and had identified themselves with it. He also considered that all of Limón's works continued to be topical because they were about human issues, and all the spectators had "their own issues."[103]

During an interview with María Elena Matadamas, Hoving said that *La Malinche* was important because it was the first time Limón "did a solo using Mexican dances, in which he allowed himself to express a series of conflicts between men, and which he experienced as a Mexican."[104]

To another interviewer, Ricardo Castillo Mireles, Hoving said that even though during the forties he and Limón had been class-mates, at the time they were not friends. However, one day Limón invited him to participate in one of his new choreographies, which happened to be *La Malinche*. "Limón and I were very different, so we spoke a lot in order to stay at the same level. He was Mexican, In-dian, Catholic, and I am Dutch" (and Hoving almost always played the "bad guy's role."). Both had just participated in one way or another in World War II, some feeling of which still remained in the piece. "It was very dramatic for someone like him to find himself dressed as a soldier. This play emerges from suffering, from injustices and cru-elty. *La Malinche* is a work that started as a solo and as a search for his Mexicanness."[105]

The piece opened at the Teatro de la Danza in Mexico City on 27 November 1981, accompanied by the *Preludio a la tarde de un fauno* and *La ópera descuartizada* by Michel Descombey and by *Kinéticas* by Bernardo Benítez. The program notes said simply that *La Malinche* depicted "a group of peasants who go from town to town depicting the conquest of Mexico. Dance-acting, half history, half folklore, evolves around one of the main personalities of the national heritage: La Ma-linche." The cast was made up of Laura Alvear, Mario Rodríguez, and Jorge Gale.[106]

To García, Lloyd's music was beautiful; it looked as if Limón had been reincarnated in Rodríguez; Alvear presented "the perfect character: repentant, suppliant, lovely": she danced with "strength and drama, and from time to time one hates her, but also feels sympathetic." Gale had a short part in which he showed his ability. The piece represented the "incipient choreographic language," "the seed" that gave life to the "fruit that we now enjoy."[107]

Castillo Mireles said that the character of Limón's Malinche contradicted the version that considered her a traitor. The choreographer had given her a more human and poetic touch, as a "conciliator" or "benevolent intermediary." The Ballet Teatro del Espacio dancers did "wonderful representations." Rodríguez had "deeply understood the internal indigenous conflict before La Malinche"; Gale was dark skinned, and because of that he could not accurately represent the Spaniard; but Alvear had been "perfect from beginning to end."[108]

According to Luis Bruno Ruiz, the second cast was of equal quality, and through this restaging one could appreciate the "intense solemnity and strong dramatic content" of Limón's works.[109]

The dance critic Patricia Cardona wrote that in *La Malinche*, Limón "limits his expressionism to a specific topic" and defines "a character or a choreographic personality that allows others to see its powerful intellect energized by a passionate nature." The piece looked naïve to her, "simple in the movement's elaboration but strong in its dramatic intention," and it was valuable for the new generations to become familiar with the choreographer, who would always be current because of his interest in the "physical form taken by pain, joy and human hope."[110]

The dance critic Alberto Dallal did not see such richness in *La Malinche*. He said that the revival was part of the "fervor for venerations and recreations that had distinguished the Mexican dance scene in recent years (perhaps more because of absences than because of reminiscences)." To him, the piece had "small success for an audience like the one from Mexico City, which at least is able to recognize when a dance is a useless repetition and not a true challenge, as he had seen pieces from the most important contemporary dance companies in the world."[111]

Josefina Lavalle had a very different opinion. She said it was important that Ballet Teatro del Espacio took one of Limón's first works and did it well. Comparing the two versions she knew, she said the Ballet Teatro del Espacio's was "almost identical to the first one showed in

Mexico" in 1951; nevertheless, she said that to compare Limón with any other dancer was unfair. She saw the dance again in 1981: "plain (not simple) in its technical aspects, with few challenges for the performers in that sense, but not in the expressiveness; nonetheless, that is how we see the dance of that time." She considers it appropriate to do revivals, as this is the only way in which an artistic work can be kept alive; it is not possible for it to be danced in precisely the same way, just as it is not possible for Bach's music to be played exactly as it was during his lifetime: "there are different interpretations" but not a failure to remember.[112]

Ballet Teatro del Espacio performed *La Malinche* in other places, including Culiacán, Limón's birthplace, in December 1981; and during the following year, at the Teatro de la Danza and the Teatro del Bosque in Mexico City; at the Festival Nacional de Danza in San Luis Potosí and the state of Baja California. In April and May 1982, Ballet Teatro del Espacio included the piece in its European tour.

Throughout Mexico and in the European cities visited during that trip, remembers Gladiola Orozco, the piece was well received; but she supposed that the audience applauded because the author was Limón, because of the story being told, and because of the character of La Malinche: "I think that it was seen with respect and pleasure, above all in Italy, to attend a Mexican play."

After these performances, Ballet Teatro del Espacio did not perform *La Malinche* again because of legal and other complications. Orozco says they wanted to keep it in their repertoire, but the requirements were too onerous. The company did not have, for example, authorization to record their version by photography or video because it would violate copyright laws, and every year Steinberg, Maxwell, and Hoving would have had to teach and supervise the details, the company assuming all the related expenses and without Lepercq's support.

Orozco considers it fair that the Limón Foundation retained the play's copyright, but at the same time a professional company like the Ballet Teatro del Espacio did not require continuous supervision, especially for such a short and simple piece. She added that the foundation lacked openness and trust, losing sight of the fact that "it is really important that a piece be presented and not forgotten."[113]

In fact, not a single work of Limón's is kept in the repertoire in Mexico, but his beautiful presence, his virile dance style, and his exciting choreography are considered a legacy for our art. Limón is still the pride and joy of Mexican dance.

NOTES

1. Jonathan Cohen, "Waldeen and the Americas: The Dance has Many Faces," in *A Woman's Gaze: Latin American Women Artists*, ed. Marjorie Agosín (Fredonia, N.Y.: White Pine Press, 1998).

2. *50 años de danza en el Palacio de Bellas Artes* (Mexico City: INBA-SEP, 1986), 2:355.

3. Ibid., 362–64. Adolph Bolm, an old acquaintance of Chávez, was invited in 1950 to teach a ballet course.

4. Carlos Monsiváis, "Notas sobre la cultura mexicana en el siglo XX," in *Historia general de México* (Mexico City: El Colegio de México, 1977), 4:414.

5. "Ley Orgánica del INBA," *Diario Oficial de la Federación*, Mexico City, 30 December 1946.

6. Robert L. Parker, "Un estudio sobre la persistencia de Carlos Chávez en el ballet," *Heterofonía*, no. 94 (July-September 1986): 24.

7. Raúl Flores Guerrero, "La danza contemporánea," in *La danza en México* (1955; reprint México: UNAM, 1980), 73–79.

8. Carlos Chávez, "La danza mexicana," in Cristina Mendoza, *Escritos de Carlos Mérida sobre el arte: la danza* (Mexico City: INBA, 1990), 285.

9. "Música. Reorganización," *Tiempo*, Mexico City, 8 September 1950, 27.

10. Miguel Covarrubias, "La danza," *México en el arte*, no. 12 (30 November 1952): 106–107.

11. Salvador Novo, "Cartas viejas y nuevas de Salvador Novo," 1951.

12. "¿Por qué no auspicia el gobierno un ballet mexicano?" *Nosotros*, 3 June 1950.

13. Rosa Reyna, "Raquel Gutiérrez," in *Una vida dedicada a la danza 1988*, Cuadernos del CENIDI Danza, no. 19 (1988): 20.

14. Miguel Covarrubias, "La danza," 107.

15. "José Limón bailarín mexicano triunfa en Estados Unidos," *Novedades*, section 3, 15 April 1949, 1.

16. Rodolfo Halffter, "La vida musical," *El Universal Gráfico*, 12 September 1950, 6.

17. Salvador Novo, "Ventana. La danza mexicana," *Novedades*, section 1, 19 September 1950, 4.

18. Wanderer, "José Limón. El primer bailarín moderno del mundo," in *México en la cultura* supplement to *Novedades*, 10 September 1950, 5.

19. Gabriel del Río, "José Limón: un gran artista," *El Universal*, section 1, 11 September 1950, 20.

20. "Ballet. Vuelta de José Limón," *Tiempo*, 22 September 1950, 26–27.

21. José Morales Esteves, "Danza. José Limón en Bellas Artes," *Excélsior*, section 3, 24 September 1950, 13.

22. Wanderer, "Pauline Koner y la danza," *México en la cultura* supplement to *Novedades*, 17 September 1950, 7.

23. "Cartelera del Palacio de Bellas Artes," *El Universal Gráfico*, 19 September 1950, 15.

24. Program for La Compañía de Danza de José Limón, Palace of Fine Arts, Mexico City, 19 September through 1 October 1950.

25. Igor Moreno, "Actividades musicales de la semana. José Limón, danzarín y coreautor," *El Nacional*, supplement, 1 October 1950, 14.

26. "Público homenaje al artista José Limón," *Excélsior*, section 2, 21 September 1950, 1–2.

27. Morales Esteves, "Danza. José Limón en Bellas Artes," 8.

28. "Gran éxito de José Limón, en Bellas Artes," *El Universal*, section 1, 25 September 1950, 13.

29. Novo, "Ventana, La danza de José Limón," 4.

30. Horacio Sánchez Flores, "Musicales. El éxito rotundo de la primer noche de José Limón y su compañía," *El Universal*, section 1, 21 September 1950, 4, 14.

31. Rodolfo Halffter, "La vida musical. Rotundo éxito de José Limón," *El Universal Gráfico*, 26 September 1950, 6.

32. Manuel Lerín, "José Limón y la danza moderna," *El Nacional*, section 1, 24 September 1950, 3, 7.

33. Manlio S. Fuentes, "Música. José Limón," *Impacto*, 30 September 1950, 80.

34. Jorge J. Crespo de la Serna, "Artes plásticas. El arte de José Limón," *Excélsior*, section 2, 30 September 1950, 2.

35. "Por nuestros teatros. Bellas Artes. El ballet de José Limón," *El Redondel*, section 2, 24 September 1950, 14.

36. S. H., "Entre músicos. Bailes clásicos y modernos," *El Redondel*, section 2, 1 October 1950, 12–13.

37. G. González y Contreras, "Teatro crítica. Compañía de danza moderna," *Impacto*, 30 September 1950, 86.

38. "Ballet. Frenesí coreográfico," *Tiempo*, 2 May 1952.

39. Igor Moreno, "Actividades musicales de la semana. El arte danzario de José Limón hizo adeptos en creciente número," supplement to *El Nacional*, 8 October 1950, 14.

40. "Notas culturales," *El Universal*, section 1, 7 September 1950, 4.

41. Program for La Compañía de Danza de José Limón.

42. "Ballet. Vuelta de José Limón," 26.

43. Novo, "Ventana, La danza de José Limón."

44. Sánchez Flores, "Musicales. El éxito rotundo de la primer noche de José Limón y su compañía," 14.

45. Gerónimo Baqueiro Fóster, "Por el mundo de la música," *El Nacional*, section 1, 23 September 1950, 8.

46. Julio Sapietsa, "El teatro en acción. Gran éxito del bailarín y coreógrafo José Limón," *El Universal Gráfico*, 23 September 1950, 10.

47. Fuentes, "Música. José Limón."

48. Wanderer, "*La pavana del Moro*," in *México en la cultura* supplement to *Novedades*, 24 September 1950, 2.

49. Halffter, "La vida musical. Rotundo éxito de José Limón," 6.

50. Junius, "La música de la semana," *Excélsior*, section 3, 24 September 1950, 6.

51. Lerín, "José Limón y la danza moderna," 7.

52. Esperanza Pulido, "Música en México," *Novedades*, section 1, 25 September 1950, 4.

53. "Por nuestros teatros. Bellas Artes. El ballet de José Limón."

54. J. N. Huerta "Palmeta," "Lo que pasa en nuestros teatros," *El Universal*, section 1, 3 October 1950, 4.

55. González y Contreras, "Teatro crítica. Compañía de danza moderna."

56. Moreno, "Actividades musicales de la semana. José Limón, danzarín y core-autor," 14.

57. Covarrubias, "La danza," 107.

58. Rosario Manzanos, "El amor total de Miguel Covarrubias y Rocío Sagaón (Entrevista)," *Proceso* 1465, 28 November 2004, 80–81; Elena Poniatowska, *Miguel Covarrubias, Vida y Mundos* (Mexico City: Ediciones Era, 2004), 13–32.

59. Margarita Tortajada Quiroz, unpublished interview with Colombia Moya, Mexico City, 30 July 2004.

60. Margarita Tortajada Quiroz, unpublished interview with Guillermo Arriaga, Mexico City, 23 July 2004.

61. Margarita Tortajada Quiroz, unpublished interview with Rosa Reyna, Mexico City, 27 July 2004.

62. Margarita Tortajada Quiroz, unpublished interview with Nellie Happee, Mexico City, 21 July 2004.

63. Margarita Tortajada Quiroz, unpublished interview with Rocío Sagaón, Mexico City, 29 July 2004.

64. Margarita Tortajada Quiroz, unpublished interview with Josefina Lavalle, Mexico City, 27 July 2004.

65. Margarita Tortajada Quiroz, unpublished interview with Farnesio de Bernal, Mexico City, 1 August 2004.

66. Margarita Tortajada Quiroz, unpublished interview with Valentina Castro, Mexico City, 29 July 2004.

67. José Rogelio Álvarez (director), *Enciclopedia de México* (México: Sabeca Internacional Investment Co., 2000), 4927.

68. Carlos Fuentes, *Todos los gatos son pardos* (Mexico City: Siglo XXI, 1979), 14.

69. Octavio Paz, *El laberinto de la soledad* (Mexico City: FCE, 1994), 80.

70. Ibid., 94.

71. Andrea Rodó y Paulina Saball, "El cuerpo ausente," *Cuerpo y Política. Debate feminista*, año 5, vol. 10 (September 1994): 81–94.

72. All the comments on these works are taken from Miguel Covarrubias, "La danza." Lucas Hoving also opened *La tertulia* (music by Juventino Rosas, orchestral version by Candelario Huízar, scenery by Antonio López Mancera).

73. Tortajada Quiroz, interview with De Bernal.

74. José Limón, quoted in Sergio Avilés Parra, "Con José Limón," in *México en la cultura* supplement to *Novedades*, 22 April 1951, 4.

75. *50 años de danza en el Palacio de Bellas Artes*, 368–369.

76. Rafael Abascal y Macías, "Miguel Covarrubias: Antropólogo," in *Miguel Covarrubias: Homenaje* (Mexico City: Fundación Cultural Televisa, A.C./ Centro Cultural Arte Contemporáneo, A.C., 1987), 156.

77. José Limón, "The Making of *Tonantzintla*" and "The Making of *Dialogues*," *Dance Magazine* 25, no. 8 (August 1951): 10–14.

78. Arthur Todd, "Mexico Responds to Modern Dance and José Limón," *Dance Observer* (March 1951).

79. Covarrubias, "La danza," 108.

80. Margarita Tortajada Quiroz, *Danza y poder* (Mexico City: INBA, 1995), 454.

81. Margarita Tortajada Quiroz, *Luis Fandiño, danza generosa y perfecta* (Mexico City: INBA, 2000), 27.

82. Pierre Bourdieu, "La dominación masculina," *La Ventana: Revista de estudios de género*, no. 3, University of Guadalajara, Mexico (July 1996): 45.

83. Judith Butler, "Variaciones sobre sexo y género: Beauvoir, Witting y Foucault," in Marta Lamas, comp., *El género: la construcción cultural de la diferencia sexual* (Mexico City: PUEG, UNAM, 1996), 311.

84. Bárbara Pollack and Charles Humphrey Woodford, "La fortaleza de una vocación," in *Dance Is Movement: A Portrait of José Limón in Words and Pictures* (Princeton: Book Company Publishers, Pennington, 1993). Reprinted in translation by Alan Stark in Margarita Tortajada, ed., *Antología José Limón*, Cuadernos del CENIDI Danza, no. 28 (Mexico City: INBA, 1994), 10.

85. John Martin, quoted in Daniel Lewis, *La técnica ilustrada de José Limón* (Mexico City: INBA, 1994), 45.

86. José Limón, quoted in Waldeen, *La danza: Imagen de creación continua* (Mexico City: UNAM, 1982), 135.

87. José Limón in Cassandra Rincón, "José Limón, el mexicano ausente: 'aquí hay talento'," *Excélsior*, 5 March 1968.

88. Judith Lynne Hanna, *Dance, Sex and Gender: Signs of Identity, Dominance, Defiance, and Desire* (Chicago: University of Chicago Press, 1988), 29.

89. Ramsay Burt, *The Male Dancer: Body, Spectacle, Sexualities* (London: Routledge, 1995), 72.

90. Risa Steinberg, quoted in Ricardo Castillo Mireles, "Al rescate de la obra de José Limón, el Teatro del Espacio," *Excélsior*, 24 November 1981, 3-B.

91. Richard Glasston, *La danza para varones como carrera* (Mexico City: INBA, 1997), 34.

92. Magda Montoya in Margarita Tortajada Quiroz, *Mujeres de danza combativa* (Mexico City: CONACULTA, 1998), 38.

93. Elissa Rashkin, "Los machos también lloran: Televisa and the Postnational Man," presentation at a conference of the Latin American Studies Association, Guadalajara, 17–19 April 1997.

94. Jean Franco, *Las conspiradoras: La representación de la mujer en México* (Mexico City: FCE, 1993), 140.

95. Ilene V. O'Malley, *The Myth of the Revolution: Hero Cults and the Institutionalization of the Mexican State, 1920–1940* (Westport, Conn.: Greenwood Press, 1986), cited by Elissa Rashkin, "Los machos también lloran."

96. Charles Ramírez Berg, *Cinema of Solitude: A Critical Study of Mexican Film, 1967–1983* (Austin: University of Texas Press, 1992), cited by Elissa Rashkin, "Los machos también lloran."

97. In Margarita Tortajada Quiroz, unpublished interview with Gladiola Orozco, Mexico City, 2 August 2004.

98. "*La Malinche*, del coreógrafo José Limón, será interpretada por el BTE," *El Día*, Culture section, 11 November 1981, 28.

99. José Enrique Gorlero, "El retorno a México de José Limón. El BTE bailará *La Malinche*," in supplement to *El Día*, 1 November 1981.

100. "¡Viva José Limón!" in *Avance*, 15 November 1981.

101. "El BTE presentará *La Malinche* de José Limón," in *El Heraldo de México*, Culture section, 14 November 1981.

102. Risa Steinberg, quoted in "Culturalísimo," *El Heraldo cultural*, 26 November 1981.

103. Raquel García Peguero, "Lucas Hoving: La raíz de Limón era México," *El Día*, Culture section, México, 22 November 1981.

104. Lucas Hoving, quoted in María Elena Matadamas, "El BTE rinde homenaje al coreógrafo José Limón," *Novedades*, Culture section, 24 November 1981, 6.

105. Lucas Hoving, quoted in Castillo Mireles, "Al rescate de la obra de José Limón, el Teatro del Espacio."

106. Program for Ballet Teatro del Espacio, Teatro de la Danza, Mexico City, 27–29 November and 3–6 December 1981.

107. Raquel García Peguero, "Triunfo total del BTE in el Teatro de la Danza," Culture section, *El Día*, 28 November 1981.

108. Ricardo Castillo Mireles, "*La Malinche*, humanizada en un ballet del bailarín y coreógrafo José Limón," *Excélsior*, 4 December 1981, 17-B.

109. Luis Bruno Ruiz, "Danza en homenaje al gran José Limón," *Excélsior*, 8 December 1981, 22, 23-B.

110. Patricia Cardona, "Durante 20 años no se incluyeron obras de José Limón en el repertorio de las compañías de danza mexicanas," *Uno más uno*, 8 December 1981.

111. Alberto Dallal, *La danza en México* (Mexico City: UNAM, 1986), 198–199.

112. Tortajada Quiroz, unpublished interview with Lavalle.

113. Tortajada Quiroz, unpublished interview with Orozco.

8. THE DIRECTOR

Thoughts on Staging José Limón's **La Malinche**

Sarah Stackhouse

Alexander Pope, in his second *Essay on Man*, wrote, "[Man is] created half to rise, half to fall." José Limón devoted his life to choreographing that thought. In many of his dramatic works man is either falling or being felled, often because of his own nature. This is true of Limón's *La Malinche*, created in 1949 from the history, sights, and sounds of Mexico stored in his memory. It is one of Limón's optimistic works, one of the few in which the fallen rise to triumph.

La Malinche is based on a Mexican theme and is, to use Louis Horst's term, an "Earth Primitive" work.[1] Limón used the naive quality of a rural band of traveling players to relate the story. His program note reads, "Malintzin, an Indian princess, was given to Cortés on his arrival in Mexico. She became his interpreter and mouthpiece. Her astuteness and complete devotion served his cause so well that he was able to conquer Mexico. She became a great lady and was baptized Doña Marina. After her death popular legend made her repentant spirit return to lament her treachery. For her there was no peace while her people were not free. During their struggles for liberation she returned as the wild Malinche to expiate her ancient betrayal."

The original cast included Limón as El Indio, Pauline Koner as La Malinche, and Lucas Hoving as El Conquistador (Cortés). Limón and Hoving were perfectly matched antagonists in their visual contrast, spatial use, and dynamic patterning. Koner harmonized with each, when partnered by them. Hoving was a tall, fair, long-limbed, northern European who seemed to take possession of the space with the angular shaping of his legs in deep plié. He accented and gave dynamic color to his phrasing with remarkable arm and hand gestures. Though he used medium or even light energy he nonetheless projected control, decision, and a sense of internal power. In contrast, Limón carried the heat of Mexico in his veins. He could be impulsive as a dancer, hurling himself through space, but he also could seem to become one with the earth, holding it down with his very weight. As is true of most of the roles Limón created for himself, in El Indio there is a sense of the nobility along with the tragedy of man. Koner was a match for both men and was able to contrast each with her incisive dancing. She too was dynamic and dramatic, a master of gesture and quick, etched movement. Wiry against Hoving's long, rangy stature, she could also meet Limón's explosive power with her condensed energy.

Norman Lloyd wrote the musical score for the completed dance. Lively and forthright, the music is in the style of a rural mariachi band. The marchlike, rhythmic music in the beginning and end contrasts marvelously with sections of lush, melodic, female vocal line.

STYLE

As in many of Limón's works, the Dionysian vies with the Apollonian, the primitive with the aristocratic, as they did in his life. *La Malinche*, with its rhythmic drive and folk quality, was part of Limón's early investigations of his Mexican memories and heritage.

I find it valuable to request that new cast members do some research, so that they begin to form an understanding of the style parameters of *La Malinche* and to fill their minds and eyes with Aztec and Mayan images. Time permitting, it's an enjoyable project to go to the library with the dancers and share our findings. We look at images of Aztec art and architecture of sixteenth-century Mexico and of more recent Mexican folk art, in particular its form and color, so relevant to the style of the dance. Also revealing are the murals of Rivera, Orozco, and Siqueiros, along with paintings depicting the Spanish conquerors, images of guerrillas of the Mexican Revolution, raptors and fighting cocks, and historical writings of the period.

In the first steps of the prologue, the *primitif* folk style of the players is prominent as they march into the plaza. They recall the painted terra-cotta figurines of Mexican folk art. Direct in their expression and movement, they have a two-dimensional sense in their predominantly frontal presentation. The style is weighted and undecorative with strong rhythmic drive. They set the stage by defining their performing space, then, one by one, they introduce their character's quality and movement motifs and give a suggestion of the drama to come.

As they become their characters and begin the drama, La Malinche and El Indio seldom turn out their legs or use spiral or twist in their movement. (The clay would shatter.) Their hands are functional, like workers' hands, and move or are held naturally with fingers together. The hands have design but are never simply ornamental. The vulnerable palm is often forward, hand slightly cupped and elbow bent, giving an obtuse angle to the arm. Their feet are usually flexed, and their leg attitudes are at a right angle or slightly more open. Foot beats, hand claps, and hand percussions on the hips and thighs suggest folk dance. It seems they are dancing with the feet of the Indian/peasant accustomed to packed earth. Limón used rhythmic counterpoint between El Indio and La Malinche like a dialogue as they reunite and later, in a lusty symmetrical dance, as they build up the physical and emotional momentum to do battle with El Conquistador.

As the story begins, El Conquistador expands into a three-dimensional quality with more sophisticated and complex movement phrases. His movements are extended and sweeping, suggesting the arrogance of the aristocracy. His use of weight projects imperious dominance and power. He doesn't use the earth as a partner in the dance, as El Indio does, but rather stabs it with his sword/cross and seems to consume it, usurp it.

Winged images appear in many of Limón's choreographic works. In *La Malinche* the raptor, the fighting cock, and the legendary eagle of Mexico's founding inform much of the movement. El Indio spreads his fingers like a bird's feathers in flight and beats his arms up and down from the shoulder in winglike fashion. At times he hovers threateningly with arms raised over his adversary, ready to swoop down for the attack.

The spatial metaphor in *La Malinche* is simple. The elements are the square of the plaza, the circling of travel, and the diagonal for confrontations. Limón used the square with a frontal, street performance orientation. In the prologue, the square and the circular space within the square are delineated. As the dancers move down the diagonal, they introduce their character's motif, then take their places in the corners to begin the drama. The players circle as though traveling from one village to another. El Conquistador uses the circle as he marches over and conquers the land. El Indio and La Malinche circle the space to gather momentum and spatial tension, like the stretch of a bowstring, to shoot down the diagonal toward El Conquistador. The diagonal provides the force of gravity and perspective to fuel all of the confrontations.

CASTING

In choosing a cast for *La Malinche*, I find that it's essential for me as setter, director, and coach to cast dancers with whom I feel a lively personal as well as artistic rapport. I want to sense their enthusiasm for the work and their desire to open up to ideas and ways of working that may be quite new to them. The process of bringing any of Limón's works to light again with a new group of dancers, professional or student, must be creative and flexible within the clarity of the stylistic framework. I need to sense that the dancers will be avid and willing to take direction and that they will bring their intelligence and artistry to recreating *La Malinche*.

When I audition dancers for *La Malinche*, the first to catch my eye are the passionate ones and those with lively, colorful, and daring kinesthetic imaginations. I want to see the dancers take a movement idea or direction and go for it, do something with it, so to speak. On the other hand, if they are trying to be correct or do what they think I want to see I feel that their artistic input could be limited. Often talented dancers may have stylistic mannerisms they are very attached to. But if I can sense that they would be amenable to direction and willing to expand their range of style to include the specific ideas of *La Malinche* I would be more likely to cast them.

Dancers in each of the roles must have well-developed rhythm and a musical ear. The architecture of the trio is important and has to have a good balance and contrast in terms of body type and size, dynamic quality, and spatial sense.

I look for an Indio with groundedness, thrust, and primitive strength. I won't often find a physique like Limón's, but a smaller dancer can move and look large if he's willing to weather the detailed coaching process. He must be able to dance "big," with an extended spatial quality—opening the joints without blocking the energy flow. Much of El Indio's dancing requires strong energy and punctuation. It's exciting to have an Indio who is clear in his understanding of the choreography, yet wild, impulsive, and spontaneous as he dances it.

Early on in the piece La Malinche needs the innocence (not foolishness) of youth. She predominantly uses free flow and round phrasing with a medium energy range and a sense of the ground under her feet. When she becomes the consort of El Conquistador, she briefly adopts his courtly manner. Later she takes on the strength of womanhood as sorrow weighs her down. Here she uses more medium to strong energy quality with spatial resistance. She evolves again as she becomes the guerrilla partner of El Indio and adopts his strong energy pattern, phrasing, and rhythmic accenting to confront and bring down El Conquistador.

El Conquistador must dominate with his powerfully directed energy and spatial voracity. He needs to be tall enough to wield the long, heavy sword. His dancing is quite vertical (not rigid)—torso unbending—though he sometimes tilts from the hip joints. His more sophisticated movement phrases need an aristocratic, assured quality. Clean but daring technique functions wonderfully here.

PREPARING THE RECONSTRUCTION

I approach each reconstruction process by watching the available films for hours. No matter how many times I've seen them, new information and revelations always appear. Next, I begin to deconvolve the many contributing elements of the choreography[2]—that is to say, to untangle the facts of the choreography from the performances seen on film, aiming at an understanding of Limón's intent. Once the intent and the facts begin to ring clear, I have the framework but also the latitude to go forward, allowing different dancers to bring their own artistry and expression to the work. It's a fascinating process though not an obvious one, as each soloist's distinct artistry colors the choreography. Therefore, the process needs to remain fluid.

There is no filmed record of a performance of the original cast members dancing *La Malinche*. But in my early days with the company I watched Limón, Hoving, and Koner for hours as they rehearsed other works. I learned a great deal from them as I absorbed their images and artistry. They were dancers of very different background and training from today's dancers. They came from an era in the development of modern dance in which individual style was more extreme, more personal than today's. Even if there were a film of the original cast, today's dancers would not be successful in attempting to do an "authentic" version. Imitation of those dancers and those performances would be disastrous and self-defeating.

Limón's choreographic process, to a great extent, made use of the particular qualities and artistry of a dancer in a role and often of the dancer's movement contributions as well. The choreography for *La Malinche* was form-fitted to Hoving and Koner and clearly contains their quality and stylistic contributions. When Limón revived a work with different dancers, he often recreated it by drawing on their particular qualities and characteristics as artists. I use his process as a guide, not to change the choreography but to allow the dancers I cast to contribute their artistry in terms of phrasing, dynamics, musicality, and interpretation. Sometimes I may mix in movement from different versions for particular dancers if it fits them and works within the context. In this way I hope to arrive at a vibrant production with new dimension, color, and timeliness. As director, however, I need to balance this evolutionary process with the need to respect what I feel was Limón's intent and to ensure the expression and clarity of the choreography. Artistry and relevancy are my aims but not authenticity, whatever that means.

The earliest film we have of *La Malinche* (1962) is one with Limón, Lola Huth, and Harlan McCallum. Another film (1968) with a cast of Juilliard School students taught and directed by Limón, is choreographically somewhat different and has, I believe, more spatial sense and clarity. It seems to me that when Limón reworked a dance in which he was not a performer, he was more aware of the integrity of movement and space. As participant he could not have sensed as clearly this critical aspect of the dance. When he could see his pieces from the outside they became, in my opinion, choreographically stronger, with the movement phrases more harmoniously related to the spatial configurations. Sometimes in reworking or rechoreographing he would eliminate some wonderful movement. Usually I base my reconstructions on Limón's later versions of a dance, but I like to consider and use some aspects of earlier versions if they function in his clearer and more mature spatial context.

In addition to the two earlier films with Limón performing or directing, Koner reconstructed, danced, and directed another filmed version (1971). In my opinion, her version is rather incoherent and remarkably different from the versions directed or danced by Limón that I watched from offstage or in the rehearsal studio. While I have learned from Koner's film, I feel it represents her choreography more than Limón's and prefer to base a reconstruction on what I experienced with him personally and in watching his films.

SETTING THE WORK

When teaching a Limón work, I begin with the basic elements: the movement material and its style parameters; the spatial aspects: patterning on the stage and the spatial relationships between and among dancers; the time aspects: rhythms and the relation of the movement to the music. This is what I recognize as the script to be established as the first level of the multilayered process involved in the rediscovery of a Limón dramatic work. Once the dancers and I have a sketch of the script in place, the dancers are freer to focus on and explore details and subtleties of expression such as musicality, phrasing, dynamics, and character.

I find it essential to lay the groundwork of this script from the outset because it provides a framework out of which the content and specificity of expression emerge and within which the dancers can stretch their creativity as artists. As abstract as it may seem, it's the sculpting of the seemingly abstract elements of time, space, and energy that evokes the aesthetic experience. We humans are deeply stirred by the pulsing and patterning of rhythm and its relation to music; by the textures and tensions of space and the bonding of body with space that gives honesty and humanity to the moving figure; by dynamic flow and accenting; and by giving in to or defying gravity. If one approaches *La Malinche* (or any of Limón's dramatic works) emotionally at first, without the framework of the script in place, the dancer's personal emotional reference could overrun essential elements of the choreographic form, generalizing or distorting the intended fabric. The subtlety and detail of the expression that Limón so beautifully wove into the choreographic fabric may be blurred or lost, and the essence and power of his intent will dissipate. The language, the script, like a grand jungle gym, defines the framework within which the dancers can explore their own artistic input.

I continue the rehearsal process by giving detailed attention to the interactions between and among dancers and to the motivation that drives them. We explore the dynamic line, the accenting, the energy flow, and phrasing with more specificity. Because of the strong rhythmic propulsion in *La Malinche*, the emphasizing of the relationship between movement and music strengthens and clarifies the marvelous counterpoint without compromising a spontaneous and visceral performance. By engaging their kinesthetic imaginations, the dancers develop dimension, color, and texture in their roles and in the work as a whole. They flesh out the script and should continue to discover its dimensions—not fix or set in stone their portrayal. With each day's rehearsal, it's necessary to reestablish the balance and integration of the form and content and to keep it all in flux.

DIRECTION AND COACHING

In terms of overall direction I want to see dancers in *La Malinche* moving to human rather than divine or archetypal images. The natural human urge to move is so touching; it is the language we all know and can read.

The archetypal approach that has sometimes been applied to directing and performing Limón works puts a mask on the performer, implies the presence of something superhuman, and holds the audience apart as observers rather than inviting them to be audience—participants in the human acts with which Limón was concerned. In my opinion, seeing the characters as archetypes makes the work look dated and robs the performers of their strongest assets on stage: their real body logic, individual character, and human understanding. I think we represent all humankind when we are truest to ourselves within the form—admittedly not an easy task, but I want to see the naked person being, not representing.

Often, dancers who have done most of their training and dancing in a particular choreographer/artist's technique and style consider these to be their means of expression and are likely to approach any dance in that same way. They may have a hard time feeling a different style; what we're familiar with is what feels right. Different style parameters initially may feel wrong or even somewhat disturbing. For instance, if one is used to doing predominantly contralateral, or twisting, movement in the torso as an essential aspect of their style, it feels very strange or wrong to keep the torso primarily in the frontal plane, the predominant element in the style for El Indio and La Malinche. The frontal orientation gives the direct, open, two-dimensional, primitive look to their movement, whereas twist gives a more sophisticated, urbane expression. Or if, as in many ballet styles, the dancer uses very little plié, the deeper knee bend in plié of Limón's style will be a challenge. When directing, I have to ask that classroom techniques, other ideas of style, and kinesthetic patterning open up to include new physical sensations and expressive possibilities. This is another process of deconvolution.

Choreography seems to me to be a process of convolution, an intertwining of many elements. Reversing this process and untangling the elements in order to understand their individual contributions and effect on the whole implies a process of deconvolution. In my experience this technique helps me and the dancers recognize and separate specific classroom techniques and styles from their artistry and adapt to the style and quality of Limón's *La Malinche*. (I never ask the dancers to throw out what they're fond of—only to allow some new experiences into their vocabulary.) Ideally in Limón's works neither the technique nor the individual stands out. Instead, the artists use their techniques, knowledge, and artistry to understand and to reveal the work.

Some Malinches may be soft and round in their movement, phrasing, and accenting, some piquant or even sharp. Either approach can be valid and beautiful when allied within the framework of the choreography. I rarely show films of previous casts because I don't want the dancers trying to do the choreography the way it was done or even to have another artist's interpretation in their eye and consciousness. As a result, much of my work in rehearsal with the dancers is to help them find the tones and textures of dancing their own body and mind within the form and style of *La Malinche*. I ask the dancers to take the movement language created by Limón and to discover and flesh out their character by attending to the way they use their weight, the space, the images, their thought and feeling. I hope as coach to enlarge upon and help shape what I find in the dancer's aesthetic sensibilities, frame of mind, and artistry within the context of Limón's choreography.

A vital aspect of discovering the dancing in Limón's dramatic works comes from the way in which the movement of the eyes and head responds to thought or external stimulus and carries the body into movement. The eyes are like a window on the thought, the mind, and the psyche of the character. Jennifer Scanlon, one of my contemporaries in the Limón Company, a reconstructor, and Alexander Technique teacher,[3] says, "Allow your thought to permeate your body" and further, "We don't change direction without a thought." Karen Donelson, a Feldenkrais teacher,[4] says, "Our eyes allow us to be present in the world" and I like to follow that with "Our eyes allow the world to be present in us." The eyes truly have to see, not just look. They may respond to a thought or to an external stimulus, but they must be responsive. The eyes guide the head; the head guides the body. When we are able to sense the motivation and the inner workings of the character, the movement becomes a powerful expression that draws the viewer in. The truth of that human physical operation allows the audience to participate, to be within the drama, and not simply to look upon physical feats being performed.

This may seem obvious, but in the learning of movement there's a tendency to jump right into the choreographed movement and not take the time to investigate how and whence the movement is generated. Dancers often keep their eyes cast down in a kinesthetic-thinking mode when learning, and therefore the need to call special attention to the eye and focus aspects of movement becomes important. When the dancers begin to find the logic and dance of the eye and head, all the body's movement becomes more organic and the expression rich and honest. This, after all, is how the human body responds to life, and it is essential for conveying the intent, content, and power of Limón's dramatic works.

Limón was an accomplished musician and one of the most musical choreographers of the twentieth century. In all of his works, the movement is so integrated with the music that it seems to be another layer of the music—and the music, another layer of the dance. Limón worked "out of his ear" and heard the choreography as much as he saw it. In *La Malinche*, the rhythmic sections, especially the canonic dialogue that reunites El Indio and La Malinche, are fast and not easy to accomplish. This duet needs to be so confident and familiar rhythmically that they can build to a wild and raucous pitch before attacking El Conquistador.

I often ask the dancers to sing with the music in melodic sections and to use some kind of vocalizing or clapping in rhythmic sections so that they will hear and acknowledge the music (not only the beat) more consciously and physically. As they do this, they begin to use the breath they find in vocalizing to realize the full scope of every phrase. As they sing they find their movement more richly related to the pulse and line of the music. If the dancer in the Malinche role sings (in rehearsal) with the vocal line, her dancing and phrasing become richly melodic. When the dancers vocalize the rhythmic sections their dancing becomes more robust, earthier, and more connected to the music. All of the dancing will come out of the music, not just go along with it (or sometimes lag behind it). The result is a broader and deeper musicality which provides space and time for rushes, suspensions, rubato, and a luscious singing quality.

The physical quality of weight is essential to the expression of Limón's characters and allows them to be real, substantive, and vulnerable. In El Indio the viewer must feel he's made of earth. When he rises he brings the earth up with him—when he falls he's absorbed back into the earth. He keeps his center of movement low in the pelvis. Even when he hovers, suspends, or beats his "wings" to lift off, he doesn't resist gravity by pulling up (raising his center of movement into the chest) but rather uses his weight as his power—his reality. His falls may be sustained or precipitous, but he doesn't fall apart. Fall or defeat may be the expression, but physically the dancer doesn't disintegrate; he still has shape. He doesn't need to prove he has weight by collapsing his joints or losing muscle guidance. If the dancer collapses, he loses momentum, the continuity of the movement phrase, and the spatial and temporal integrity. Collapse may be the desired illusion, but it's not the dancer's reality. It is distinctly not in Limón's range of movement qualities and doesn't provide the image of weight.

Another element in achieving the sense of weight is the ability to stretch the timing of the movement phrase within the musical framework. That is to say, the dancer must distribute the movement in time (musicality!) and space in order to truly make use of the music's texture, quality, and expression. The dancer must imagine that the space, time/music, and choreographed movement go together to form a three-dimensional elastic fabric. Each of the elements helps hold the others together and apart and is rooted in gravity. Without that full use of space as well as time, there is a tendency to rush, thus conveying a sense of lightness. The dancers' strength and weight lie with the music's pulse. They are neither drumming out the beat, nor looking like a dancing conductor, nor distributing time and space equally. Rather they are working with and within the musical framework. Indeed, dynamic and time contrasts are essential to dramatic and compelling dancing. There is room for personal musicality—but the pulsing of the time framework has to remain alive in the dancer and be felt by the viewer. Losing that continuity, dancers lose the space/time fabric, their strength and connection to gravity, and the expressive moment. The dancer can hold to gravity when needed or make use of it for gathering power to fly but, in a Limón work, can never ignore it.

In all of Limón's dramatic and abstract works, the dancers need to extend the sense of their body's connection with the space. In finding textures and tensions in the space, they will expand the range of textures, tensions, and expressivity of their body. When this happens, the dancers sense a partnership with the space that is as ever-present as the other side of their skin. The studio and the stage are full of space to be moved through, leaned upon, enfolded, surrounded by, and danced with. The dancers find themselves dancing the space rather than the body, which, perhaps surprisingly, gives the very human expression that Limón was after. The character, the dancer, the expression are revealed and draw us in.

The extraordinary artistic heritage that Limón bequeathed us through his dancing and choreography consists of an expansiveness of body movement, mind, and spirit. He offered us the struggles and glories of human existence and revealed his subjects through three-dimensional substance and familiarity. Winning or losing, falling and rising, his characters remain profoundly vital, big as life. Though they often meet their undoing, they do so with power and passion. In *La Malinche*, the fallen El Indio and La Malinche rise to become a fighting machine to triumph over El Conquistador. After their victory El Indio forgives La

Malinche, and in the epilogue even El Conquistador is up and marching again as they all return to their traveling player personae and are off to the next village, hopefully with their pockets full of coins.

NOTES

1. Louis Horst (1884–1964) was a pianist, composer, and dance composition teacher. He served as the musical director for the Denishawn Company as well as the Graham Company and School. He also worked with Doris Humphrey, Charles Weidman, Agnes DeMille, and Anna Sokolow, among others.

2. In the *Dictionary of Geological Terms, deconvolution* is defined as "Any number of mathematical processes designed to restore a wave shape to the form it had before it underwent a convolution." It seems to me that choreography is a convolution, and certainly the untangling of all of the various elements that go into it requires a tremendous process of deconvolution.

3. The Alexander Technique "is a practical technique for changing your reaction to a given stimulus." Jeremy Chance, *The Alexander Technique* (London: Thorsons, 2001).

4. "The Feldenkrais Method is a form of sensory motor learning connecting intention with action." Karen Donelson, personal conversation, May 14, 2007.

BIBLIOGRAPHY

Online Sources

American Masters. Diego Rivera. http://www.pbs.org/wnet/americanmasters/data
base/rivera_d.html (accessed 7-28-2005).

Culture Shock: Flashpoints: Visual Arts: Diego Rivera's Man at the Crossroads. http://
www.pbs.org/wgbh/cultureshock/flashpoints/visualarts/diegorivera_a.html
(accessed 7-29-2005).

Dance History Archives-José Limón. http://www.streetswing.com/histmai2/
d2limon1. htm (accessed 7-29-2005).

Diego Rivera, Chapingo (Capilla Riveriana). http://www.chapingo.mx/academicos/
capilla/Mprin/ (accessed 7-29-2005).

Diego Rivera: Man at the Crossroads. http://www.fbuch.com/crossroads.htm (accessed 7-28-2005).

Diego Rivera Web Museum: Biography. http://www.diegorivera.com/bio/ (accessed 7-29-2005).

Doris Humphrey. http://doris-humphrey.biography.ms/ (accessed 7-29-2005).

Edificio Principal y La Capilla. http://www.chapingo.mx/academicos/capilla/
Nrev/ NE.htm (accessed 7-29-2005).

Hammer, Zachary. *José Limón, a Dancing Man.* http://people.smu.edu/zhammer
(accessed 7-28-2005).

José Clemente Orozco. Vida Y Obra. Biography and Works. http://www.colegiona-
cional.org.mx/Orozco.htm (accessed 7-29-2005).

Limón (José) Photographs, Biography. http://digilib.nypl.org/dnyaweb/dhc/findaid/
limon@Generoic_BookTextview/125 (accessed 7-29-2005).

Martínez, Glenn A. *Mojados, Malinches, and the Dismantling of the United States/
Mexico Border in Contemporary Mexican Cinema.* http://webpub.allegheny.edu/
group/LAS/LatinAmIssues/Articles/Vol14/LAI_vol_14_section_II.html

McCaa, Robert. The Geometry of Gender among Aztecs: 'Earthly Names,' Marriage, and the Household. *http://www.hist.unm.edu/~rmccaa/AZTCNAM2/
nahuanms.htm (accessed November 23, 2000).*

National Palace, Mexico City. http://www.interamericaninstitute.org (accessed
7-29-2005).

Pauline Lawrence Limón Collection. "Visiones Prohispanistas y Proindigenistas
de la Conquista de México." http://digilib.nypl.org (accessed 7-29-2005).

Weidman (Charles) Papers, Biography. http://digilib.nypl.org/dynaweb/dhc/
findaid/weidman/GenericBookTextView136 (accessed 7-29-2005).

Printed Materials, Notes,
Photographs, and Interviews

Abascal y Macías, Rafael. *Miguel Covarrubias: Antropólogo*. Mexico City: Fundación Cultural Televisa, A.C./Centro Cultural Arte Contemporáneo, 1987.

Alamán, Lucas. *Disertaciones Sobre la Historia de la Republica Megicana, Desde la Época de la Conquista Que los Españoles Hicieron, a Fines del Siglo Xv y Principios del XVI, de las Islas y Continente Americano, Hasta la Independencia*. 3 vols. Mexico City: J. M. Lara, 1844–1849.

Alarcón, Norma. "Chicana Feminist Literature: A Re-Vision through Malintzin / or Malintzin: Putting Flesh Back on the Object." In *This Bridge Called My Back: Writings by Radical Women of Color*, edited by Cherrie Moraga and Gloria Anzaldúa, 182–190. New York: Kitchen Table Press, 1983.

———. "Traddutora, Traditora: A Paradigmatic Figure of Chicana Feminism. Cultural Critique." *The Construction of Gender and Modes of Social Division* 13 (Fall 1989): 57–87.

Alberó de Villava, Helena. *Malintzin y el señor Malinche*. Mexico City: Edamex, 1995.

Alberti Manzanares, Pilar. "El Concepto Sobre la Mujer Azteca Deducido a Través de las Diosas en México Prehispánico." Ph.D. dissertation, Universidad Complutense de Madrid, 1993.

Alva Ixtlilxochitl, Fernando de. *Obras Históricas*. Edited by Edmundo O'Gorman. Mexico City: UNAM/IIH, 1975.

———. *Historia de la Nación Chichimeca* (composed between 1610 and 1640). Edited by Germán Vázquez. Madrid: Historia 16, 1985.

Anawalt, Frances Berdan, and Patricia Anawalt, eds. *Codex Mendoza*. Berkeley: University of California Press, 1992.

Anawalt, Patricia Reiff. *Indian Clothing before Cortes*. Norman: University of Oklahoma Press, 1981.

Anderson, Arthur J. O. "Aztec Wives." In *Indian Women of Early Mexico*, edited by Stephanie Wood, Susan Schroeder, and Robert Haskett, 55–85. Norman: University of Oklahoma Press, 1997.

Anzaldúa, Gloria. *Borderlands/La Frontera: The New Mestiza*. San Francisco: Aunt Lute Books, 1987.

Avilés Parra, Sergio. "Con José Limón." *México en la cultura de Novedades*, April 22, 1951, 4.

Baas, Jacquelynn. "Interpreting Orozco's Epic." *Dartmouth Alumni Magazine*. January/February 1984.

Balderrama, Francisco E., and Raymond Rodriguez. *Decade of Betrayal: Mexican Repatriation in the 1930s*. Albuquerque: University of New Mexico Press, 1995.

Bantel, Linda, and Marcus B. Burke. *Spain and New Spain, Mexican Colonial Arts in Their European Context*. Corpus Christi: Art Museum of South Texas, 1979.

Baqueiro Fóster, Gerónimo. "Por el Mundo de la Música." *El Nacional*, September 30, 1950, 8.

Barbosa Sánchez, Araceli. *Sexo y Conquista*. Mexico City: UNAM, 1994.

Bell, Karen Elizabeth. "Kingmakers: The Royal Women of Ancient Mexico." Ph.D. dissertation, University of Michigan, 1992.

Berdan, Frances F. *The Aztecs of Central Mexico: An Imperial Society*. New York: Holt, Rinehart and Winston, 1982.

Berg, Charles Ramírez. *Cinema of Solitude: A Critical Study of Mexican Film, 1967–1983*. Austin: University of Texas Press, 1992.

Blanco, Iris. "Participación de las Mujeres en la Sociedad Pre-Hispánica." In *Essays on La Mujer*, edited by Rosaura Sanchez and Rose Martinez Cruz, 48–81. Los Angeles: Chicano Studies Center Publications, 1977.

Bourdieu, Pierre. "La Dominación Masculina." *La Ventana. Revista de estudios de género* 3 (July 1996).

Bourque, Linda Brookover. *Defining Rape*. Durham: Duke University Press, 1989.

Bouvier, Virginia M. *Women and the Conquest of California, 1542–1840: Codes of Silence*. Tucson: University of Arizona Press, 2001.

Brenner, Anita. *The Wind That Swept Mexico*. George R. Leighton, photographs. Austin: University of Texas Press, 1971.

Brown, Betty Ann. "Seen but Not Heard: Women in Aztec Ritual—The Sahagún Texts." In *Text and Image in Pre-Columbian Art: Essays on the Interrelationship of the Verbal and Visual Arts*, edited by Janet C. Berlo, 119–154. Oxford: BAR Press, 1983.

Brownmiller, Susan. *Against Our Will: Men, Women, and Rape*. New York: Simon and Schuster, 1975.

Brumfiel, Elizabeth M. "Weaving and Cooking: Women's Production in Aztec Mexico." In *Engendering Archaeology: Women and Prehistory*, edited by Joan Gero and Margaret Conkey, 224–251. Oxford: Basil Blackwell, 1991.

———. "Figurines and the Aztec State: Testing the Effectiveness of Ideological Domination." In *Gender and Archaeology*, edited by Rita P. Wright, 143–166. Philadelphia: University of Pennsylvania Press, 1996.

———. "Asking About Aztec Gender: The Historical and Archaeological Evidence." In *Gender in Pre-Hispanic America: A Symposium at Dumbarton Oaks*, edited by Cecelia F. Klein, 57–85. Washington, D.C.: Dumbarton Oaks Research, 2001.

Burkhart, Louise. *The Slippery Earth: Nahua-Christian Moral Dialogue in Sixteenth-Century Mexico*. Tucson: University of Arizona Press, 1989.

———. "Mexica Women on the Home Front: Housework and Religion in Aztec Mexico." In *Indian Women of Early Mexico*, edited by Stephanie Wood, Susan Schroeder, and Robert Haskett, 25–54. Norman: University of Oklahoma Press, 1997.

Burt, Ramsay. *The Male Dancer: Body, Spectacle, Sexualities*. London: Routledge, 1995.

Bustamante, Carlos Maria. *Cuadro Histórico de la Revolución Mexicana (1823–1832)*. 5 vols. Mexico City: Instituto Cultural Helénica; Fondo: de Cultura Económica, 1985.

Butler, Judith. "Variaciones Sobre Sexo y Género: Beauvoir, Witting y Foucault." In *El Género: La Construcción Cultural de la Diferencia Sexual*, edited by Marta Lamas. Mexico City: PUEG, UNAM, 1996.

Cardona, Patricia. "Durante 20 Años No Se Incluyeron Obras de José Limón en el Repertorio de las Compañías de Danza Mexicanas." *Uno más uno*, December 8, 1981.

Carrasco, Pedro. "Royal Marriages in Ancient Mexico." In *Explorations in Ethnohistory: Indians of Central Mexico in the Sixteenth Century*, edited by H. R. Harvey and Hanns J. Prem, 41–82. Albuquerque: University of New Mexico Press, 1984.

———. "Indian-Spanish Marriages in the First Century of the Colony." In *Indian Women of Early Mexico*, ed. Susan Schroeder, Stephanie Wood, and Robert Haslett. Norman: University of Oklahoma Press, 1957.

Carrera, Magali Marie. "The Representation of Women in Aztec-Mexica Sculpture." Ph.D. dissertation, Columbia University, 1979.

Caso, Alfonso. *The Aztecs: People of the Sun*. Translated by Lowell Dunham. Norman: University of Oklahoma Press, 1958.

Castañeda, Antonia. "Presidarias y Pobladoras: Spanish-Mexican Women in Frontier Monterey, Alta California, 1770–1821." Ph.D. dissertation, Stanford University, 1990.

———. "Sexual Violence in the Politics and Policies of Conquest: American Women and the Spanish Conquest of Alta California." In *Building with Our Hands: New Directions in Chicana Studies*, edited by Adela de la Torre and Beatríz M. Pesquera, 15–33. Berkeley: University of California Press, 1993.

Castellanos, Rosario. *El eterno femenino*. Mexico City: Fondo de Cultura Económica, 1975.

Castillo Mireles, Ricardo. "Al Rescate de la Obra de José Limón, El Teatro del Espacio." *Excélsior*, November 24, 1981, 3.

———. "La Malinche, Humanizada en un Ballet del Bailarín y Coreógrafo José Limón." *Excélsior*, December 4, 1981, 17.

Chance, Jeremy. *The Alexander Technique*. London: Thorsons, 2001.

Charlot, Jean. *Mexican Mural Renaissance*. New York, 1979.

Chavero, Alfredo. *Historia Antigua y de la Conquista*, vol. 1 in *México a Través de los Siglos*, ed. Vicente Riva Palacio. 4 vols. Mexico City: G. S. López [1940].

———. *Xochitl: drama en tres actos y en verso*. 3d ed. Mexico City : G. A. Esteva, 1878.

Chávez, Carlos. "La Danza Mexicana." In *Escritos de Carlos Mérida Sobre el Arte: La Danza*, edited by Cristina Mendoza. Mexico City: Instituto Nacional de Bellas Artes, 1990.

Cheron, Philippe. *El Árbol de Oro: José Revueltas y el Pesimismo Ardiente*. Ciudad Juárez, Mexico City: Universidad Autónoma de Ciudad Juárez, 2003.

Clavijero, Francisco Javier. *Historia Antigua de México*. Prólogo de Mariano Cuevas. Mexico City: Editorial Porrua, 1976.

Clendinnen, Inga. *Aztecs: An Interpretation*. Cambridge: Cambridge University Press, 1991.

Cline, S. L. *Colonial Culhuacan, 1580–1600: A Social History of an Aztec Town*. Albuquerque: University of New Mexico Press, 1986.

Codex Mendoza. Frances Berdan and Patricia Anawalt, eds. 4 vols. Berkeley: University of California Press, 1992.

El Códice Gracida-dominicano sobre la Danza de Ya-ha-zucu hoy Cuilapan, ed. Jesús Martínez Vigil. 2d ed. [Oaxaca de Juárez, Mexico]: Instituto Oaxaqueño de las Culturas: Casa de la Cultura Oaxaqueña, 1995.

Cohen, Jonathan. "Waldeen and the Americas: The Dance has Many Faces." In *A Woman's Gaze: Latin American Women Artists,* edited by Marjorie Agosín (Fredonia, N.Y.: White Pine Press, 1998).

Copel, Melinda Susan. "José Limón, Modern Dance and the State Department's Agenda: The Limón Company Performances in Poland and Yugoslavia: 1957." In *Dancing in the Millennium, Proceedings of the Society for Dance History 2000,* 2000.

———. "The State Department Sponsored Tours of José Limón and the Modern Dance Company, 1954 and 1957: Modern Dance, Diplomacy, and the Cold War." Ed.D. thesis, Temple University, 2000.

Costa Lima, Lucia da. "Performing Latinidad: Dances and Techniques of José Limón." In *Dancing in the Millennium, Proceedings of the Society of Dance History Scholars,* 115–118, 2000.

Cotera, Martha P. *Diosa and Hembra: The History and Heritage of Chicanas in the U.S.* Austin: Information Systems Development, 1976.

Covarrubias, Miguel. "La Danza." *México en el arte* 12 (1952): 106–107.

Crespo de la Serna, Jorge J. "Artes Plásticas: El Arte de José Limón." *Excélsior,* September 30, 1950.

Cypess, Sandra Messinger. *La Malinche in Mexican Literature: From History to Myth.* Austin: University of Texas Press, 2000.

Dallal, Alberto. *La Danza en México.* Mexico City: UNAM, 1986.

De Castillo, Adelaida R. "Malintzin Tenépal: A Preliminary Look into a New Perspective." In *Essays on La Mujer,* edited by Rosaura Sánchez and Rosa Martinez Cruz, 124–149. Los Angeles: University of California, Chicano Studies Center Publications, 1977.

Delancy, Patty. "José Limón's *La Malinche.*" The hydra quality in Brazil: A case study of class, gender and qualidade in the northeast. Dissertation 1994.

Delgado, Jaime. "El Amor en la América Prehispánica." *Revista de Indias* (1969): 151–171.

D'Harnoncourt, René. "Mexican Arts." *American Magazine of Art* (January 1931).

Díaz del Castillo, Bernal. *Historia Verdadera de la Conquista de la Nueva España.* 2 vols. Mexico City: Editorial Aramor, 1955.

Dunbar, June, ed. *José Limón: The Artist Reviewed.* Singapore: Harwood Academic Publishers, 2000.

Durán, Fray Diego. *Historia de las Indias de Nueva España y Islas de Tierra Firme.* 2 vols. Mexico City: Editorial Porrua, 1967.

"Estas Son las Leyes Que Tenían los Indios de la Nueva España." In *Nueva Colección de Documentos para la Historia de México, Pomar-Zurita-Relaciones Antiguas (Siglo XVI),* edited by Joaquín García Icazbalceta. Mexico City: Editorial Salvador Chávez Hayhoe, 1941.

Evans, Susan. "Sexual Politics in the Aztec Palace: Public, Private, and Profane." *Res* (1998): 167–183.

———. "Aztec Noble Courts: Men, Women, and Children of the Palace." In *Royal Courts of the Ancient Maya*, edited by Takeshi Inomata and Stephen D. Houston, 237–273. Boulder: Westview Press, 2001.

Ferguson, George. *Signs and Symbols in Christian Art*. New York: Oxford University Press, 1961.

Florentine Codex. Edited by Arthur J. O. Anderson and Charles E. Dibble. Vol. 14. Salt Lake City: School of American Research and University of Utah Press, 1950–1982.

Flores Guerrero, Raúl. "La Danza Contemporánea." In *La Danza en México*, 73–79. Mexico City: UNAM, 1980.

Florescano, Enrique. "Quetzalcóatl: Un Mito Hecho de Mitos." In *La Sociedad y Sus Mitos*, edited by Enrique Florescano, 1995.

Foulkes, Julia L. *Modern Bodies: Dance and American Modernism from Martha Graham to Alvin Ailey*. Chapel Hill: University of North Carolina Press, 2002.

Franco, Jean. *Las Conspiradoras: La Representación de la Mujer en México*. Mexico City: FCE, 1993.

———. *Plotting Women*. New York: Columbia University Press, 1989.

Frye, David L. *Indians into Mexicans: History and Identity in a Mexican Town*. Austin: University of Texas Press, 1996.

Fuentes, Carlos. *Todos Los Gatos Son Pardos*. Edited by Siglo. Mexico City, 1979.

Fuentes, Manlio S. "Música. José Limón." *Impacto*, 30 September 1950.

Gamio, Manuel. *Forjando Patria* (1916). Prólogo de Justino Fernandez. Mexico City: Porrúa, 1982.

Garafola, Lynn. "Works Choreographed by José Limón." In *Unfinished Memoir*, 1999.

García, Matt. *A World of Their Own: Race, Labor, and Citrus in the Making of Greater Los Angeles, 1900–1970*. Chapel Hill: University of North Carolina Press, 2001.

García Canclini, Néstor. *Culturas Híbridas: Estrategias Para Entrar y Salir de la Modernidad*. Mexico City: Grijalbo, 2001.

Garcia Icazbalceta, Joaquin. *Opúsculos y Biografias*. Mexico City: UNAM, 1973.

García Peguero, Raquel. "Lucas Hoving: La Raíz de Limón Era México." *El Día*, November 22 1981.

Garcia-Quintana, Josefina. *El Lienzo de Tlaxcala*. Mexico City: Cartón y Papel de México, 1983.

Garza Tarazona de González, Silvia. *La Mujer Mesoamericana*. Mexico City: Editorial Planeta Mexicana, 1991.

Gibson, Charles. *Tlaxcala in the Sixteenth Century*. Stanford: Stanford University Press, 1967.

Gillespie, Susan D. *The Aztec Kings: The Construction of Rulership in Mexica History*. Tucson: University of Arizona Press, 1989.

Glantz, Margo, ed. *La Malinche, Sus Padres y Sus Hijos*. Mexico City: UNAM, 1994.

Glasston, Richard. *La Danza Para Varones Como Carrera*. Mexico City: Instituto Nacional de Bellas Artes, 1997.

Goldsmith Connelly, Mary. "Barriendo, Tejiendo y Cocinando: El Trabajo Doméstico en la Sociedad Azteca." In *Chalchihuite: Homenaje a Doris Heyden*, edited by María de Jesús Rodríguez-Shadow and Beatriz Barba de Piña Chán, 213–225. Mexico City: INAH, 1999.

González Hernández, Cristina. *Doña Marina (La Malinche) y la Formación de la Identitdad Mexicana.* Madrid: Encuentro, 2002.

González y Contreras, G. "Teatro Crítica: Compañía de Danza Moderna." *Impacto,* September 30, 1950.

González Torres, Yolotl. "El Panteón Mexica." *Antropología e historia* 25 (1979): 9–19.

Gorlero, José Enrique. "El Retorno a México de José Limón. El BTE Bailará La Malinche." *El Día,* November 1, 1981.

Gorsline, Douglas. *What People Wore.* New York: Viking Press, 1952.

Graff, Ellen. *Stepping Left: Dance and Politics in New York City, 1928–1942.* Durham: Duke University Press, 1997.

Greenblatt, Stephen. *Marvelous Possessions: The Wonder of the New World.* Chicago: University of Chicago Press, 1991.

Gruzinski, Serge. *Painting the Conquest: The Mexican Indians and the European Renaissance.* Paris: Unesco, Flammarion, 1992.

H. S. "Entre Músicos. Bailes Clásicos Y Modernos." *El Redondel,* October 1, 1950, 12–13.

Halffter, Rodolfo. "La Vida Musical." *El Universal Gráfico,* September 12, 1950, 6.

———. "La Vida Musical. Rotundo Éxito de José Limón." *El Universal Gráfico,* September 26, 1950, 6.

Hanna, Judith Lynne. *Dance, Sex and Gender: Signs of Identity, Dominance, Defiance, and Desire.* Chicago: University of Chicago Press, 1988.

Harris, Max. "Moctezuma's Daughter: The Role of La Malinche in Mesoamerican Dance." *The Journal of American Folklore* 109, no. 432 (1996): 149–177.

Hassig, Ross. *Aztec Warfare: Imperial Expansion and Political Control.* Norman: University of Oklahoma Press, 1988.

———. "The Maid of the Myth: La Malinche and the History of Mexico." *Indiana Journal of Hispanic Literatures* 12 (1998): 101–133.

Heinzelman, Kurt. *The Covarrubias Circle: Nickolas Muray's Collection of Twentieth-Century Mexican Art.* Harry Ransom Humanities Research Center Imprint Series. Austin: University of Texas Press, 2004.

Hellbom, Anna-Britta. *La Participación Cultural de las Mujeres Indias y Mestizas en el México Precortesano y Postrevolucionario.* Stockholm: Ethnographical Museum, 1967.

Hemming, John. *The Conquest of the Incas.* New York: Harcourt Brace Jovanovich, 1970.

Hernandez, Sonia. *"Malinche in Cross-Border Historical Memory."* This volume.

Herren, Ricardo. *La Conquista Erótica de las Indias.* Barcelona: Planeta, 1991.

Horn, Rebecca. "Gender and Social Identity: Nahua Naming Patterns in Postconquest Central Mexico." In *Indian Women of Early Mexico,* edited by Stephanie Wood, Susan Schroeder, and Robert Haskett. Norman: University of Oklahoma Press, 1997.

Huerta, J. N. "Palmeta, Lo Que Pasa en Nuestros Teatros." *El Universal,* October 3, 1950, 4.

Hurtado, Albert L. *Intimate Frontiers: Sex, Gender, and Culture in Old California.* Albuquerque: University of New Mexico Press, 1999.

Hutton, Patrick. *History as an Art of Memory*. Hanover: University of New England Press, 1993.

Jewell, Edward. "The Realm of Art: Orozco's New Murals at Dartmouth." *New York Times*, February 25 1934, 12X.

Joyce, Rosemary A. *Gender and Power in Prehispanic Mesoamerica*. Austin: University of Texas Press, 2000.

Junius. "La Música de la Semana." *Excélsior*, September 24, 1950, 6.

Kamen, Henry. *Philip of Spain*. New Haven: Yale University Press, 1997.

Kartunnen, Frances. *Between Worlds: Interpreters, Guides, and Survivors*. New Brunswick: Rutgers University Press, 1994.

————. "Rethinking Malinche." In *Indian Women of Early Mexico*, edited by Stephanie Wood, Susan Shroeder, and Robert Haskett. Norman: University of Oklahoma Press, 1997.

Keen, Benjamin. *The Aztec Image in Western Thought*. New Brunswick: Rutgers University Press, 1971.

Kellogg, Susan. "Aztec Inheritance in Sixteenth-Century Mexico: Colonial Patterns, Prehispanic Influences." *Ethnohistory* 33, no. 3 (1986): 313–330.

————. "Kinship and Social Organization in Early Colonial Tenochtitlán." In *Ethnohistory*, edited by Ronald Spores, 103–121. Austin: University of Texas Press, 1986.

————. *Law and the Transformation of Aztec Culture, 1500–1700*. Norman: University of Oklahoma Press, 1995.

————. "From Parallel and Equivalent to Separate but Unequal: Tenochca Mexica Women, 1500–1700." In *Indian Women of Early Mexico*, edited by Stephanie Wood, Susan Schroeder, and Robert Haskett, 123–143. Norman: University of Oklahoma Press, 1997.

————. *Weaving the Past: A History of Latin America's Indigenous Women from the Prehispanic Period to the Present*. New York: Oxford University Press, 2005.

Klein, Cecilia. "Rethinking Cihuacoatl: Aztec Political Imagery of the Conquered Woman." In *Smoke and Mist: Mesoamerican Studies in Memory of Thelma D. Sullivan*, edited by J. Kathryn Josserand and Karen Dakin, 237–277. Oxford: BAR Press, 1988.

————. "The Shield Women: Resolution of an Aztec Gender Paradox." In *Current Topics in Aztec Studies: Essays in Honor of Dr. H. B. Nicholson*, edited by Alana Cordy-Collins and Douglas Sharon, 39–64. San Diego: San Diego Museum Papers, 1993.

————. "Fighting with Femininity: Gender and War in Aztec Mexico." *Estudios de Cultura Náhuatl* 24 (1994): 219–253.

Klor de Alva, Jorge. "Sahagún and the Birth of Modern Ethnography: Representing, Confessing, and Inscribing the Native Other." In *The Works of Bernardino de Sahagún, Pioneer Ethnographer of Sixteenth-Century Aztec Mexico*, edited by Klor de Alva et al. Austin: University of Texas Press, 1988.

Knight, Alan. "Racism, Revolution, and Indigenismo: Mexico, 1910–1940." In *The Idea of Race*, edited by Richard Graham. Austin: University of Texas Press, 1990.

Koner, Pauline. *Solitary Song*. Durham: Duke University Press, 1989.

Ladd, Doris M. *Mexican Women in Anahuac and New Spain: Aztec Roles, Spanish*

Notary Revelations, Creole Genius. Austin: Institute for Latin American Studies, University of Texas, 1979.

Lafaye, Jacques. *Quetzalcóatl and Guadalupe: The Formation of the Mexican National Consciousness 1531–1813.* Translated by Benjamin Keen. Chicago: University of Chicago Press, 1976.

Lanyon, Anna. *Malinche's Conquest.* St. Leonards, NSW, Australia: Allen and Edwards, 1999.

Lerín, Manuel. "José Limón y la Danza Moderna." *El Nacional,* September 24, 1950, 3–7.

Lewis, Daniel. *The Illustrated Dance Technique of José Limón.* New York: Harper and Row, 1984.

———. *La Técnica Ilustrada de José Limón.* Mexico City: Instituto Nacional de Bellas Artes, 1994.

Lewis, Laura A. "Temptress, Warrior, Priestess or Witch? Four Faces of Tlazolteotl in the Laud Codex." In *Códices y Documentos Sobre México: Segundo Simposio,* edited by Constanza Vega Sosa, Salvador Rueda Smithers, and Rodrigo Martínez Baracs. Mexico City: INAH and Dirección General de Publicaciones del Consejo Nacional para la Cultura y las Artes, 1997.

[Lienzo de Tlaxcala] Homenaje a Cristóbal Colón: antiguedades mexicanas / publicadas por la Junta Colombina de México en el cuarto centenario del descubrimiento de América . . . Mexico City: Oficina Tipográfica de la Secretaría de Fomento, 1982. Nettie Lee Benson Latin American Collection, University of Texas Libraries, University of Texas at Austin.

Lienzo de Tlaxcala. N.p., ca. 1890. Believed to be the Cahuantzi plates.

Limón, José. *Limón Manuscript(S).* New York: New York Public Library.

Limón, José. "The Dance: A Visitor in Mexico." *New York Times,* July 22 1957.

———. "The Making of *Tonantzintla* and the Making of *Dialogues.*" *Dance Magazine,* August 1951, 10–14.

———. "Composing a Dance." *Juilliard Review* (Winter 1955): 18.

———. "Rebel and the Bourgeois." In *The Vision of Modern Dance in the Words of Its Creators,* edited by Jean Morrison Brown. Princeton: Princeton Book Co., 1979.

———. "Limón Journal" 3 (Fall 1998).

———. *An Unfinished Memoir.* Edited by Lynn Garafola. Hanover and London: Wesleyan University Press, University Press of New England, 1999.

Limón, Pauline Lawrence. "Pauline Lawrence Limón Manuscripts." In *Public Library Dance Collection,* Folders 193, 97, 98. New York.

Lipsett-Rivera, Sonya. "The Intersection of Rape and Marriage in Late-Colonial and Early-National Mexico." *Colonial Latin American Historical Review* 6, no. 4 (1997): 559–590.

Lloyd, Margaret. *The Borzoi Book of Modern Dance.* Dance Horizons, 1974 ed. New York: Knopf, 1949.

Lloyd, Norman. "Composing for the Dance." *Dance Observer* (October 1972): 118.

Lockhart, James. *The Nahuas after the Conquest: A Social and Cultural History of the Indians of Central Mexico, Sixteenth through Eighteenth Centuries.* Stanford: Stanford University Press, 1992.

Lockhart, James, Susan Schroeder, and Doris Namala, eds. *Annals of His Time: Don Domingo de San Antón Muñón Chimalpahin Quauhtlehuanitzin*. Stanford: Stanford University Press, 2006.

López Austin, Alfredo. "La Sexualidad entre los Antiguos Nahuas." In *Familia y Sexualidad entre Nueva España*. Mexico City: Fondo de Cultura Económica, 1982.

———. "La Parte Feminina del Cosmos." *Arqueología Mexicana* 5, no. 29, Special Issue (1998): 6–13.

López de Gómara, Francisco. *Historia de la Conquista de México*. 2 vols. Mexico City: Editorial Pedro Robredo, 1943.

López de Meneses, Amada. "Tecuichpochtzin, Hija De Moteczuma (1510?–1550)." *Revista de Indias* 9 (1948): 471–496.

MacLachlan, Colin. "The Eagle and the Serpent: Male over Female in Tenochtitlan." *Proceedings of the Pacific Coast Council of Latin American Studies* 5 (1976): 45–56.

Malachi Roth, Ute Hagen, and Isaiah Shaffer. *Limón: A Life Beyond Words*. Frenchtown, N.J.: Dance Conduit/Antidote Films, 2003.

Marcus, George, and Michael M. Fischer. *Anthropology as Cultural Critique: An Experimental Moment in the Human Sciences*. Chicago: University of Chicago Press, 1986.

Martin, John. "José Limón Comes into His Own-Helen Tamiris and 'It's up to You.'" *New York Times*, April 4, 1943.

Martínez-Marín, Carlos. "History of the Lienzo de Tlaxcala." In *El Lienzo de Tlaxcala*. Mexico City: Cartón y Papel de México, 1983.

Matadamas, María Elena. "El BTE Rinde Homenaje al Coreógrafo José Limón." *Novedades*, November 24, 1981.

Maturo, Carol L. "Visual Communication: Props and Costumes." This volume.

———. "Malinche and Cortés, 1519–1521: An Iconographic Study," Vol. 1. Ph.D. dissertation, University of Connecticut-Storrs, 1994.

McCaa, Robert. "Matrimonio Infantil, Cemithualtin (Familias Complejas) y el Antiguo Pueblo Nahua." *Historia Mexicana* (1996): 3–70.

McCafferty, Sharisse D., and Geoffrey D. McCafferty. "Powerful Women and the Myth of Male Dominance in Aztec Society." *Archaeological Review from Cambridge* 7 (1988): 45–59.

———. "The Metamorphosis of Xochiquetzal: A Window on Womanhood in Pre- and Post-Conquest Mexico." In *Manifesting Power: Gender and the Interpretation of Power in Archaeology*, edited by Tracy L. Sweely. London: Routledge, 1999.

Medina, Pilar. "José Limón en la Danza Mexicana." In *La Danza en México*, edited by Leopoldo Sánchez et al. Culiacán, Sinaloa: Colegio de Sinaloa, 1999.

Menéndez, Miguel Ángel. *Malintzin en un fuste, seis rostros, y una sola máscara*. Mexico City, 1964.

Meyer, Michael C., and William L. Sherman. *The Course of Mexican History*. New York, 1979.

Molina Enriquez, Andres. *Los Grandes Problemas Nacionales*. Mexico City: Imprenta de A. Carranza e hijos, 1909.

Monsiváis, Carlos. "Notas Sobre la Cultura Mexicana en el Siglo Xx." In *Historia General de México*. Mexico City: El Colegio de México, 1977.

———. "Sociedad y Cultura." In *Entre la Guerra y la Estabilidad Política: El México de los Cuarenta*, edited by Rafael Loyola, 270. Mexico City: Grijalbo-CNCA, 1990.

———. "La Malinche y el Primer Mundo." In *La Malinche, Sus Padres y Sus Hijos*, edited by Margo Glantz. Mexico City: UNAM, 1994.

Morales Esteves, José. "Danza. José Limón en Bellas Artes." *Excélsior,* September 24, 1950.

Moreno, Igor. "Actividades Musicales de la Semana. El Arte Danzario de José Limón Hizo Adeptos en Creciente Número." *El Nacional,* October 14, 1950, 14.

———. "Actividades Musicales de la Semana. José Limón, Danzarín Y Coreautor." *El Nacional,* October 14, 1950, 14.

Motolinía, Fray Toribio (de Benavente). *Memoriales o Libro de las Cosas de la Nueva España y los Naturales de Ella*. Mexico City: UNAM, 1971.

Muñoz Camargo, Diego. "Historia de Tlaxcala." In *Historia 16*. Madrid, 1986.

Nash, June. "The Aztecs and the Ideology of Male Dominance." *Signs* 4, no. 2 (1978): 349–362.

Nicholson, H. B. "Religion in Pre-Hispanic Central Mexico." In *Archaeology of Northern Mesoamerica*, edited by Gordon F. Ekholm and Ignacio Bernal, 395–446. Austin: University of Texas Press, 1971.

Norte, Tigres Del. *Caben Dos Patrias en el Mismo Corazón*. Fonavisa, 1997.

Novo, Salvador. "Ventana, La Danza de José Limón." *Novedades,* September 21, 1950, 4.

———. "Ventana. La Danza Mexicana." *Novedades,* September 19, 1950, 4.

———. "Cartas Viejas y Nuevas de Salvador Novo." Mexico City, 1951.

———. *Cuauhtémoc, Pieza en un Acto*. Mexico City, 1962.

Núñez Becerra, Fernanda. *La Malinche: De la Historia al Mito*. Mexico City: INAH, 1996.

Offner, Jerome A. *Law and Politics in Aztec Texcoco*. Cambridge: Cambridge University Press, 1983.

O'Malley, Ilene V. *The Myth of the Revolution: Hero Cults and the Institutionalization of the Mexican State, 1920–1940*. Westport Conn.: Greenwood Press, 986.

Parker, Robert L. "Un Estudio Sobre la Persistencia de Carlos Chávez en el Ballet." In *Heterofonía*, no. 94 (July-September). Mexico City: Instituto Nacional de Bellas Artes, 1986.

Paz, Octavio. *The Labyrinth of Solitude*. Translated by Lysander Kemp. New York: Grove Press, 1960.

———. *El Laberinto de la Soledad*. Mexico City: FCE, 1994.

———. "Triunfo Total del BTE en El Teatro de la Danza." *El Día*, November 28, 1981.

Pellicer, Carlos. *Mural Painting of the Mexican Revolution*. 2d ed. Mexico City: Fondo Editorial de la Plástica Mexicana, 1985.

Pereyra, Carlos. *Hernán Cortés*. Madrid, 1931.

Pérez-Rocha, Emma. *Privilegios en Lucha: La Información de Doña Isabel Moctezuma.* Mexico City: INAH, 1998.

Peterson, Jeanette. "¿Lengua o Diosa? The Early Imaging of Malinche." In *Chipping Away on Earth: Studies in Prehispanic and Colonial Mexico in Honor of Arthur J. O. Anderson and Charles E. Dibble,* edited by Eloise Quiñones Keber, 187–202. Lancaster, Calif.: Labyrinthos, 1994.

Pollack, Barbara, and Charles Humphrey Woodford. *Dance Is a Moment: A Portrait of José Limón in Words and Pictures.* Pennington, N.J.: Princeton Book Co., 1993.

———. "La Fortaleza de Una Vocación." In *Cuadernos del Cenidi Danza,* edited by Margarita Tortajada. Mexico City: Instituto Nacional de Bellas Artes, 1993.

Pomar, Juan Bautista. "Relación de Tezcoco." In *Nueva Colección de Documentos para la Historia de México,* edited by J. García Icazbalceta, 1–69. Mexico City: Imprenta de Francisco Díaz de León, 1891.

Poniatowska, Elena. *Miguel Covarrubias, Vida y Mundos.* Mexico City: Ediciones Era, 2004.

Pratt, Mary Louise. "Yo Soy La Malinche: Chicana Writers and the Poetics of Ethnonationalism." *Callaloo* 16, no. 4 (1993): 860.

Pulido, Esperanza. "Música en México." *Novedades,* September 25, 1950, 4.

Quezada, Noemí. "Creencias Tradicionales Sobre Embarazo y Parto." *Anales de Antropología* 14 (1977): 307–326.

Quiñones Keber, Eloise. "Reading Images: The Making and Meaning of the Sahaguntine Illustrations." In *The Works of Bernardino de Sahagún,* edited by Klor de Alva et al. Austin: University of Texas Press, 1988.

———. "Painting Divination in the Florentine Codex." In *Representing Aztec Ritual: Performance, Text, and Image in the Work of Sahagún,* edited by Eloise Quiñones Keber, 252–276. Boulder: University Press of Colorado, 2002.

Quiñonez, Naomi Helena. "Hijas de La Malinche: The Development of Social Agency among Mexican American Women and the Emergence of First Wave Chicana Cultural Production." Ph.D. dissertation, Claremont Graduate School, 1997.

Rashkin, Elissa. "Los Machos También Lloran: Televisa and the Postnational Man." Paper presented at the Reunión de Latin American Studies Association, Guadalajara, Guadalajara, Mexico, April 17–19, 1997.

Rebolledo, Efren. "El Águila Que Cae (1916)." Introd. edición y bibliografía por Luis Mario Schneider. In *Obras Completas.* Mexico City: Instituto Nacional de Bellas Artes, Departamento de Literatura, 1968.

Rebolledo, Tey Diana. "Women Singing in the Snow: A Cultural Analysis of Chicana Literature." In *Infinite Divisions: An Anthology of Chicana Literature,* edited by Rebolledo and Eliana S. Rivero. Tucson: University of Arizona Press, 1995.

Revueltas, José. *El Luto Humano.* Mexico City: Editorial México, 1943.

Reyna, Rosa. "Raquel Gutiérrez, Una Vida Dedicada a la Danza 1988." *Cuadernos del CENIDI Danza,* no. 19 (1988): 20.

Rincón, Cassandra. "José Limón, El Mexicano Ausente: 'Aquí Hay Talento.'" *Excélsior,* March 5, 1968.

Río, Gabriel del. "José Limón: Un Gran Artista." *El Universal*, September 11, 1950, 20.

Robertson, Donald. *Mexican Manuscript Painting of the Early Colonial Period: The Metropolitan Schools*. New Haven: Yale University Press, 1959.

Rodó, Andrea, and Paulina Saball. "El Cuerpo Ausente." *Cuerpo y Política. Debate feminista* 10 (September 1994): 81–94.

Rodríguez-Shadow, María J. *La Mujer Azteca.* 3d ed. Mexico City: Universidad Autónoma del Estado de México, 1997.

Rosaldo, Renato. "When Natives Talk Back: Chicano Anthropology since the Late Sixties." In *The Renato Rosaldo Lectures, 1985*. Tucson: Mexican American Studies and Research Center, 1985.

Ruiz, Felipe González. *Doña Marina, La India Que Amó a Cortés*. Madrid: Ediciones Morata, 1944.

Ruiz, Luis Bruno. "Danza en Homenaje al Gran José Limón." *Excélsior*, December 8, 1981, 22–23.

Ruiz, Viki. "'Star-Struck' Acculturation, Adolescence, and Mexican American Women 1920–1950." In *Building with Our Hands: New Directions in Chicana Studies*, edited by Beatríz M. Pesquera and Adela de la Torre. Berkeley: University of California Press, 1993.

Sahagún, Bernardino de. *Primeros Memoriales.* Paleography and translation by Thelma O. Sullivan, rev. H. B. Nicholson. Norman: University of Oklahoma Press, 1997.

Sanchez, George J. *Becoming Mexican American: Ethnicity, Culture, and Identity in Chicano Los Angeles, 1900–1945*. New York: Oxford University Press, 1993.

Sánchez Flores, Horacio. "Musicales. El Éxito Rotundo de la Primer Noche de José Limón y Su Compañía." *El Universal*, September 21, 1950, 4, 14.

Sapietsa, Julio. "El Teatro en Acción. Gran Éxito del Bailarín y Coreógrafo José Limón." *El Universal Gráfico*, September 23, 1950, 10.

Schroeder, Susan. "The Noblewomen of Chalco." *Estudios de Cultura Náhuatl* 22 (1992): 45–86.

Seed, Patricia. *To Love, Honor and Obey in Colonial Mexico: Conflicts over Marriage Choice, 1574–1821*. Stanford: Stanford University Press, 1988.

Sierra, Justo. *Historia de México: La Conquista.* Madrid: s.n., 1917.

Smith, Bradley. *Mexico, a History in Art.* Garden City, N.Y.: Harper and Row, 1968.

Somonte, Mariano G. *Doña Marina, "La Malinche."* Mexico City: n.p., 1969.

Sousa, Lisa M. "Women in Native Societies and Cultures of Colonial Mexico (Nahua, Mixtec, Zapotec, Mixe)." Ph.D. dissertation, UCLA, 1998.

Stackhouse, Sarah. *Thoughts on Setting José Limón's La Malinche.* Philadelphia: Society of Dance History Scholars, 2002.

Stern, Steve J. *Peru's Indian Peoples and the Challenge of Spanish Conquest: Huamanga to 1640.* 2d ed. Madison: University of Wisconsin Press, 1993.

Storm, Deliah Anne. "Retextualized Transculturations: The Emergence of La Malinche as Figure in Chicana Literature." Ph.D. dissertation, University of Illinois at Urbana-Champaign, 1994.

Strate, Walter, photographer. New York City: Limón Foundation Archives.

Suárez de Peralta, Juan. "Tratado del Descubrimiento de las Indias: Noticias de Nueva España" (1589). Nota preliminaria de Federico Gómez de Orozco. Mexico City: Secretaría de Educación Pública, 1949.

Sullivan, Thelma D. "Tlazolteotl-Ixcuina: The Great Spinner and Weaver." In *The Art and Iconography of Late Post-Classic Central Mexico,* edited by Elizabeth Hill Boone, 7–35. Washington, D.C.: Dumbarton Oaks, 1982.

Tafolla, Carmen. "Yo Soy La Malinche." In *Infinite Divisions,* edited by Rebolledo and Rivero. Tucson: University of Arizona Press, 1995.

Todd, Arthur. "Mexico Responds to Modern Dance and José Limón." *Dance Observer* (1951).

Todorov, Tzvetan. *The Conquest of America: The Question of the Other.* New York: Harper and Row, 1984.

Toor, Frances. *A Treasury of Mexican Folkways.* New York: Crown Publishers, 1947.

Toro, Alfonso. *Compendio de Historia de México Escrita Para Uso de las Escuelas Preparatorias de la Republica.* Mexico City: Sociedad de Edición y Librería Franco-Americana, 1926.

Tortajada Quiroz, Margarita. "Mujeres de Danza Combativa." *CONACULTA,* 1998.

———. *Danza Y Poder.* Mexico City: Instituto Nacional de Bellas Artes, 1995.

———. *Luis Fandiño, Danza Generosa y Perfecta.* Mexico City: Instituto Nacional de Bellas Artes, 2000.

———. Unpublished interview with Rocío Sagaón, 2004.

———. Unpublished interview with Colombia Moya, 2004.

———. Unpublished interview with Farnesio de Bernal, 2004.

———. Unpublished interview with Gladiola Orozco. Mexico City, 2004.

———. Unpublished interview with Guillermo Arriaga, 2004.

———. Unpublished interview with Josefina Lavalle, 2004.

———. Unpublished interview with Nellie Happee, 2004.

———. Unpublished interview with Rosa Reyna, 2004.

———. Unpublished interview with Valentina Castro, 2004.

Townsend, Camilla. *Malintzin's Choices: An Indian Woman in the Conquest of Mexico.* Albuquerque: University of New Mexico Press, 2006.

Tozzer, Alfred M. "Landa's *Relación de las Cosas de Yucatán.*" In *Peabody Museum Papers.* Cambridge, Massachusetts: Peabody Museum of Archaeology and Ethnology and Harvard University, 1941.

Vasconcelos, José. *La Raza Cósmica; Misión de la Raza Iberoamericana.* Paris: Agencia mundial de librería, 192.

Vachon, Ann. "Limón in Mexico; Mexico in Limón." In *José Limón: The Artist Reviewed,* edited by June Dunbar. New York: Routledge, 2002.

———. (Producer), and Malachi Roth (Director). *Limón: A Life Beyond Words.* New York: Antidote International Films, 2004.

Vetancurt, Agustín. *Teatro Mexicano [1697–1678].* Facsimile edition. Mexico City: Editorial Porrua, 1971.

Waldeen. *La Danza. Imagen de Creación Continua.* Mexico City: UNAM, 1982.

Wanderer. "José Limón. El Primer Bailarín Moderno del Mundo." *México en la cultura de Novedades,* September 10, 1950, 5.

———. "La Pavana del Moro." *México en la cultura de Novedades,* September 24, 1950, 2.

———. "Pauline Koner y la Danza." *México en la cultura de Novedades,* September 17, 1950, 7.

Williams, Adrianna. *Covarrubias,* ed. Doris Ober. Austin: University of Texas Press, 1994.

Williams, William Carlos. *In the American Grain.* New York: New Directions, 1956.

Wood, Stephanie. "Sexual Violation in the Conquest of the Americas." In *Sex and Sexuality in Early America,* edited by Merril D. Smith, 9–34. New York: New York University Press, 1998.

Wright de Kleinhans, Laureana. "Caonianal, Tenepal or Malinal." In *Mujeres Notables Mexicanas.* Secreatría de Instrucción Pública y Bellas Artes, Mexico, 1910.

Wurm, Carmen. *Doña Marina, La Malinche: Eine Historische Figur Und Ihre Literarische Rezeption.* Frankfurt am Maim: Vervuert Verlag, 1996.

Periodicals and Miscellaneous

"Ballet. Frenesí Coreográfico." *Tiempo,* May 2, 1952.

"Ballet. Vuelta de José Limón." *Tiempo,* September 22, 1950, 26–27.

"El BTE Presentará La Malinche de José Limón." *El Heraldo de México,* November 14, 1981.

"Cartelera del Pba." *El Universal Gráfico,* September 19, 1950, 15.

50 Años de Danza en El Palacio De Bellas Artes. Vol. 2. Mexico City: Instituto Nacional de Bellas Artes-SEP, 1986.

"Culturalísimo." *El Heraldo cultural,* November 26, 1981.

"Dartmouth Scored in Alien Art Row." *New York Times,* June 10, 1933, 15.

"Enciclopedia de México." In *Sabeca Internacional Investment Co.,* edited by José Rogelio Álvarez. Mexico City, 2000.

"Gran Éxito de José Limón, en Bellas Artes." *El Universal,* September 25, 1950, 13. "José Limón Bailarín Mexicano Triunfa en Estados Unidos." *Novedades,* April 15, 1949, 1.

"La Malinche del Coreógrafo José Limón, Será Interpretada por el BTE." *El Día,* November 11, 1981.

"Ley Orgánica del Inba." In *Diario Oficial de la Federación.* Mexico City, 1946.

Limón Programs. New York: New York Public Library, 1941.

Malintzin en un Fuste, Seis Rostros, y Una Sola Mascara. Mexico City, 1964.

"The Mexican Exhibition." *American Magazine of Art.* January 1931, 3.

"Música. Reorganización." *Tiempo,* September 8, 1950.

"Notas Culturales." *El Universal,* September 7, 1950, 4.

"Por Nuestros Teatros. Bellas Artes. El Ballet de José Limón." *El Redondel,* September 24, 1950.

"Por Qué No Auspicia el Gobierno un Ballet Mexicano?" *Nosotros*, June 3 1950.

"Program of the José Limón Dance Company." Mexico City: Palace of Fine Arts Mexico City, 1950.

"Programa de Mano del Ballet Teatro del Espacio." Mexico City: Teatro de la Danza, 1981.

"Público Homenaje al Artista José Limón." *Excélsior*, September 21, 1950.

"Viva José Limón!" *Avance*, November 15, 1981.

CONTRIBUTORS

Shelley C. Berg, an Associate Professor and Director of Graduate Studies in Dance at Southern Methodist University, earned her Ph.D. in Performance Studies from New York University. She teaches dance history, dance criticism, and ballet. Berg graduated from the Royal Ballet School, London, and has danced professionally with London Festival Ballet, Slovene National Ballet in Yugoslavia, and Les Grands Ballets Canadiens of Montreal. She has also been a dance consultant to the dance panel for the National Endowment for the Arts. Her publications include *Le Sacre du printemps: Seven Productions from Nijinsky to Martha Graham* and numerous articles for *Dance Chronicle*. Berg served as president of the Society of Dance History Scholars (2001–2005).

Patty Harrington Delaney is an Associate Professor and Coordinator of Graduate Studies in the Dance Division at Southern Methodist University, where she teaches Labanotation, composition, and American musical theater history. She is a Professional Certified Notator whose Labanotation scores include José Limón's *La Malinche*, Leni Wylliams's *Sweet in the Morning*, and Pilobolus's *Alraune*. Professor Delaney's interactive educational DVD on *La Malinche* won a Silver Award at the 2004 Houston International Film Festival, and her character analysis of *La Malinche* was published in *Dance Chronicle*. She is a member of the boards of the Dance Notation Bureau and the International Council of Kinetography Laban/Labanotation. Her choreographic credits include numerous musical productions, television commercials, corporate industrials, and concert works. She was a member of the regional modern dance company Dancers Unlimited, where she performed the works of such renowned artists as Bill Evans and Moses Pendleton.

Sonia Hernandez, a native of the Rio Grande Valley, is Assistant Professor of History at the University of Texas-Pan American. She was a 2005–2006 Northeast Consortium for Faculty Diversity Dissertation

Fellow, Northeastern University, Boston, 2003 William and Flora Hewlett Fellow in the Oaxaca Summer Institute, and received both the Murray Miller Scholarship for 2001–2002, and the Mexican American Graduate Fellowship from the Center for Mexican American Studies at the University of Houston. She is currently revising her dissertation on the Mexican northeast entitled, "Mexicanas and Mexicanos in a Transitional Borderland, 1880–1940," for publication.

Susan Kellogg holds a Ph.D. in Anthropology from the University of Rochester and currently serves as Professor and Chair of the History Department at the University of Houston. She has published extensively in Mesoamerican ethnohistory, women's and gender history of the Americas as well as cultural studies. Her many publications include a comprehensive survey of the history of native women in Latin America, *Weaving the Past: A History of Latin America's Indigenous Women* (Oxford University Press, 2005); *Dead Giveaway* (with Matthew Restall), which examines indigenous practices before and after the Conquest in social, economic, and political contexts; and *Law and the Transformation of Aztec Culture, 1500–1700* (University of Oklahoma Press, 1995), an extensive examination of the Spanish impact on Aztec family and property rights.

David LaMarche is the Music Director of the Limón Dance Company and Conductor and Music Administrator of American Ballet Theatre. Previously as Music Director of the Dance Theatre of Harlem, he toured five continents and performed with the company in historic engagements at the Kirov Theater and the Johannesburg Auditorium in South Africa. He has worked as Guest Conductor with the New York City Ballet, the San Francisco Ballet, the Joffrey Ballet, Het National Ballet of the Netherlands, and Les Grands Ballet Canadiens. He has composed and arranged several scores for the ballet and has recently recorded his song cycle based on poems of Edna St. Vincent Millay. LaMarche is a graduate of Boston University and a native of Rhode Island.

Carol Maturo is the author of "Malinche and Cortés, 1519–1521: An Iconographic Study," a 1994 doctoral dissertation at the University of Connecticut, Storrs, under Hugh M. Hamill. She has lectured on the iconography of Malinche and Cortés at Connecticut State University as well as at the American Association of Teachers of Spanish and Portuguese, Connecticut Humanities Council, and Connecticut Council of Language Teachers.

Patricia Seed is Professor of History at the University of California, Irvine, and the author of *Ceremonies of Possession in Europe's Conquest of the New World*. She has also written two prize-winning books: a comparative history of European colonialism's impact on the indigenous people of the New World, *American Pentimento: The Invention of Indians and the Pursuit of Riches* (winner of the 2003 Prize in Atlantic History) and *To Love, Honor, and Obey in Colonial Mexico, 1564–1821* (1989 Bolton Prize), as well as dozens of articles on Latin American and comparative world history. She danced for seventeen years, performed with the Steffi Nossen Dance Company, and choreographed for her university dance troupe before beginning a career in academia.

Sarah Stackhouse danced with the Limón Dance Company from 1958 to 1969 as a principal dancer and partner to Limón. She was also a member of the American Dance Theatre at Lincoln Center, Alvin Ailey American Dance Theater, Louis Falco and Dancers, The Workgroup—directed by Daniel Nagrin—and Annabelle Gamson Dance Solos, Inc. She has given residencies, staged, and directed many of Limón's major works for classical and modern companies throughout Europe, Mexico, China, and India and has served as an American Cultural Specialist for the Cultural Programs Division of the U.S. Department of State, lecturing and teaching in Rome, Perugia, and Florence, Italy. She has taught at the Juilliard School, the American Dance Festival, and the Conservatory of Dance at Purchase College—SUNY, N.Y. Her writings have appeared in two books, *East Meets West in Dance: Voices in the Cross-Cultural Dialogue* and *José Limón: The Artist Reviewed*. Her paper "The Moor's Pavane—Notes on the Characters, Casting, and Scenes" is included in the Labanotation score of this Limón work.

Margarita Tortajada Quiroz received her Ph.D. from Universidad Autónoma Metropolitana in Mexico City and is Researcher Level II of the National Researchers System (SNMI). She has worked at the Dance Research, Documentation, and Information National Center "José Limón" (CENIDIDanza), National Institute of Fina Arts (INBA) since 1988. Her seven books on dance include *Danza y poder* (Dance and Power) (1995); *La danza escénica de la Revolución Mexicana, nacionalista y vigorosa* (*Theatrical Dance of the Mexican Revolution, Vigorous and Nationalist*) (2000); *Danza y género* (Dance and Genre) (2001); *Frutos de mujer: Las mujeres en la danza escénica* (Women's Productions: Women in Theatrical Dance) (2001) and has edited an anthology on José Limón and translated Daniel Lewis's *The Illustrated Technique of José Limón* in Spanish. Contributor to Taryn Benbow-Pfalzgraf (editor), *International Dictionary of Modern Dance* (Detroit, New York, London: St. James Press, 1998). She composed nine essays on Mexican modern dance and Mexican dancers. She is presently writing an article on the professional dancers' perspectives on injury. Currently she teaches Mexican dance history at the Contemporary Dance School, Ministry of Culture of Mexico City.

INDEX